Haynes for HOME DIY

Lawnmower
Manual

**DIY maintenance, repair and renovation
of rotary and cylinder lawnmowers**

3rd Edition

ABCDE
FGHIJ
KLMNO
PQRS

1st edition published 1980 & 1985 - by M. C. Crawley and J. M. F. Parker
2nd edition published 1995 - updated by George Milne
3rd edition published 2000 - updated by Andrew Shanks and Martynn Randall
Reprinted 2002

Published by:
Haynes Publishing
Sparkford, Yeovil, Somerset BA22 7JJ, UK

British Library Cataloguing-in-Publication data:

A catalogue record for this book is available from the British Library

ISBN 1 85960 337 8

Printed in the USA.

ACKNOWLEDGEMENTS

The authors and publishers would like to thank the following for all their help: Rochford Garden Machinery for the loan of lawnmowers and engines and continual support throughout the project; Pete Loxton from Loxton Garden Machinery; Ian Jones at the British Agricultural & Garden Machinery Association.

Contents

WARWICKSHIRE COLLEGE LIBRARY

Safety first   Page   4

General information
Introduction   Page   5
Lawnmowers covered   Page   5
Warranty considerations   Page   5
Engine identity   Page   6
Ordering spare parts   Page   7
Buying decisions   Page   8
Using the mower   Page   9
Overhaul   Page   10
Mistakes to avoid   Page   15

General procedures
Using the mower   Page   17
Storage at end of season   Page   18
Dismantling   Page   18
Cleaning and inspecting parts   Page   19
Reassembly   Page   27
Sharpening blades   Page   28
Routine maintenance   Page   30
Fault-finding   Page   31

Engine dismantling and reassembly
Briggs & Stratton MAX 4hp 4-stroke engine   Page   33
Briggs & Stratton Intek/Europa OHV 4-stroke engine   Page   45
Briggs & Stratton Quantum 55 'L' Head 4-stroke engine   Page   59
Briggs & Stratton I/C horizontal crank 'L' Head 5 hp 4-stroke engine Page   73
Briggs & Stratton 35 Sprint/Classic 2.6 kW 4-stroke engine   Page   83
Honda GV100 4-stroke engine   Page   93
Honda GXV120 4-stroke engine   Page 111
Honda OHC GCV135 4.5 hp (3.3 kW) 4-stroke engine   Page 135
Tecumseh LAV 1 53 4-stroke engine   Page 149
Tecumseh 3.5 hp/Vantage 35 4-stroke engine   Page 163
Tecumseh MV100S 2-stroke engine   Page 177

Which engine is fitted?   Page 187

Glossary   Page 192

Safety first

Mow safely

- [ ] Read the operation and instruction books before using the mower.
- [ ] Never run an engine in an enclosed space.
- [ ] Check oil levels prior to each cut or at least weekly.
- [ ] Switch off the engine before refilling the petrol tank.
- [ ] Wear trousers and hard shoes when operating rotary mowers.
- [ ] Familiarise yourself with the operating controls especially 'Operator Proximity Controls'.
- [ ] Remove all debris from the area.
- [ ] Do not use a lawnmower with a 4-stroke engine on slopes greater than 30 degrees.
- [ ] Never tilt a rotary mower when the engine is running. The body cannot give protection from the rotating blades. The high rotational speed of the cutter blade means that the blade continues to rotate after the engine is switched off.
- [ ] Never use a rotary mower with a damaged body or guards.
- [ ] If a rotary mower is used without the grass collector, make sure that the deflector plate is in the down position to protect the operator from stones, dust and other debris.
- [ ] Remove any build-up of grass, leaves or any other combustible material from the silencer area.
- [ ] Check whether the silencer has a spark arrestor if you are operating in an area where a fire could be started.
- [ ] For under deck inspection of rotary mowers, always tilt the front wheels upwards, dropping the handles to the ground. Do not tip mower sideways as this can flood the air filter.
- [ ] If a rotary mower starts vibrating, stop the engine immediately and investigate.
- [ ] Check the cutter blade bolt and all other nuts and bolts are secure.
- [ ] Before working on any mower, disconnect the plug lead and tie it back so that it cannot touch the sparking plug.
- [ ] Never renew one blade only on a rotary mower. Retain balance by renewing the set using new bolts and fittings.
- [ ] Check that any part of the engine is cool before grasping it.

Work safely

- [ ] Before draining oil, make sure it has cooled sufficiently not to scald you.
- [ ] Don't siphon toxic liquids such as fuel by mouth and don't allow them to remain on your skin. Store petrol in approved metal or high impact plastic petrol containers.
- [ ] Don't inhale clutch lining dust.
- [ ] Don't turn the engine over unless the spark plug lead is detached and retained out of the way.
- [ ] Don't use petrol for cleaning parts, unless it is specified.
- [ ] Don't allow spilled oil or grease to remain on the floor – wipe it up before someone slips on it.
- [ ] Don't use ill-fitting spanners or tools which may slip and cause injury or damage parts.
- [ ] Don't attempt to lift a heavy component beyond your capability – get help.
- [ ] Don't rush to finish a job, or take unverified short cuts.
- [ ] Do take care when attempting to slacken a stubborn nut or bolt. It is generally better to pull on a spanner, rather than push. Then if slippage occurs you will fall away rather than towards the mower.
- [ ] Do wear eye protection when using power tools such as grinders, sanders and drills.
- [ ] Do use a barrier cream on your hands prior to undertaking dirty jobs – it will protect your skin from infection and make cleaning your hands easier.
- [ ] Do keep loose fitting clothing and long hair well out of the way of moving parts.
- [ ] Do keep your work place tidy – it could be dangerous to fall over tools and components left lying around.
- [ ] Do exercise caution when compressing springs for removal or installation. Apply and release tension progressively and use tools that preclude violent escape of the spring and other components.
- [ ] Do carry out work in a systematic sequence, checking as you go.
- [ ] Do check that everything is assembled correctly and tightened afterwards.
- [ ] If despite following all these precautions, you are unfortunate enough to hurt yourself, seek immediate medical assistance.

Chapter 1
General information

Introduction
Lawnmowers covered
Warranty considerations
Engine identity
Ordering spare parts
Buying decisions
  Cylinder mowers
  Rotary lawnmowers
  Rotary versus cylinder

Using the mower
  Preparing to mow
  Setting mower height
  Mowing angles
  Frequency of mowing

Overhaul
  Which tools?
  Buying tools
  Storage and care of tools
  Special factory tools
  Advance preparations
  Tight spots
Mistakes to avoid

Introduction

The sale of lawnmowers has become an international business and there is a very wide range of models available. The UK market alone accounts for 250,000 units and these are spread among many manufacturers. Previous editions of the *Lawnmower Manual* selected the most popular 12 petrol-driven lawnmowers on the market and gave detailed overhaul information on each.

Today, it would be a very small retail showroom indeed that held just 12 models. A visit to a retail garden machinery retailer has become a daunting experience with line after line of lawnmowers on display. Many manufacturers offer many more than a dozen models in their ranges and these will include several distinct families of lawnmower types.

This new version of the Haynes *Lawnmower Manual* has additional information about how to choose the lawnmower best suited to your needs. The manual explains what is actually meant by the advertising copy in the manufacturers' catalogues and will help in the identification of those features that will be helpful and those that can be managed without.

The social trend has been towards more gardens for more people. Even in the smallest gardens, there are considerations to be borne in mind when choosing the right lawnmower. For all sizes of gardens, there are choices to be made that relate to life style and the desired appearance of your garden.

A manual from Haynes, the world's largest publisher of owners' workshop manuals, would not be complete without detailed technical guidance as to how to maintain, repair and overhaul your lawnmower. This latest version of the *Lawnmower Manual* differs from previous editions in its concentration on engines for detailed overhaul guidance. This is because the global nature of the lawnmower market has seen the emergence of a handful of world leaders in suitable engine technology. Thus the detailed overhaul guidance for engines included in this manual covers the majority of lawnmower models produced over the last ten years that remain in use today. The manual can be seen as an indispensable companion to the Owner's Handbook that comes with all new mowers.

Since the previous *Lawnmower Manual* was published, many innovations in design and facilities have been introduced to the market. There are now rotary lawnmowers whose rear roller gives a 'striped' appearance and there are types that can mulch, collect and work in long, wet grass. All new mowers now have safety controls known by the standard of 'Operator Proximity Controls' that prevent the machine running away from the operator or from being operated unless that user has a grip on the controls. The manual explains all these new features and weighs their importance according to the user's needs.

Lawnmowers covered

The lawnmowers covered in this manual include those fitted with the petrol engines to be found in the Engine Overhaul chapters. The information provided in early chapters is of a general nature and applies to the majority of lawnmowers on the market whether or not they are powered by the engines that feature in the overhaul section.

Warranty considerations

Following the lead of the automobile market, lawnmower manufacturers compete with each other to offer extended warranties on their products. Be very wary of the small print, however, because some warranties involve taking the mower back to the supplying dealer for service if the extended warranty is to remain valid. Other manufacturers warrant the main body of the mower for an extended period but only warrant the engine for a shorter period – typically 3 years for the body and 1 year for the engine. Before undertaking any repair work beyond routine maintenance, do check with the supplying dealer about the warranty situation.

The purpose of a warranty is to cover the unexpected due to poor manufacture in the first place; warranties very rarely cover breakdown that results from normal, responsible use. It is not unknown for manufacturers to accept liability for inbuilt shortcomings in design even when a recall has not been requested – check first with the supplying dealer before undertaking any serious overhaul work.

Current legislation requires all warranties to be transferable to second or successive owners during the warranty period. If there is no reason for there to be a problem, there will be no reluctance to transfer the warranty, so make sure that you have this undertaking from the original supplying dealer in writing before purchasing any secondhand machine – whether buying privately or through a dealer.

Engine identity

To determine what repair information and specifications to use, and to purchase replacement parts, you'll have to be able to

Typical Briggs & Stratton model identification number

accurately identify the engine you're working on. Every engine, regardless of manufacturer, comes from the factory with a model number (MN) stamped or cast into it somewhere. The most common location is on the shroud used to direct the cooling air around the cylinder (look for the recoil starter - it's normally attached to the shroud as well). On some engines, the number may be stamped, cast into or attached to the main engine casting and may not be visible, especially if the engine is dirty.

The position of the model identification number (MN) differs with the manufacturer as does the interpretation of the number.

Briggs & Stratton

Briggs & Stratton stamp the MN on the engine cooling shroud and it is the first 5 or 6 numbers that are relevant – the term 'Model' aligns with this part of the MN.

The MN may be interpreted by reference to the chart below.

The first one or two digits give the displacement of the engine in cubic inches (cu. in.). If the displacement in cubic centimetres (cc) is important for you to know, the conversion factor is 16.387 (e.g. 8 cu. in. is approximately 131 cc). The digit following the displacement code indicates the 'Basic Design Series' and may be interpreted as an engine family designation that defines configuration, cylinder type and ignition system.

The second digit after the displacement code defines the orientation of the crankshaft, the carburettor type and also the governor operation.

The third digit after the displacement gives the bearing type or gear reduction or the orientation of the auxiliary drive.

The fourth digit after the displacement defines the engine's starter type.

BRIGGS & STRATTON MODEL NUMBER KEY

Displacement (cubic inches)*	First Digit After Disp. Basic Design Series	Second Digit After Disp. Crankshaft/ Carburettor/ Governor	Third Digit After Disp. Bearings/ Reduction gears/ Auxiliary drive	Fourth Digit After Disp. Starter type
6	0	0	0 = Plain bearing	0 = No starter
8	1	1 = Horizontal (Vacu-Jet)	1 = Flange mount plain bearing	1 = Rope starter
9	2			
10	3	2 = Horizontal (Pulsa-Jet)	2 = Ball bearing	2 = Rewind starter
13	4			
	5	3 = Horizontal (Flo-Jet; pneumatic governor)	3 = Flange Mount ball bearing	3 = Electric (110-volt; gear drive)
	6			
	7	4 = Horizontal (Flo-Jet; mechanical governor)	4	4 = Electric starter/ generator (12-volt; belt drive)
	8			
	9			
		5 = Vertical (Vacu-Jet)	5 = Gear reduction (6 to 1)	5 = Electric starter only (12-volt; gear drive)
		6	6 = Gear reduction (6 to 1; reverse rotation)	6 = Wind-up starter
		7 = Vertical (Flo-Jet)	7	7 = Electric starter (12-volt; gear-drive with alternator)
		8	8 = Auxiliary drive perpendicular to crankshaft	8 = Vertical-pull starter
		9 = Vertical (Pulsa-Jet)	9 = Auxiliary drive parallel to crankshaft	

*Cubic inches x 16.387 = Cubic centimetres (cc)

Tecumseh

Tecumseh stamp the engine number either on the engine cooling shroud or on a tag attached to the crankcase. The number is made up of a MODEL/SPEC. NO. (M/S No.) followed by the serial number which is prefixed 'SER'. The MODEL group of letters and numbers gives information about the engine's general specification and its cubic capacity. The SPEC No. provides detailed information about variations on the standard engine and this number will need to be quoted when ordering parts. Finally, the SERIAL No. gives year, day and manufacturing plant information about the engine.

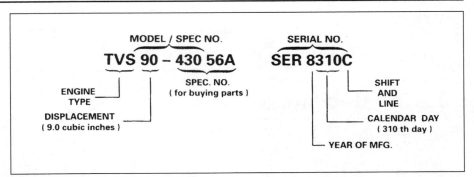

Typical Tecumseh model identification number

Honda

Honda engines covered in the overhaul section are all from the 'G' series of engines rated up to 5.5 hp. The model number is stamped into the side of the crankcase for engines with a vertical crankshaft orientation and the serial number is stamped into the end of the crankcase. For horizontal crankshaft engines, the Model and Serial numbers are both stamped on the crankcase furthest away from the cylinder head.

Typical Honda model identification number – vertical shaft engine

Typical Honda serial number – vertical shaft engine

Ordering spare parts

To ensure that the correct parts are ordered, both the Model Designation of the lawnmower and also the Model and Serial number of the engine will generally be required. It is helpful to keep a note of these numbers handy when ordering. Where a spare part to replace a worn or damaged part is required, it will help the service dealer or agent if the complete assembly is taken to his service depot. It is possible that the new part will form part of a new assembly that replaces the original. Dealers' parts stock records are retained today on microfiche or computer records and sight by the service dealer of the original part and assembly will help to ensure that the correct part can be ordered.

Buying decisions

The bright and glossy new mowers in the dealer's showroom make an impressive but confusing sight. Choosing the one most suited to your needs is based, however, on very logical considerations.

Advances in the design of lawnmowers using rotary (i.e. horizontal cutter blade) action have meant that these designs have overtaken the traditional cylinder mower in the market. The great majority of mower sales are now of the rotary type due to the added versatility that they offer.

Cylinder mowers

Cylinder mowers cut grass by a scissor technique. A rotating cylinder with five or more spiral set blades cuts the grass against a cutter bar. A fine finish results and the heavy rear roller both levels the ground as well as giving a 'striped' appearance to the grass as the grass stems lie in opposing directions. The drive train for the cutting cylinder and drive train for the heavy rear roller is complex and, generally, the whole unit will be extremely sturdy. The lawn best suited to a cylinder mower will be flat and without any steep inclines. Cylinder mowers are prone to damage of the cylinder and cutter bar by small stones or even cricket boot studs and professional help will be needed to regrind the cutting bar and cylinder blades.

Perhaps the greatest disadvantage of a cylinder mower is an inability to cut long grass and inevitable clogging when cutting wet grass. For those of us with the time to cut the lawn twice a week or at least every 5 days, a cylinder mower certainly gives the finest results.

Cylinder mowers are available with different numbers of blades on the cylinder from 3 to 12 giving from 52 cuts per metre up to 146 cuts per metre. For domestic use, cutting widths range from 30 cm to 60 cm and at an average speed of between 2 and 4 mph, the narrowest cut width would suit an area half the size of a tennis court while the widest will cope comfortably with three times this area.

A innovation on cylinder mowers is a cassette system enabling the cutter cylinder to be exchanged with a scarifier, the latter being used to remove matted, dead grass as well as moss and other weeds. A further feature to look for is a cylinder disengagement facility which enables just the rear roller to be driven while the blades are not engaged.

Rotary mowers

The cutting action of a rotary lawnmower is by a rotating cutter blade set at right angles to the vertical axis of the engine. There are three basic types.

Hover mowers need no wheels as they are supported on a cushion of air created by the spinning impeller. Petrol-powered hover mowers are all of the mulching type, i.e. the grass is not collected. Cutting widths range from 38 to 50 cm and cutting heights range from 10 to 34 mm.

Wheeled rotary lawnmowers are either of the 'Push' or 'Self-propelled' kind. For the smaller garden or where there are few slopes, the lower price of a push mower should be considered. Where there are slopes or rougher areas of the garden and if cutting may be of long or wet grass, a self-propelled mower would be favoured.

Wheeled rotary mowers have a wheel at each corner and the cutting width is approximately the same as the track width. If the garden design includes many flower beds, the wheels can drop over the grass verge and the edges will be scalped. In this case, the choice might well be for a rotary mower with a rear roller.

Rear roller type rotary lawnmowers have two important advantages. They overcome the problem of the scalping of the lawn edge and they also provide the 'striped' appearance that was once the province of the cylinder mower.

Features to look out for on rotary mowers are:

- ☐ Simple height-of-cut adjustment.
- ☐ Simple removal of the grass collection bag.
- ☐ Easy switching between collection, mulching and side discharge.
- ☐ Disengagable cutter drive.
- ☐ Disengagable traction drive.

Rotary versus cylinder

Rotary

- Relatively few moving parts hence cheaper for given width of cut.
- Engine must operate near full throttle hence greater wear, more noise (especially blade noise) and greater fuel consumption.
- Cutters are cheap to replace and easy to sharpen and maintain.

- Will cut longer, wetter, rougher grass than cylinder mower.

- Perform better than cylinder mowers on inclines, subject to any lubrication limitations.
- Cutting height easily adjusted.
- Can be used to clean up autumn leaves and debris.

- Stones and hard objects do less damage to cutters, which are more easily repaired.
- Out of balance cutter causes serious engine damage.
- Noisy.

Cylinder

- Complicated drive arrangements hence greater expense.
- Engine can operate at any speed desired and mower still cuts. Smaller engine can cope with given width of cut.
- Cutter system more complicated, adjustment much more critical, maintenance of cutting edges needs professional attention. Properly adjusted they have a longer life than rotary cutters.
- Will cut to a better finish, but only cope with much shorter grass than rotary mowers.
- May be fitted with scarifier cartridge in place of cutter cylinder (models from Atco Qualcast).
- Not good on slopes due to roller skidding, higher risk of tipping over.
- Cutting height adjustment not easy on most types and requires use of tools; some recent types (eg Atco Commodore) now have easy knob-type adjuster.
- Stones, etc trapped between cylinder and stationary blade easily ruin cutter system. Regrinding is a professional job.
- More all-round maintenance because of chains and drives.
- Quiet.

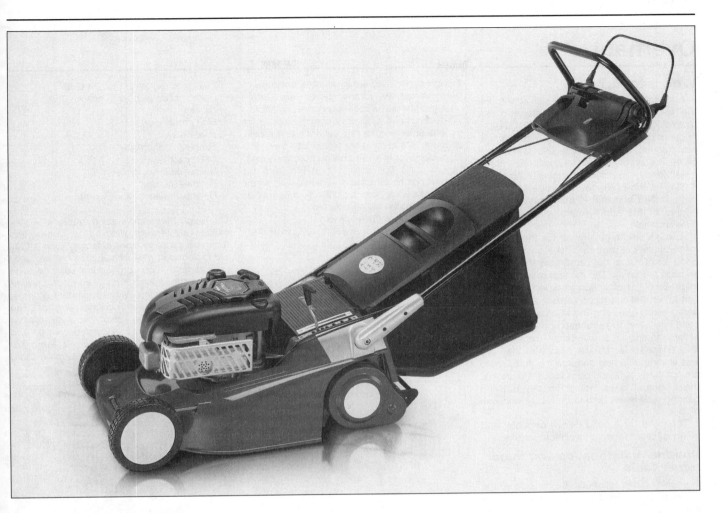

Using the mower

Note: *Only those aspects of grass care connected with the use of mowers are dealt with here.*

Preparing to mow

1 Damage to blades should be avoided. On cylinder mowers they affect the cutting, on rotaries they may affect the balance as well and cause vibration and engine wear.

2 It is good practice to rake or brush the area before mowing to remove harmful objects such as stones, hard twigs and parts of toys.

3 Grass is best not cut while wet. Not only will it not cut well, but wet grass cuttings and mud are even worse for mowers than dry grass cuttings and earth.

Setting mower height

1 Coarse grass is best for wear, fine grass for appearance. Longer grass at about 13 to 20 mm (½ to ¾ in) will better withstand the attacks of feet, children, pets and bicycles.

2 Closer cut grass is better for appearance, at say 7 to 10 mm (¼ to ⅜ in). Closer cutting is suitable only for close growing, dense grass, otherwise it will look sparse and lack colour when short, because of too much earth showing.

3 If the grass is appreciably long, the general opinion is that it is best to cut it in two goes 3 to 4 days apart; the mower will give a better finish used this way. It has been said that as a general rule do not cut more than ⅓ of its length in one go.

4 However, there is an advantage to cutting heavily and cutting short if the area is getting coarse in its growth. Cutting short favours the finer grasses which do not grow well when shaded by long, broader grasses. It may be worthwhile keeping the area short for a month or so to see if the ratio of fine to coarse improves and gives a more pleasing appearance.

Mowing angles

1 Rotary mowers will cut grass sticking up in all directions. Cylinder mowers sometimes miss small clumps growing at an awkward angle.

2 Every other mowing it can pay to use a different pattern, going crossways and diagonally, finishing up by going over again in the usual directions and sequence to give a uniform finish. This can deal with the thicker tufts better, as well.

3 Cylinder mowers sometimes miss clumps because the bottom blade needs resetting. Without the 'scissors' action against the blades of the cylinder, clean, uniform, and complete cutting cannot take place.

Frequency of mowing

1 It is advisable not to mow too frequently in dry weather. If the box is left off a cylinder mower the cuttings help the dryness by forming a mulch. Remember also that dry weather means dust, and dust means more wear. If you live in a dry area, check air and fuel filters more frequently.

2 At the first spring cut, set blades high. Later, cut every week while grass grows. Cut twice a week, if weather permits, during the peak growing period.

Overhaul

Which tools?

In an ideal world, it would be possible to list the tools required for each stage of an overhaul. Unfortunately, mower design appears to be in a constant state of change, with frequent re-tooling for smaller parts. Even on such a simple matter as spanners it is not possible to be specific: an engine of American design which is made in Europe may have both unified and metric bolts, and the next engine of the same make will be slightly different again.

Readers who regularly service their cars or motorbikes will probably have a reasonably good kit of tools, but remember that mower engines are small. The owners of motorbikes might be better off in some respects.

It is not difficult to go all round the engine and mower, checking the fit of your tools, in case you need to purchase something extra before starting on an overhaul. Use socket or ring spanners whenever possible, they are less likely to slip and damage the nuts. There are not many nuts and bolts inside the engine, the principal ones being on the big-end bearing, and these tend to be robust because of their function.

The need for a solid bench or table, and plenty of clean rags, goes without saying.

Routine maintenance and minor repair tools

The tools on this list should be considered the minimum required for doing routine maintenance, servicing and minor repair work. Incidentally, if you have a choice, it's a good idea to buy combination spanners (ring and open-end combined in one spanner); while more expensive than open-end ones, they offer the advantages of both types. Also included is a complete set of sockets which,

though expensive, are invaluable because of their versatility (many types are inter-changeable and accessories are available). We recommend $\frac{3}{8}$ in drive over $\frac{1}{2}$ in drive for general small engine maintenance and repair, although a $\frac{1}{4}$ in drive set would also be useful (especially for ignition and carburettor work). Buy 6-point sockets, if possible, and be careful not to purchase sockets with extra thick walls – they can be difficult to use when access to fasteners is restricted.

> Safety goggles/face shield
> Combination spanner set ($\frac{1}{4}$ to $\frac{7}{8}$ in or 6 to 19 mm)
> Adjustable spanner – 10 in
> Socket set (6-point)
> Reversible ratchet
> Extension – 6 in
> Universal joint
> Spark plug socket (with rubber insert)
> Spark plug gap adjusting tool
> Feeler gauge set
> Standard screwdriver ($\frac{5}{16}$ in x 6 in)
> Standard screwdriver ($\frac{3}{8}$ in x 10 in)

> Phillips screwdriver (no. 2 x 6 in)
> Combination (slip-joint) pliers – 6 in
> Oil can
> Fine emery cloth
> Wire brush
> Funnel (medium size)
> Drain pan
> Starter clutch spanner*
> Flywheel holder*
> Flywheel puller or knock-off tool*

*Although these tools are normally available exclusively through distributors/dealers (so technically they're 'special factory tools'), they are included in this list because certain tune-up and minor repair procedures can't be done without them (specifically contact breaker points and flywheel key replacement on most Briggs & Stratton and Tecumseh engines). The factory tools may also be available at hardware and lawn and garden centres and occasionally you'll come across imported copies of the factory tools – examine them carefully before buying them.

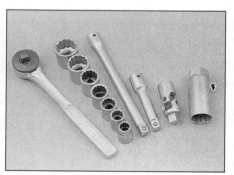

One of the most important items you'll need is a face shield/safety goggles – fortunately, it'll also be one of the least expensive.

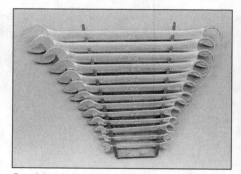

Combination spanners – buy a set with sizes from $\frac{1}{4}$ to $\frac{7}{8}$ in or 6 to 19 mm.

Adjustable spanners are very handy – just be sure to use them correctly or you can damage fasteners by rounding off the hex head.

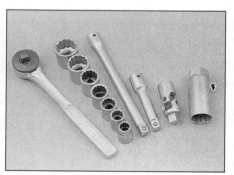

A $\frac{3}{8}$ in drive socket set with interchangeable accessories will probably be used more often than any other tool(s) (left-to-right; ratchet, sockets, extensions, U-joint spark plug socket) – don't buy a cheap socket set.

A spark plug adjusting tool will have several wire gauges for measuring the electrode gap and a device used for bending the side electrode to change the gap – make sure the one you buy has the correct size wire to check the spark plug gap on your engine.

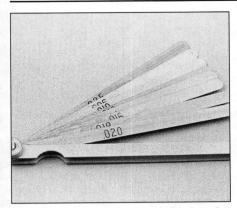

Feeler gauge sets have several blades of different thicknesses – if you need it to adjust contact breaker points, make sure the blades are as narrow as possible and check them to verify the required thickness is included.

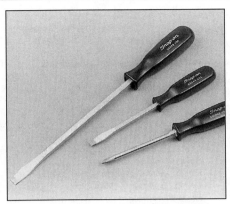

The routine maintenance tool kit should have $5/16$ x 6 in and $3/8$ x 10 in standard screwdrivers, as well as a no. 2 x 6 in Phillips screwdriver.

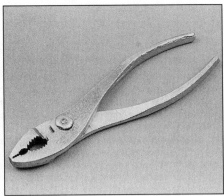

Common slip-joint pliers will be adequate for almost any job you end up doing.

A shallow pan (for draining oil/cleaning parts with solvent), a wire brush and a medium size funnel should be part of the routine maintenance tool kit.

To remove the starter clutch used on Briggs & Stratton engines, a special tool (which is turned with a spanner) will be needed.

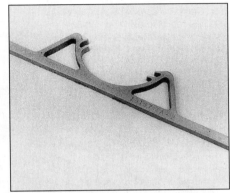

Briggs & Stratton also sells a special flywheel holder for use when loosening the nut or starter clutch.

The flywheel on a Briggs & Stratton engine can be removed with a puller (shown here) . . .

. . . or, although it's not recommended by the factory, a knock-off tool, which fits on the end of the crankshaft (Tecumseh flywheels can also be removed with one of these tools).

Many Tecumseh and Honda engines require a three jaw puller like the one shown here for flywheel removal.

Repair and overhaul tools

These tools are essential if you intend to perform major repairs or overhauls and are intended to supplement those in the *Routine maintenance and minor repair* tool kit.

The tools in this list include many which aren't used regularly, are expensive to buy, or which need to be used in accordance with their manufacturer's instructions. Unless these tools will be used frequently, it's not very economical to purchase many of them. A consideration would be to split the cost and use between yourself and a friend or neighbour.

Ring spanners
Torque spanner (same size drive as sockets)
Ball pein hammer – 12 oz (any steel hammer will do)
Soft-face hammer (plastic / rubber)
Standard screwdriver (1/4 in x 6 in)
Standard screwdriver (stubby – 5/16 in)
Phillips screwdriver (no. 3 x 8 in)
Phillips screwdriver (stubby – no. 2)

Hand impact screwdriver and bits
Pliers – self-locking
Pliers – needle-nose
Wire cutters
Cold chisels – 1/4 and 1/2 in
Centre punch
Pin punches (1/16, 1/8, 3/16 in)
Line up tools (tapered punches)
Scribe
Hacksaw and assortment of blades
Gasket scraper
Steel rule/straight edge – 12 in
A selection of files
A selection of brushes for cleaning small passages
Small extractor set
Spark tester
Compression gauge
Ridge reamer
Valve spring compressor
Valve lapping tool
Piston ring removal and installation tool
Piston ring compressor
Cylinder hone
Telescoping gauges

Micrometer(s) and/or dial/Vernier calipers
Dial indicator
Tap and die set
*Torx socket(s)**
Tachometer, or strobe timing light with rpm scale

* *Some Tecumseh two-stroke engines require a Torx socket (size E6) to remove the connecting rod cap bolts. If you're overhauling one of these engines, purchase a socket before beginning the disassembly procedure.*

One of the most indispensable tools around is the common electric drill. One with a 3/8 in capacity chuck should be sufficient for most repair work – it'll be large enough to power a cylinder surfacing hone. Collect several different wire brushes to use in the drill and make sure you have a complete set of sharp bits (for drilling metal, not wood). Cordless drills, which are extremely versatile because they don't have to be plugged in, are now widely available and relatively inexpensive. You may want to consider one, since it'll obviously be handy for non-mechanical jobs around the house and workshop.

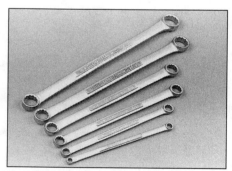

A set of ring spanners will complement the combination spanners in the routine maintenance tool kit.

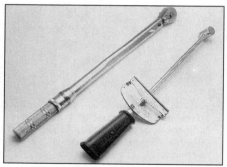

A torque spanner will be needed for tightening head bolts and flywheel nuts (two types are available: click type – left; beam type – right).

A ball-pein hammer, soft-face hammer and rubber mallet (left-to-right) will be needed for various tasks (any steel hammer can be used in place of the ball-pein hammer).

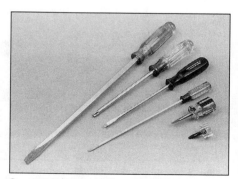

Screwdrivers come in many different sizes and lengths.

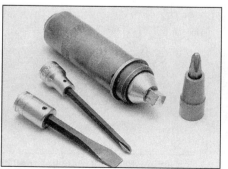

A hand impact screwdriver (used with a hammer) and bits can be very helpful for removing stubborn, stuck screws (or screws with deformed heads).

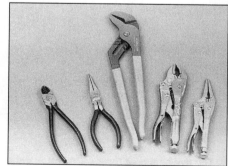

As you can afford them, 'water-pump', needle-nose, self-locking and wire cutting pliers should be added to your tool collection.

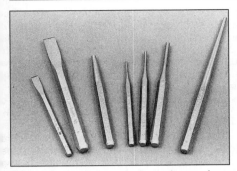

Cold chisels, centre punches, pin punches and line-up punches (left-to-right) will be needed sooner or later for many jobs.

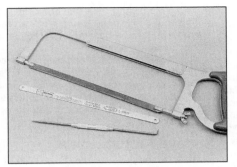

A scribe is used for making lines on metal parts and a hacksaw and blades will be needed for dealing with fasteners that won't unscrew.

A gasket scraper is used for removing old gaskets from engine parts after disassembly – scouring pads can be used to rough up the gasket surfaces prior to reassembly.

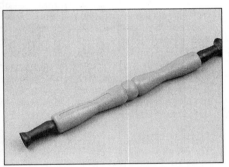

Files must be used with handles and should be stored so they don't contact each other.

A selection of nylon/metal brushes is needed for cleaning passages in engine and carburettor parts.

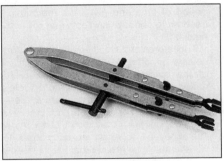

A valve spring compressor like this is required for side valve Briggs & Stratton engines.

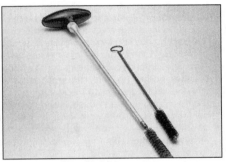

A valve lapping tool will be needed for any four-stroke engine overhaul.

Some overhead valves (OHV) 4-stroke engines require a tool like this to compress the springs so the valves can be removed.

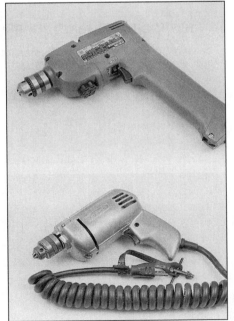

An electric drill (both 230-volt AC and cordless types are shown here).

Piston ring compressors come in many sizes – be sure to buy one that will work on your engine.

Some Tecumseh two-stroke engines require a No. 6 Torx socket for the removal of the connecting rod bolts during an engine overhaul.

Buying tools

For the do-it-yourselfer just starting to get involved in small engine maintenance and repair, there are a number of options available when purchasing tools. If maintenance and minor repair is the extent of the work to be done, the purchase of individual tools is satisfactory. If, on the other hand, extensive work is planned, it would be a good idea to purchase a modest tool set. A set can usually be bought at a substantial saving over the individual tool prices (and they often come with a tool box). As additional tools are needed, add-on sets, individual tools and a larger box can be purchased to expand the tool selection. Building a tool set gradually allows the cost to be spread over a longer period of time and gives the mechanic the freedom to choose only tools that will actually be used.

Tool stores and small engine distributors or dealers will often be the only source of some of the overhaul and special factory tools needed, but regardless of where tools are bought, try to avoid cheap ones (especially when buying screwdrivers, spanners and sockets) because they won't last very long. The expense involved in replacing cheap tools will eventually be greater that the initial cost of quality tools.

Storage and care of tools

Good tools are expensive, so it makes sense to treat them with respect. Keep them clean and in usable condition and store them properly. Always wipe off dirt, grease and metal chips before putting them away. Never leave tools lying around in the work area.

Some tools, such as screwdrivers, pliers, spanners and sockets, can be hung on a panel mounted on the garage or workshop wall, while others should be kept in a tool box

or tray. Measuring instruments, gauges, cutting tools, etc. must be carefully stored where they can't be damaged by weather or impact from other tools.

When tools are used with care and stored properly, they'll last a very long time. However, even with the best of care, tools will wear out if used frequently. When a tool is damaged or worn out, replace it; subsequent jobs will be safer.

Special factory tools

Each small engine manufacturer provides certain special tools to distributors and dealers for use when overhauling or doing major repairs on their engines. The distributors and dealers often stock some of the tools for the do-it-yourselfer and independent repair shops. A good example would be tools like the starter clutch spanner, flywheel holder and flywheel puller(s) supplied by Briggs & Stratton, which are needed for relatively simple procedures such as contact breaker points (they're required to get the flywheel off for access to the ignition parts). If the special tools aren't used, the repair either can't be done properly, or the engine could be damaged by using substitute tools. Fortunately, the tools mentioned are not very expensive or hard to find.

Other special tools, like bushing drivers, bushing reamers, valve seat and guide service tools, cylinder sizing hones, main bearing repair sets, etc. are prohibitively expensive and not usually stocked for sale by dealers. If repairs requiring such tools are encountered, take the engine or components to a dealer with the necessary tools and pay to have the work done, then reassemble the engine yourself.

Advance preparations

Check round your machine before starting

any work, identifying the major parts. Read this Chapter for general procedures for dismantling, cleaning, inspection for wear, and reassembly advice. Go through the Chapter covering your particular machine; many of the photographs show tools being used and the techniques of fitting parts.

These preparations will give a good idea of the tools and special materials such as gasket jointing compounds you will need. Also when to lubricate and when not, and what to use. It is assumed you will have engine oil, if you have a 4-stroke engine, and this can be used on all metal-to-metal surfaces when parts are assembled together. With a 2-stroke, light machine oil should be used, not engine oil which tends to be too heavy and has other disadvantages.

Tight spots

We were surprised by how tight some of the crossheaded bolts were, and found an impact screwdriver helpful on numerous occasions.

Some flywheels were on tight, and usually required a puller. It should be noted that legged pullers are not recommended by many manufacturers. All can supply their own flywheel puller, often a very simple device consisting of a flat bar with bolts which are tightened slowly in turn until the seal between the flywheel and the crankshaft gives. The techniques given in this manual will work again and again without trouble, but some experience with such tools is needed: if in doubt, get the manufacturer's special tool.

'Release' fluids can be invaluable with really obstinate nuts and bolts and screws or those in awkward places, liable to get corroded.

A plastic or hide mallet is essential, to minimise the risk of damage during certain dismantling tasks.

Mistakes to avoid

Every mower service station has a chamber of horrors where damaged, worn out, or downright dangerous parts are thrown, discarded from mowers brought in for overhaul or repair. Service engineers are no longer surprised by what they find and the owners have not looked to see what has happened and so never know. The mower is returned (if worth repairing, of course), together with an unavoidably large bill which would have been much smaller had the mower received regular maintenance. This section shows a small collection of such horrors.

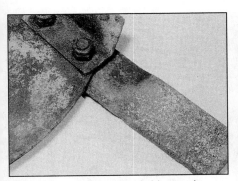

1 Grassed areas are best raked or swept before mowing. This does two things: it prepares the grass for cutting and it clears stones and other hard objects which can damage the cutting edges or can be thrown out at a dangerously high speed and cause injury. This bottom blade from a cylinder mower has been badly bent by striking a rock or concrete path at speed, through careless handling. It will no longer be in contact with the cutting cylinder blades all along its length and will cut unevenly.

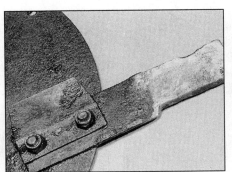

2 This cutting disc from a rotary mower shows two defects. First, the grass deflectors mounted on top of the blades have been battered out of shape. Because they were not working properly, the mower deck kept getting clogged up with grass, making cutting inefficient and putting extra load on the engine as well.

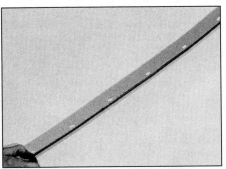

3 Secondly, the hopelessly blunt and chipped cutting edges gave poor cutting action. The engine was being run at full throttle all the time to try to compensate and even then the grass was being torn off rather than cut. If some time had been spent straightening and sharpening, results would have been transformed, and the engine could have been run at about 3/4 throttle. Less trouble and wear and tear all round.

4 Here the cutting edge is reasonably good but the blade has been chipped. There was other damage elsewhere and a noticeable lack of balance in the cutting disc, causing vibration and damage to the engine.

5 An almost unbelievable example of neglect. This disc has four fixing points for two cutters and two grass deflectors. Running with only one cutting blade caused very serious vibration. Perhaps the owner was a pneumatic drill operator and felt more at home with it working like this. Engine wear is shown later, the result of far less out of balance effects than this. (See the crankshaft wear picture.)

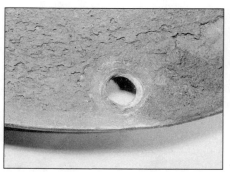

6 While still on cutting discs, never use one with elongated fixing holes, it is very dangerous. The blades can work loose and fly off, and remember they are travelling at an average speed of 200 miles per hour when rotating and will travel quite a distance if they get past the guards. Fit a new disc, and always use new bolts and fittings, even if the old blades are re-usable.

7 When a cutting disc or a cutter bar on a rotary mower is out of balance it is trying to shake the end of the engine crankshaft to-and-fro all the time. If this goes on, both crankshaft and bearings will be worn on two sides, one more than the other, usually. This main journal has become deeply grooved round one half-circle . . .

8 . . . in just the same way as the bearing in the crankcase into which it fits. Here the wear is obvious, but long before it gets so bad, the state of wear can be detected by running a finger nail along the bearing surface.

9 The tremendous twisting action to the out of balance cutters is shown on this crankshaft, worn round one half-circle at one end and the opposite half-circle at the other.

10 Wear on this crank pin had a simple cause, lack of lubrication. The oil in the sump was very dirty and there was not much of it. It is good practice to top up the sump every time the mower is used, and to change the oil at the recommended intervals. Oil is cheap, repairs are not.

11 Keep a lookout for wear and act before trouble develops. This belt on a cylinder mower is showing cracks on the edge running in the grooves of the pulleys and soon will start to disintegrate.

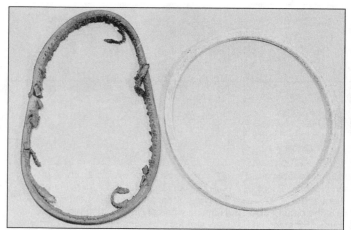

12 Here is a really bad case alongside a new belt for comparison. If you spot trouble before it goes too far a belt cannot snap and leave you with an unusable mower on the first fine Sunday for weeks.

13 Investigate any unusual noise or action. Here, the owner could have noticed how the cylinder mower was snatching as the drive took up, so that the mower gave a jerk forwards. The holes in the large sprocket are getting enlarged because the bolts are slack, also the chain is slack and snatches as the clutch is engaged. The small sprocket is showing signs of wear, which will not do the second chain much good.

Chapter 2
General procedures

Contents

Using the mower
Before
Starting
After
Storage at end of season
Dismantling
Flywheels
Recoil starters
Cleaning and inspecting parts
Air filters
Fuel filters
Carburettors
Spark plugs and valves
Reed valves

Cylinder head
Piston and rings
Crankshaft and camshaft
Engine castings
Lubrication system
Points
    Briggs & Stratton points
    Tecumseh points
Electronic ignition
Reassembly
Lubrication
Fitting
Tightening
Testing and carburettor adjustments

Sharpening blades
Rotary cutters
    Sharpening
    Balancing
Cylinder cutters
    Bottom blade
    Lapping
Routine maintenance
Fault-finding
Mower will not start
Mower starts, but gives low power
Mower runs unevenly
Engine misses when driving mower
Engine knocks

Using the mower

Before

1 Check for loose parts, including the cutter bar fixing bolts and blade fixing bolts on rotaries.
2 If necessary, lightly lubricate the external parts of the clutch and throttle hand controls and the carburettor linkage, to ensure free movement.
3 On cylinder mowers, lubricate the bearings of the cutting cylinder and roller. If there is no oiling hole, tilt the mower to get oil to run in.
4 Top up the sump (4-stroke). Remember that oil is not only essential for avoiding undue engine wear, it helps to cool a hard-working engine.
5 Top up the petrol tank with petrol (4-strokes) or petrol-oil mixture in the recommended proportions (2-strokes).
Note: *If it is necessary to turn the mower over, remember to turn off the petrol and remove the tank or empty it. Drain the oil or tip the mower backwards. If the mower is electric start, remove the battery.*

Starting

1 If of the self-propelled type, ensure clutch is disengaged.
2 Set choke (unless automatic choke). Use carburettor tickler or priming button.
3 Set control to start position, or set throttle about $\frac{1}{3}$ way open.
4 Pull starter.

After

1 Clean grass cuttings and dirt from cooling fins and other parts of engine.
2 Rotary mowers: scrub out the under-deck with water and a stiff brush until down to metal.
3 Cylinder mowers: brush off all cuttings and dirt. Use a wet brush for the more awkward areas.
Note: *This takes very little time if done after every cutting – the juice from grass and other green-stuff is corrosive and very difficult to remove when left.*

Storage at end of season

1 Turn petrol off and run the engine until it stops, to clear the petrol line.

2 Remove, drain, and dry out the petrol tank thoroughly. In steel tanks, put in about a tablespoon of light oil, replace the petrol cap and turn the tank in all directions to spread the oil. Empty out the excess and replace the cap. This light coating of oil will discourage rust formation.

Note: *Trying to use last season's petrol causes many failures to start in the spring!*

3 4-strokes: drain the oil sump thoroughly and refill with fresh oil to the normal level.

4 Remove the spark plug, pour in one tablespoon of light oil (2-strokes) or engine oil (4-strokes). Use the starter to turn over the engine five or six times to circulate the oil, then replace the spark plug.

5 Thoroughly clean the complete mower. Remove all covers and clean out all grass and dirt. Lubricate all external moving parts and turn them to circulate the lubricant thoroughly to help prevent rust.

6 Wipe over all metal parts of the mower with an oily rag to reduce rusting.

7 Remove or fold the handles and raise the mower off the floor to let air circulate, using bricks or pieces of wood. Choose a spot as dry and well-ventilated as possible.

8 Cover with an old sheet or similar fabric. Do not use plastic bags or sheets as they cause condensation with changes of temperature.

9 4-strokes: turn the engine so that it is left on compression (both valves closed). Sticking valves cause failure to start in the spring.

Note: *If the above seems arduous, a very well-known and long-established mower manufacturer says that failure to prepare for storage in the winter will cause more damage to the mower than a season's hard use.*

Dismantling

The instructions given in the sections dealing with individual engines include guidance on dismantling and show tools in use, but problems can still arise with parts which are so tight or badly stuck or contaminated that they cannot be shifted. Remember that if the force applied is concentrated in one spot and applied in one short sharp action, success can often be achieved.

The application of great strength or violent hitting usually results in something getting broken; skill sensibly applied is the answer. For example, one can lean heavily on a blade type screwdriver and try to turn it with both hands and not succeed. A flat-nosed punch placed against one end of the slot in the screwhead and a positive tap with a hammer will often suffice; if not, try alternate ends, several times. The use of 6-point sockets will usually undo rounded bolts and nuts.

Cylinder heads should be eased off carefully, using a tool on both sides. Tap lightly all round with a soft mallet first, to break the seal. The same applies to flywheels, especially those on a tapered shaft. The shock from a series of quite light taps will usually break the grip and other methods will then have a chance, for example, pullers (see *Flywheel* below).

Heat can work wonders. A gas torch can be used for a few moments to expand the area gripping a shaft, followed by tapping with a soft mallet, but apply the heat very briefly, especially if vulnerable parts such as electrical fittings and connections are underneath.

Accurately applied heat can be useful. Small screws and bolts can be heated up with a solder gun without too much affecting the surrounding area. This is a good way of releasing screws held with Loctite: the reed valves in 2-stroke engines are often mounted with this, and the screws secured with it as well.

The stems of exhaust valves may have got so gummed up that the valves can not be drawn up out of their guides. Clean the stems with a fine abrasive tape or a file. Then, when removed, finish off cleaning them so that they will not get gummed up so quickly when replaced.

Mention is made repeatedly of making notes during dismantling. So many changes take place in mower design that this is essential to avoid mishaps when reassembling: your mower may have an older type (or the latest type) of fitting. A piece of card can be useful: the parts can be taped in their correct sequence on to it, to be cleaned at leisure later. In the case of parts such as valves and bolts, a simple sketch of the top of the engine can be made, holes made in the card, and each placed in its correct position.

Flywheels

Removing the flywheel from the crankshaft is a common task in small engine repair. The flywheel is usually located on the crankshaft by a key and tightened onto a taper which is usually very tight and requires considerable force to remove. This ideally can be achieved by use of manufacturer's recommended pullers, many of which are simple devices consisting of a metal plate with bolts which screw into the flywheel, then nuts are tightened evenly to push the plate onto the crankshaft which forces the flywheel from the taper. Most manufacturers advise against the use of legged pullers.

An alternative method is as follows. Remove flywheel nut and washer then replace the nut until it is flush with the end of the crankshaft then lever the flywheel gently away from the engine. Now tap the end of the crankshaft sharply with a soft faced hammer. Be careful to hit it squarely or damage will be done to the crankshaft. This should free the flywheel from its taper. This method is not recommended by manufacturers but works well if applied correctly. If in doubt obtain the correct puller for your engine.

Recoil starters

These are dealt with in the specific engine chapters, as there are wide variations in their details. However, when renewing starter cords or fitting new handles to most starters that require a knot to secure them, the figure of eight knot is the most effective method, and less likely to pull through. Heat seal the end of the cord to prevent fraying, by holding it momentarily in a naked flame.

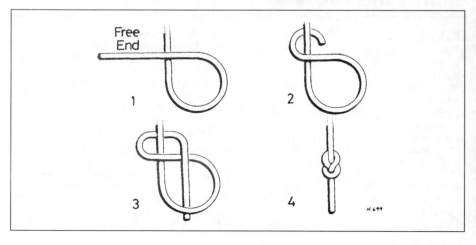

Cleaning and inspecting parts

Air filters

Perhaps the commonest type is oiled polyurethane foam. The block of foam plastic should be cleaned in petrol, squeezed dry, a tablespoon of engine oil placed over one face, and gently squeezed to work the oil all through it. Never run an engine with the foam not oiled: one calculation shows that when oiled its efficiency is about 95%, without oil 20 to 25%. A similar type uses oiled aluminium foil.

Another widely used type has a paper element. To clean, it should be tapped gently for a few minutes. Never apply a liquid cleaner. If it looks grubby, far better for your engine and yourself to fit a new one, they are not expensive.

In the case of mowers with snorkels, a good guide to the efficiency of the air filter is whether there is dust in the tube. If so, clean it out and fit a new element, the old one is useless.

1 The next two designs of filter were not fitted to any of the mowers in this manual, but may be encountered. The first has two dry pads...

2 ... the air passing through a labyrinth...

3 ... and a domed section. The technique is pre-filtering and a turbo action is imparted to the air, which throws dirt aside before the air is allowed to enter the carburettor.

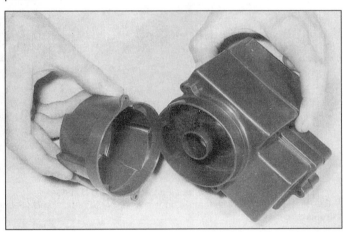

4 The second one has an oil bath; the correct level of oil is marked in the container...

5 ... into which fits a metal or plastic stocking, the whole sealed off with a lid.

Fuel filters

One of the commonest is a simple wire gauze, fitted in the petrol tap or in the petrol line. Clean by washing it in clean petrol; do not try to brush or use an air blast: it is easily damaged. Larger mowers sometimes have a petrol filter with a replaceable element.

'In-line' type filters must be fitted the correct way round, an arrow will indicate direction of flow. When re-fitting a used filter, check the direction as incorrect fitment would allow trapped sediment to pass to the carburettor.

Tapered filters (usually in sintered metal) should have the point of the taper towards the fuel flow to present maximum surface area.

Carburettors

Clean all parts in clean petrol. If metal parts will not clean, use a solvent. Do not use a solvent on plastic parts, Do not use wire to clean jets.

1 Examine all needles of float valves, and of the mixture and slow running jets, as applicable according to the carburettor design. Look very closely then run a finger nail along the slope of the needle point. If ridged, replace the needle and its seat, the latter of which is usually a screw-in fitting.

2 This needle is quite badly ridged and should be replaced and a new seating to match screwed into the top plate. Check that the needle is not bent.

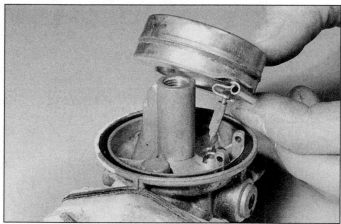

3 This type of carburettor has a different needle and float arrangement, but the same principles apply to needle and seating replacement.

4 Some carburettors are fitted with a removable bowl. This is held in position over the float by a central bolt, and incorporates a tickler in the base. Check the condition of the rubber washer of the tickler and that the tickler works freely. Check the condition of fibre washers in the bowl.

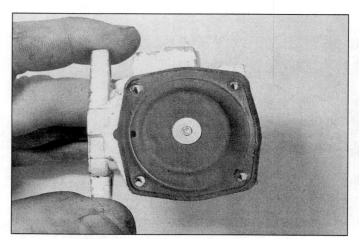

5 In diaphragm-type carburettors, visually check the state of the diaphragm. It must be in good condition and not hardened or cracked. If it is defective, replace it.

6 Always renew all gaskets and O-rings where fitted on a carburettor. The manufacturers usually supply a complete carburettor kit containing all the parts they recommend renewing as a matter of routine, when overhauling.

Spark plugs and valves

Clean with wire brush, never in a sandblasting machine; some engine manufacturers warn that its use will invalidate their guarantee. It is almost impossible to get all the abrasive particles out of the plug. If plug points are worn, or the porcelain insulation around the centre terminal is cracked or damaged, fit a new plug. It is probably better to fit a new plug even if it was renewed not long ago.

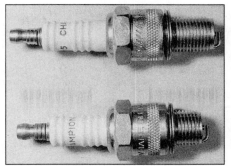

1 Be sure to get the correct plug type. Plugs have different reaches, as shown here, and the use of one with an incorrect reach may foul the engine parts. They also have different performance features, so the manufacturer's recommendations should always be followed.

2 If your engine has been performing badly, giving little power, and its exhaust valve looks like this, an overhaul is overdue.

3 This is slightly better, but the sloping face which gives the seal with its seat in the cylinder head is uneven and marked.

4 If the margin, the vertical piece above the slope, is not worn down to 0.40 mm (0.016 in), and the valve is otherwise in good condition, with the stem not worn or bent, it will be worth regrinding the valve and its seat.

5 The tool is rotated to-and-fro between the palms of the hands, and the valve lifted and turned round slightly every 15 to 20 rotations, to even out the grinding all round. Coarse grinding paste is used first, then when an even face starts to appear, it is cleaned off and fine paste used.

6 This valve being refitted has an even, very fine, smooth face all round and will seal well. Because metal has been removed, the valve will be sitting slightly lower and the valve clearance between the end of its stem and the tappet must be checked...

7 ... with a feeler gauge (doing this before the spring is fitted is easier). Make sure the valve is pressed home (by hand, or with the valve spring). If the gap is smaller than that specified for the engine, the stem of the valve must be ground down to give the correct figure.

8 Drill a hole in a block of wood, taking care to keep it at right angles, and use it like this. Rub slowly on the grinding block, and pause frequently: too fast and too long at one time may overheat the stem and destroy its temper, and it may then wear more rapidly. Note that one thumb is keeping the stem hard against the grinding block while the other hand slides the wood block to-and-fro. The hole in the wood keeps the stem vertical all the time.

Reed valves

Many 2-strokes have reed valves which consist of thin flexible springs looking rather like the blades of a feeler gauge. If cleaning is needed it should be carried out very carefully. The blades should have a gap under them, they spring slightly outwards from their mounting, the gap usually being around 0.125 to 0.25 mm (0.005 to 0.010 in). If they are bent or kinked, or the gap is greater than this, replacements should be fitted. Reed valves close off the crankcase from the carburettor inlet manifold while the new petrol and air mixture is being moved to the combustion chamber and the exhaust gases are being discharged, so their operation is important to the efficiency of the engine. Some 2-stroke engines have a three-port arrangement in the cylinder and do not need reed valves.

Cylinder head

Various tools have been suggested for cleaning off cylinder block surfaces, heads and the tops of valves and pistons: a coin, which is relatively soft and, used with care, should not damage even aluminium engines; an old blunt screwdriver can also be used with a little pressure. Possibly the best of all is a wire brush in a drill head, with plenty of oil. The series of surfaces, fitted with a gasket ready to receive the cylinder head, is in perfect condition and was prepared by this last method. Never use caustic soda solution. It will dissolve aluminium and produce an explosive gas.

Piston and rings

1 Pistons should be cleaned off, the rings removed by easing them gently out of their grooves, and the grooves cleaned with an old piece of piston ring ground down to a chisel edge. Clean also the back of the piston rings. Great care is necessary, as the cast iron rings are very brittle.

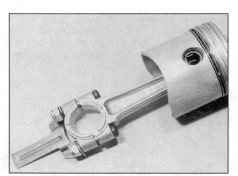

2 These grooves are clean, the bottom oil ring has been fitted and the parts assembled to check for wear. Always note which way round the piston fits in the cylinder, which end of the gudgeon pin is at which side of the piston, and which way round the connecting rod fits inside the piston. This rod has identification marks one side; mark that side of the piston (inside) if there is no way of identifying it. The two halves of the split big-end bearing must go together the same way they came off.

3 Note that the two piston rings do not have their gaps in line with one another: one faces the camera, the other is at the top at about 90°. With three sets of rings, stagger them at about 120°, evenly round the piston. The pistons of most 2-strokes (but not all) have pegs in their ring grooves so that the rings will only fit in one position and cannot move when fitted: this is to prevent them from fouling the ports inside the cylinder.

Note: *The gudgeon pin on some engines is a tight fit and the piston needs warming up in hot water before the pin will go in; do not strike or use force, pistons can be fairly fragile, and it is easy to bend the connecting rod.*

4 Note the three ports of this 2-stroke engine cylinder. Note also they have been cleaned in preparation for the rebuild. A piston ring is being measured with a feeler gauge: as it wears, the gap between its ends increases. Technical Data in each chapter gives the limits at which new rings should be fitted.

5 A safe way to insert a ring for measurement in the cylinder bore is vertically, then turn it carefully while inside the cylinder. A good method for getting it level in the bore is to insert the piston upside down and push the ring into position for measurement. Usually the place to measure is with the ring about 19 mm (0.75 in) below the top but on Victa 2-strokes it should be near the bottom of the cylinder. For Victa, it is recommended not to fit new piston rings only, always a new piston and rings.

Important: *If in any doubt about the state of the cylinder, piston and rings, or any similar group of parts, take the complete set and the cylinder block to your service station. They have special tools for accurate measurement and can, if necessary, supply complete sets of matched parts to the manufacturer's specification, to suit the condition of your engine. This applies also to the crankshaft and camshaft.*

Crankshaft and camshaft

1 Examine the bearing surfaces on the crankshaft and camshaft. If there is grooving through wear or lack of lubrication causing an accumulation of dirt in the bearings, run a fingernail along. If grooving is only just detectable, it may be left as it is, but if grooved badly as on the crankpin in the photograph, take the advice of your service agent. Crankshafts can be reground and a connecting rod supplied to fit, in most cases but it may be cheaper to replace the engine – your service dealer will advise.

Important: *Never fit a new crankshaft or a reground crankshaft in the original bearings.*

2 Note the soft aluminium plates in the vice to protect the surfaces of the crankshaft. Never clamp a part in a vice without protection.

3 Examine the bushes (or ball-bearings) in which the shafts run. They should be a close fit and not show wear. Clean ball-bearings in solvent to remove all lubrication, then spin them close to the ear: they should run reasonably freely and without noise when unloaded. Renew a bearing if it shows undue movement along the axis (along the length of the shaft when fitted), or is noisy. If plain bushes are used in the crankcase for the shafts, and these are worn, it is uneconomic to repair them.

4 Examine the lobes of the cams, which should be of uniform shape, not worn. Examine the gears of the camshaft and crankshaft for wear: is there undue play/backlash between them?

Engine Castings

Check engine castings for cracking and stripped threads – threads can be restored by fitting the correct size of thread insert but cracked castings should be replaced.

Lubrication system

1 Always renew oil seals: sometimes there is a dust cover on the outside. Note very carefully which way round it fits. If inserted the wrong way the engine sump will empty itself quite rapidly, in all probability making a horrible mess of the mower (and of the engine if the leak is not noticed soon enough).

2 Examine very closely all bearing bushes, big-end bearings and connecting rods, to look for oilways drilled in them. Make sure these are clear after cleaning the part; quite often the dirt is washed into the oilway and sits there, blocking the oil and causing rapid wear of the parts not receiving lubrication. There are always oilways in engines with oil pumps, and shafts are sometimes drilled through, end-to-end, as a passage for the oil.

3 Check self-aligning bearings are free to rock in all directions, and grease them well. They are often used to give freedom of movement to a drive shaft and its connection with a driven shaft: as when an engine crankshaft is driving a chain sprocket shaft of a cylinder mower, for example.

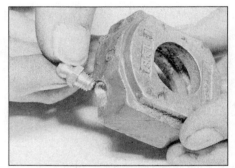

4 Cylinder mowers have numerous oiling points to lubricate the bearings of the cutting cylinder, roller and other parts. As shown here, it is sometimes possible to tap a thread in the oiling hole and fit a nipple. Use of a grease gun has advantages in that it forces the grease or oil on to the moving surfaces and at the same time helps to force the dirt and other contaminations away from the outside of the bearing. Furthermore, the admission point of the lubricant will be sealed off automatically.

5 Always treat the springs of starters with respect. If they come out they will unwind very rapidly and can cause injury. This spring is in a container: keep it in the container if it is necessary to remove it from the housing. Put a strip of wood across and tie round to prevent any possibility of its unwinding.

6 In numerous places in the manual it is advised to mark the position of the contact breaker mounting plate before any dismantling, immediately the flywheel has been removed. This position determines the time that the spark will jump the terminals of the spark plug and fire the petrol-air mixture. Precise timing is essential for correct engine operation. A worn flywheel-to-crankshaft key can affect timing and cause poor ignition. Fit a new key if wear is present.

Electronic ignition

Engines fitted with electronic ignition have no contact breaker points and therefore do not need to have their ignition timed. The spark is triggered automatically every time the magnetic mass built into the flywheel rotates past the solid state ignition assembly. The positioning of the latter is built into the engine and the ignition system is non-adjustable.

Points

Check the gap between the contact breaker points if the engine is fitted with a conventional breaker ignition. The gap should be 0.51 mm (0.020 in) or as recommended by the engine manufacturer. Before checking the gap make sure the points are clean, i.e. there is not a pip on one point and a crater on the other. Small pips and craters can be cleaned off using a fine carborundum stone, but if large ones are present, fit new points. If new points quickly develop a new pip and crater, the condenser is weak and should be renewed. If the spark at the plug appears weak and yellowish rather than strong and blue, this could also mean a weak condenser. This is often confirmed by the engine starting when cold but misfiring and refusing to spark as it gets hotter. The fibre heel of the moving point should be lubricated with a small blob of grease where it bears on the cam sleeve. On most engines the contact breakers are located underneath the flywheel. Refer to the relevant engine chapter for instructions on removing flywheels.

Briggs & Stratton points

1 Fit the capacitor under the clamp, but leave the clamp untightened. Push the fibre cam follower rods alongside and push it home

2 Fit the coil spring over the centre contact of the capacitor. Fit the post; the lug in the boss fits into the slot of the post

3 Fit the end of the moving contact arm into the slot of the post and hook the coil spring into the arm and over the second post.

4 Feed the wire from the magneto, with the earthing wire, through the centre post of the capacitor, which is held by a small coil spring. The cable slots into the casting.

5 Check the points gap. This should be 0.51 mm (0.020 in). The easiest way to position the engine on compression (both valves closed) with the points fully open is to turn it by means of the flywheel, which will have to be removed to adjust the fixed contact to the required setting.

6 Setting completed. Note the key in the keyway of the shaft, needed to turn the shaft by the flywheel. Always use an aluminium key, never a steel one.

7 Fit the contact breaker cover.

Tecumseh points

1 Fit the contact breaker assembly. Line up with the marks made when dismantling, and tighten it down.

2 Slide the contact breaker cam over the shaft. Fit the fixed contact but do not tighten.

3 Fit the moving contact assembly. The plastic mounting fits into a recess, the cam follower over the pivot on the fixed contact assembly.

4 Turn the crankshaft until the follower is exactly on top of the cam lobe. Move the fixed contact until the gap is 0.51 mm (0.020 in). Tighten the fixed contact locking screw.

5 Recheck the contact breaker gap. Connect the brown wire, the black wire and the black shorting out wire to the terminal post.

6 Fit the cover and secure it with the clip.

Reassembly

Lubrication

1 All rotating and rubbing surfaces of the engine and mower must be lubricated during their assembly, unless instructions are to the contrary. Ball-bearings and roller bearings must be greased. Plain bearings, shafts, gudgeon pins, big-end bearings, piston rings must be oiled: use engine oil for 4-strokes, light machine oil for 2-strokes. If this is not done, considerable wear will be caused during the first run up of the engine; if the worst does not happen, such as a partial seizure.

2 Oil seals must be oiled before insertion, and before passing the shaft through. If this is not done, it is possible to split the lip of the seal, so that it will no longer embrace the shaft closely all round, and the oil will get through. In passing, it may be mentioned that seals have a right way and a wrong way of being fitted: this will have been noted with the old seal. Sometimes the seals have instructions printed on one surface.

3 Drive chains on cylinder mowers should be thoroughly cleaned, then regreased. Belts should not be lubricated; if noisy, use French chalk dusted on the rubbing surfaces. Remember that chains and belts which are adjusted too tightly will absorb engine power, besides wearing the chain and sprockets, or belt and pulleys, unnecessarily rapidly. If no specific figure is given, about 13 mm (0.5 in) slack in the middle of the longest run is a general guide. With spring-loaded idlers taking up the slack, of course, adjustment is automatic, and some models have these on chains and belts.

4 The assembly of cylinder mowers gives an excellent opportunity to grease all the working parts very thoroughly. This not only lubricates the rubbing surfaces but helps to keep out grass juices, grit and other contaminants.

Fitting

As when dismantling, reassembly needs careful attention and slow, gentle handling. Force is seldom needed and never sensible, whereas a sharp tap at the right places, once everything is lined up in the correct position, is strength used intelligently. If anything will not go together, and one hits a positive obstruction, stop and investigate.

Tightening

1 It is possible to find the correct degree of torquing, or exact amount of tightening required, for most nuts and bolts, but few owners will have tools of the sizes required if they have any at all. Figures have been given for the more important fasteners.

2 The technique of tightening correctly without a torque wrench is to be aware of the feel you are getting from the spanner. Tighten first as far as is easy, until a definite stop is felt. Then give a firm, steady pull as far as it feels it wants to go. A violent jerk is not the action, because momentum can carry you too far; simply keep a firm grip and firm pressure until the fixing feels firm.

3 On rotary mowers, the bolts fixing the cutter bar or the disc, and the blades on discs, require somewhat greater force, but again, not a violent pull. Just a more positive tightening action.

4 When there are a number of bolts or nuts to the fixing, tighten them in turn, quite lightly, then more firmly, then tightly. On cylinder heads, tighten in turn diagonally and work round the head, crossing from side-to-side.

5 Be sure to fit shakeproof washers if they were found when dismantling. At some points on some engines slotted locking plates with ears (tabs) are used under nuts or bolt heads: this is the case with some oil spoilers on big-ends. Turn the ears up against one face, after tightening.

6 After tightening, always check the freedom of moving parts, to be sure there is no binding. After tightening big-end bearings, for example, check that the connecting rod can be slid slightly from side-to-side along the crankpin: and when released, it should fall down below the crankpin by its own weight, quite freely.

7 Check the freedom of the camshaft and crankshaft in their bearings, before connecting them up, engaging the gears, and so forth. Common sense, in short, is a good guide to good rebuilding.

Testing and carburettor adjustments

1 Mower engines are relatively simple mechanisms and do not have many adjustments. One reassembles them the way they were, with the throttle, governor, and other controls in the same positions.

2 These are permanent settings, for the most part. Certainly the governor connections should not be disturbed, but having overhauled the engine it is likely to perform in a different manner from that when it was last used. One item which may need attention is the carburettor.

3 Some carburettors have no adjustment while some have just one adjustment, the idler screw. This spring-loaded screw presses on the carburettor control, to which the cable throttle control is fitted, and determines the speed of the engine when the hand throttle is closed. Run the engine until thoroughly warm, and adjust to give a reliable tickover.

4 Other carburettors may have one or two more adjusters, also spring-loaded. One is likely to have most effect when the engine is running about half speed, fairly fast, the other on tickover. The latter, slow-running control of the petrol supply is normally left alone. Run the engine until really warm, from 3 to 5 minutes, depending on the weather.

5 Remember not to screw the adjusting screw in tightly, you can damage the seating. Be gentle. With the engine running fairly fast, screw in until it will go no further or until the engine starts to falter or stalls, whichever happens first. Then turn it in the opposite direction until the engine starts to 'hunt' with an uneven beat, counting the number of turns. Finally, set the screw half way between the two positions.

6 The above procedure takes care of variations in the condition of engines, the effect of fitting new parts, and other variables, and will normally result in a satisfactory adjustment. If, however, the engine seems to lack power under load, unscrew a further $\frac{1}{4}$ turn to give a slightly richer mixture.

7 Some operating instructions issued with the mower give quite explicit guidance on adjusting the carburettor: if so, then obviously that advice must be followed. A crude guide is that if the engine lacks power, the mixture is too weak (too little petrol in the petrol-air mixture), if it seems to run roughly and /or produce smoke, especially on speeding up, and the exhaust system gets clogged quickly with soft carbon, the mixture is too rich.

Note: *The above procedure follows an overhaul, when it is known that valve clearances (on a 4-stroke) and contact breaker and spark plug gaps have just been set. At any other time, remember that satisfactory running may be impossible unless these are correct.*

Sharpening blades

Rotary cutters

Examine cutting edges regularly. This will not only enable you to check their condition but also to look for corrosion of the cutting area as well as nicks or more serious damage to the blades themselves. Small nicks can be filed away but, with larger ones, resharpening is not really practical as so much of the metal has to be removed right along the blade edge: more seriously, balance will be affected and the other side must then be attended to both for safety and for the sake of avoiding engine damage through vibration.

Rotary cutters take many forms. Some cutter bars have an integral sharpened edge at each end, others have cutting blades bolted on. Cutting discs may have two blades, three blades or two blades plus two grass deflectors. In all cases, these are bolted on. Some blades are triangular, giving three cutting edges which can be used in turn as they get blunted.

It is very important for safety to inspect all bolts and fittings very carefully. Any looseness must be investigated: is the locknut losing its grip? Is the shakefree washer (if fitted) too flattened or blunted to do its job? Is there any sign of the bolt hole becoming enlarged? If the enlargement is unmistakable then it is likely that the bolts will work loose again, despite the use of locknuts or other locking devices: a new disc is the only safe step here.

It goes without saying that the central fixing bolt holding the bar or disc to the end of the engine crankshaft must always be checked. Most of them are tightened down on a Belleville washer, with the domed surface always on the bolt head side. These washers are not merely washers, they are also springs, because of their shape, and the important advantage of this is that when parts settle down during the running of the mower, the Belleville washer still retains its pressure on the bolt and prevents it from loosening any further. Another advantage is that if the cutter strikes a heavy object it is free to give and spin round under the washer, which still retains its grip and continues to hold the cutter and make it turn again once the obstruction has been cleared.

Sharpening

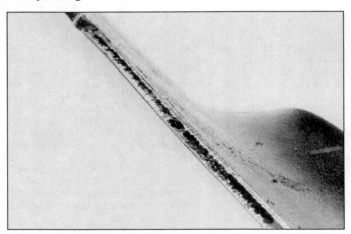

1 Sharpen to an angle of 30°, and keep the angle even all along the cutting edge, as shown here. Note that the back of the blade is turned up to form a grass deflector.

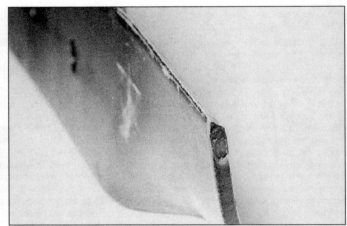

2 Do not sharpen to a point as this will quickly burr over and give a poor cutting edge. Leave a slight shoulder of about 0.4 mm (0.16 in) as shown here. This will wear back to give a good, long lasting edge.

Balancing

Whatever the type of cutter, the general procedure is the same. One needs a thin steel rod, the smaller the better: this is supported firmly in a horizontal position and the bar or disc balanced on it through its fixing hole, as shown in the illustrations. For best results the rod must be of much smaller diameter than the hole, and of course it must be straight.

Having been thoroughly cleaned, the bar or disc is supported on the rod. First, test the dimensions. Fix a thin strip of metal or other suitable pointer alongside the tip of one of the blades so that it just touches. Turn the bar or disc a half-circle until the other cutter is against the pointer. The difference should not be more than 1.50 mm (0.06 in).

Before correcting any difference, check the balance. Set the blades at the same height, with the bar parallel with the floor, and release gently. Unless the cutter bar or disc has been damaged, it is most likely that the longer side will dip towards the floor, showing it is out of balance. If so, make a few strokes of a file across the end of the longer part and recheck balance. Keep doing this until it no longer dips when released. As a check, turn it through a half-circle and check the balance again.

If the dimensions were correct, which is usually the case, but there is indication of being out of balance, file off the back of the bar or cutter, not the end. The secret with the filing is a little at a time. The better the all-round balance you can get, the more smoothly will the mower run and the less wear and strain there will be on the engine.

With a disc with four fittings, say two cutters and two grass deflectors, balance with the cutters only and then with the deflectors only. A disc with three blades is more difficult, but do a particularly careful check on their dimensions first. Then spin the disc several times to check whether it always tends to settle with one blade nearer the bottom. If so, it is likely that the disc assembly is slightly heavier at that point.

Important: *Bent blades, uneven length fittings or bars, and bent bars, are best discarded and new ones obtained and fitted.*

Cylinder cutters

No instructions have been given for regrinding the blades of cutting cylinders, because this is one operation which can only be carried out satisfactorily on a machine made specially for the purpose, such as those used in lawnmower repair establishments. It is worth considering the requirements for correct grinding.

The cutting cylinder may have anything from 3 blades, as on the smallest lightweight machines, to 12 blades on larger models in the higher price brackets. The blades may be straight or slightly curved: either way, they are set at an angle to the axle of the cylinder. All these blades do the cutting by a scissor action against the bottom blade. As each cylinder blade comes round and strokes the bottom blade, it is in contact with it at only one point at any given moment. Contact must therefore be maintained between the angled blade on the cylinder and the straight bottom blade all along its length, otherwise there will be gaps in the cutting.

Another way of looking at it is from either end, along the axle. Every part of every blade must describe a perfect circle of exactly the same diameter as it spins, so that all the blades together are rather like a cylinder (hence the name) whose outside edge is always in contact with the bottom blade. And this is only the start.

The surface of the cutting edge of the bottom blade is at an angle. Each blade on the cylinder must therefore be ground at the same angle. Multiply these requirements by from 3 to 12 times, and one would have to be a masochist to want to attempt doing the job at home.

The special grinding machines referred to can be adjusted to an accuracy of at least 0.4mm (0.016 in). The cutting cylinder is supported in its own bearings, so that it spins as precisely as it does when in the mower. A grinding wheel, set at the required angle and driven by an electric motor, is mounted alongside on an accurate slide and passes from end-to-end of the cylinder, which is steadily spinning. The cylinder has been sprayed with paint all over, so that as the grinding progresses it is easy to be sure when all the nicks and jags on the blades have been ground off, as only a straight, smooth and paint-free edge can then be seen. When all blades have a complete cutting edge, smooth and clean and sharp, the machine is set to make several passes, grinding in both directions: this evens out any differences between the cutting edges and removes any slight roughness; it also dresses the grinding wheel itself in readiness for the next cylinder.

Bottom blade

It is possible to regrind a bottom blade which is in good condition although this is seldom worthwhile. To obtain the best performance from the refurbished cylinder it is best to renew the blade. During use of a mower it may happen that a bottom blade, if rather lightweight and struck by some object, becomes bowed or dished. Obviously in this condition the scissor action cannot be complete at all points and poor cutting will result. It is sometimes possible to insert shims at its mounting points so that when screwed down it tends to straighten out.

Set the bottom blade so that it only just makes contact with the cylinder blades as the latter rotate. Too firm a contact wears both blade and cylinder cutting edges, causes noisy operation and puts an extra load on the engine.

To check cutting efficiency, hold a single thickness of thin paper across the bottom blade cutting edge, so that it points more-or-less at the cylinder axle, then carefully turn the cylinder by hand. Be very careful as the blades are sharp enough to cause serious injury. Scissor action between fixed and moving blades should cut the paper. Repeat at various points along the bottom blade, using all the cylinder blades. Ideally, the paper should be cut at any point along the bottom blade by any cylinder blade.

Some users may prefer to have a very slight clearance between the bottom blade and the cylinder blades; this gives very quiet operation while still giving a good cut, provided the blades are sharp.

Lapping

Grinding leaves slight roughness on one edge, which will be taken off against the bottom blade during mowing, the blade being further adjusted after 'running in'. If preferred, the cutting cylinder can be lapped.

Lapping compound can be obtained; it is usually oil mixed with grit, sizes between 100 and 300 microns, for this purpose. It is applied to the blades and the cylinder is turned backwards, in the opposite direction to mowing. Usually this can be done by fitting a brace on a nut on its shaft and turning by hand. Both the blades on the cylinder and the bottom blade and all fittings must be cleaned thoroughly afterwards as the grit will quickly damage moving parts such as bearings and chains. The bottom blade is set close for the operation, and after cleaning is readjusted and a paper cutting test carried out as described under the previous heading.

Lapping can also be used to sharpen up a slightly dulled set of blades. It can improve matters and give better mowing for a time, but cannot compensate for any nicks or chips in the blades; only grinding will remove these. Patent devices for 'grinding' at home, the 'work of a few minutes' and 'saving yourself mower repair depot charges' are really a variation of lapping and subject to the same limitations of being a temporary solution which has to be repeated after a comparatively short time. Only a grinding machine will give durable resharpening which will result in a high quality finish to a lawn.

Routine maintenance

Every month or every 12 hours operation

Important: *New 4-stroke mowers should have the sump drained and refilled with fresh oil after the first 2 to 3 hours operation.*

☐ Remove the spark plug and clean the electrodes with a wire brush. Reset gap to 0.76 mm (0.030 in), or as recommended by manufacturer.

☐ Check condition of electrical leads and for looseness.

☐ Rotary mowers: check cutting edges of cutter bar or disc blades. File down small nicks only. If large nicks are evident, remove cutter assembly and check balance.

☐ Check the security of all nuts and bolts.

☐ Cylinder mowers: check the setting of the bottom blade to ensure it has the correct 'scissors' action with the blades of the cutting cylinder.

☐ If necessary, lubricate the moving parts of the height adjusters and controls.

Every two months or every 25 hours operation

☐ Service the air filter.

☐ Clean the contact breaker points (unless electronic ignition). Turn the engine to give the widest gap and reset this to correct figure.

☐ 4-strokes: Drain and refill the oil sump.

☐ Check the fuel filter (if fitted). If a filter is not fitted, remove the top of carburettor and check for dirt.

☐ Run the engine for 3 to 5 minutes until it has thoroughly warmed through. Check the idling and speeding up response and adjust the carburettor, if necessary.

☐ Remove cutter bar or disc and check the balance.

☐ Adjust the hand control settings if necessary, including clutches on cylinder mowers, and self-propelled mowers.

☐ Adjust the chains or belts on cylinder mowers and self-propelled mowers, if necessary.

☐ Lubricate all mower parts as appropriate, including the height adjustment.

☐ Check the blades are not bent (cylinder mower).

☐ Check the condition of the blade edges on cylinder mowers. If necessary, lap the edges by turning the cylinder backwards (with a handbrace on the shaft or other means), having lapping compound on the bottom blade and the bottom blade set close. When the edges have improved, clean off all compound very thoroughly and reset the bottom blade.

☐ Grease the chains (if fitted). Inspect the condition of any drive belts to check for cracking.

Important: *In dusty operating conditions, more frequent servicing of the air and fuel filters, and changing of the engine oil, will be needed.*

End of season or every 75 hours operation

☐ Check engine compression (use a screw-in compression tester). If not very satisfactory, consider overhaul.

☐ Remove cylinder head (obtain new gasket). Remove carbon deposits. Inspect valves and consider regrinding; adjust tappet clearance (4-strokes).

☐ 2-strokes: clean out ports with a wooden tool and blow out all carbon. Wipe clean carefully.

☐ Check the starter mechanism and renew the cord, if necessary. On models which have sharp pawls gripping a cup (without recesses, the non-ratchet type), sharpen up the pawls with a file, to improve the grip.

☐ Drain oil sump (4-strokes) very thoroughly. Refill with fresh oil of the recommended viscosity.

☐ Dismantle and clean out the carburettor, fitting new gaskets when reassembling.

☐ Dismantle and clean out the fuel tap. Clean the fuel filter, if fitted.

☐ Check and clear the vent hole in the petrol tank cap.

☐ If there is a valve on the crankcase breather in the valve chest, check whether it works freely. If not, dismantle, clean, and renew parts if necessary, and refit using a new gasket set.

☐ Air filter: fit a new paper cartridge, or if polyurethane foam or stocking and dry element type, wash and if still looking dirty consider obtaining a replacement.

☐ Check the condition of the cutting blades on rotary mowers and consider fitting a new set (with new bolts and fittings, never the old set) or consider dismantling cylinder mower to send the cutting cylinder away for regrinding.

☐ Check the wear of all bearings in the mower and consider what action is to be taken. New bearings can be fitted, and plain bushes usually can be reamed out and fitted with new insert bushes. If the hole in the bush has worn oval or the wear is offset, fit a new bush, as hand reaming a new hole concentrically is extremely difficult.

Fault-finding

Notes
- It is assumed that starting procedures were correct.
- It is assumed the starter is turning the engine over smartly. If not it should be removed and the starter fault rectified.
- Always have a fire extinguisher to hand.
- Do not work in a confined or enclosed space.

Mower will not start
- Check that the shorting-out strip is not touching the top of the plug.
- If the shorting out connection is at the carburettor, check this does not foul any part and provide a way to earth.
- Check the spark plug, remove and inspect.
- If wet, petrol is getting there.
- Hold spark plug with screw portion against engine and spin with starter. If no spark, remove the lead and hold it about 1.50 to 2.00 mm (0.06 to 0.08 in) from a clean part of the top of the cylinder head, and spin again. If there is a spark, the plug is faulty and needs renewing.
- If no spark, check the contacts in the contact breaker for correct gap and make sure points are clean.
- Check the connections through the ignition system, for loose wires or screw fittings.
- If the mower still will not start, change the capacitor.
- If the plug is dry and there is a spark, check that there is petrol in the tank, check the fuel filter is not blocked, and check petrol line right through.
- If the plug is wet and there is a spark check that the air cleaner is not choked.

Important: *Never run the engine without the air cleaner, even for a few moments.*
- If the air cleaner is clear, check the choke setting.
- Check the carburettor adjustments.
- Check exhaust muffler is not blocked especially on 2-stroke engines.

Mower starts, but gives low power
- Dirty air filter.
- Governor sticky or movement blocked.
- Fuel restricted.
- Throttle or mixture controls incorrectly set.
- Blocked exhaust ports (2-strokes) or carbon in exhaust muffler.
- Mower parts clogged with grass, etc.
- Badly adjusted chains or belts, and/or clutch out of adjustment, causing drag; tight chains and belts consume power.
- Poor crankcase seal (2-strokes).
- Faulty reed valve, or dirty reed valve (2-strokes).

Mower runs unevenly
- Incorrect mixture setting, probably too rich.
- Loose dirt in fuel line.
- Sticky carburettor controls.
- Blocked exhaust system.
- Loose hand controls or cables which move with movements of mower.
- Reed valve choked (2-strokes).

Engine misses when driving mower
- Dirty spark plug: clean and then reset gap. Renew, if in poor condition.
- Pitted contact breaker points: file smooth or renew points, and reset gap.
- Contact breaker moving point arm is sticky: remove and clean pivot, lubricate with one drop of machine oil.
- Valve clearance incorrect, or weak valve springs (4-strokes).
- Carburettor adjustment incorrect, probably richer mixture needed.
- Reed valve choked (2-strokes).

Engine knocks
- Carbon in combustion chamber.
- Flywheel loose: remove starter and check that key in keyway of shaft is correctly located. Check Belleville washer has domed side uppermost and retighten securing nut.
- Check for wear on main and connecting rod bearings.

Note: *If after checks performance still seems poor, the engine may need overhauling. A quick check on compression is as follows:*

2-strokes
Turn the engine slowly, one complete revolution. Repeat several times. There should be a distinct resistance to turning, but much more resistance during one half-turn than during the other half-turn.

4-strokes
Spin the engine the opposite way to normal running (anti-clockwise viewed from the flywheel end in the case of Briggs & Stratton engines). There should be a sharp rebound.

Notes

Chapter 3
Briggs & Stratton MAX 4hp 4-stroke engine

Model/spec. number on engines: 110700, 111700, 112700, 114700

Mower application

Every effort has been made to make the list of models that use this engine as comprehensive as possible. Due to model and engine supply changes, you may have a mower that is not listed. Refer to *Engine Identity* on page 6 to identify the engine that you have, or contact an engine supply dealer to assist with identification.

Atco	Hayter Harrier 2	Husqvarna
Flymo	Hayter Hawk	Mountfield Emperor
Hayter Harrier	Hayter Hunter 48	Mountfield Empress

Technical data

Spark plug gap	0.75 mm (0.030 in)
Armature air gap	0.25 to 0.36 mm (0.010 to 0.014 in)
Valve clearance:	
Inlet	0.13 to 0.18 mm (0.005 to 0.007 in)
Exhaust	0.23 to 0.28 mm (0.009 to 0.011 in)
Breather disc valve clearance	1.10 mm (0.043 in)
Wire gauge must not enter space between valve and body	
Ring gap not to exceed:	
Compression rings	0.80 mm (0.031 in)
Oil ring	1.14 mm (0.045 in)
Cylinder wear:	
Rebore if oversize is greater than	0.08 mm (0.003 in)
Or ovality greater than	0.06 mm (0.0024 in)
Oil	SAE 30 or SAE 10W-30
Oil capacity	0.6 litres

Dismantling

Read Chapter 2 for hints and tips on dismantling and reassembly before starting to dismantle. The information given there will assist an orderly and methodical approach to engine overhaul.

1 Remove battery.
2 Unclip starter cord from handle.
3 Disconnect the electrical connection from starter.
4 Remove air filter.
5 Remove power drive belt cover.
6 Remove the two bolts securing the power drive shaft bearing under the cover.
7 Tip mower backwards to stand on grass deflector.
8 Remove cutter bar and friction disc. A puller may be needed, take care not to bend the disc.
9 Remove Woodruff key from crankshaft.
10 Remove engine drain plug, drain oil into suitable container, refit the drain plug.
11 Remove throttle cable, noting the position of it.
12 Undo three engine mounting bolts and remove engine, support the engine while undoing the last bolt to avoid it falling out,

release belt from power drive pulley as you are removing the engine.
13 Remove starter cover.
14 Remove fuel tank assembly held by three small bolts and one larger one, disconnect fuel pipe from tap.
15 Remove engine cowl and dipstick tube.
16 Remove battery charging coils, note the small spacer under the coil on the back bolt.
17 Take off air filter housing, disconnect engine breather pipe from rear.
18 Unhook stop wire from throttle control plate.
19 Unbolt and remove electric starter unit.
20 Remove carburettor and throttle control plate, carefully noting positions and order of governor links and spring.
21 Remove ignition coil.
22 Remove mesh screen from starter clutch.
23 Unscrew and remove starter clutch, flywheel may be jammed with screwdriver in starter teeth against rear post. Turn starter with large stilsons or special removing tool. Remove washer.
24 Remove flywheel *(see advice in Chapter 2)*.
25 Remove exhaust screen then bend back locking tabs and remove two exhaust mounting bolts.

26 Remove engine breather from valve chest, note steel plate attached to top bolt.
27 Slacken and remove remaining cylinder head bolts, remove cylinder head and gasket.
28 Turn the engine over and remove power drive cover and gasket.
29 Remove shaft retainer from slot then shaft may be slid inwards to give access to sump bolt inside sump.
30 Clean any rust or debris from the crankshaft with emery cloth to avoid damaging the seal when you take the sump off.
31 Remove six sump bolts, remove sump.
32 Remove camshaft with governor and oil slinger, make notes of any shims that may be on the end of the camshaft.
33 Remove cam followers.
34 Remove big end cap.
34 Remove any carbon from top of cylinder bore and push piston out through the top, taking care not to damage the bore. Remove crankshaft. Remove valve springs using special valve tool or spanner head, push plate up valve stem and pull towards notch to release. **Note:** *exhaust valve spring is longer than inlet spring.*
36 Finally, remove the valves.

Reassembly

1   Clean all parts in paraffin or engine degreaser, remove all traces of old gaskets from mating faces of sump, engine block and cylinder head. Do this very carefully so as not to damage the aluminium castings. Clean carbon from valves, exhaust port and piston crown, and lap in valves as explained in Chapter 2 but do not refit the springs yet as the valve clearances will have to be checked later.

2   Check the condition of all bearings in the engine (pictures show bearing locations) and check the crankshaft for wear on big end and main bearing journals as described in Chapter 2.

3   Check condition of cylinder bore for deep scratches. Check castings for cracks and also check condition of crankshaft seals and power take-off (PTO) shaft seal.

5 Carefully remove piston rings noting which way up they were and the position in the grooves. Slide them one by one about 25 mm (1 in) down cylinder bore and check that the gap between the ends of the rings does not exceed the limits in the specifications; replace the rings if the ring gap is excessive.

6 Check small end bearing for wear by holding the piston in one hand and twisting the connecting rod in the other. The piston should slide freely on the pin but not rock. If worn, the connecting rod and gudgeon pin must be replaced.

4 Refit gear on power take-off shaft. Roll pin goes through the gear and hole in the shaft, locking the two together.

7 Lubricate the main bearing in the crankcase and the tapered end of the crankshaft with engine oil. Fit crankshaft into the crankcase.

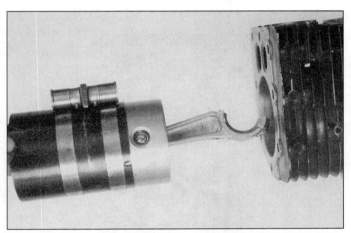

8 Lubricate piston and cylinder bore and refit piston. A piston ring clamp will have to be fitted to compress the piston rings before sliding the piston into bore. The open end of the big end cap should face the valves as shown in this picture. Lower piston carefully into the bore taking care not to scratch it. Push piston out of clamp with hammer handle. This should happen reasonably easily; if any obstruction is felt stop to investigate the cause.

9 Oil the big end bearing and refit big end cap.

10 Be sure to tighten securely as there are no locking tabs. Rotate the crankshaft to check for free movement.

11 Lubricate and refit cam followers making sure they are replaced in their original holes.

12 Rotate crankshaft so timing dimple in the gear is facing towards the camshaft bearing hole.

13 Fit camshaft so that the timing marks in crankshaft and camshaft align – remembering any shims that were on the camshaft when dismantled.

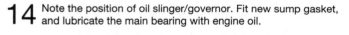

14 Note the position of oil slinger/governor. Fit new sump gasket, and lubricate the main bearing with engine oil.

15 Slide the sump gently down the crankshaft. Make sure the oil slinger and camshaft are in their correct positions and the locating dowels line up with their holes.

16 Fit the sump bolts, the short one goes into the hole beside the power take-off gear. Tighten the bolts evenly to avoid cracking or distorting the sump.

17 Slide the power take-off shaft carefully and twist it to engage gear.

18 The shaft locating plate may now be placed in its slot to lock the shaft in position.

19 Fit a new gasket and secure the power take-off cover with the four small bolts.

20 Check valve clearances. The valve must be held down firmly in its seat with the piston at top dead centre on the firing stroke (with both valves closed). Feeler gauge should slide between valve stem and cam followers without moving the valve. Clearances are given in specifications at the beginning of this chapter. If the clearance is too small, the end of the valve stem must be filed off slightly to give the correct gap (as described in Chapter 2).

21 Refit valve springs.

22 Remove all the carbon from the cylinder head using a soft scraper or wire brush to avoid scratching the aluminium. Place a new gasket on the cylinder. Fit the cylinder head but leave out the bolts as shown; these will be used to secure the carburettor later.

23 Remove the carburettor from throttle control plate (2 bolts), check condition of 'O' ring between plate and carburettor. Check condition of the needle valve, mixture screw and float. Clean all parts in petrol and blow through jets. Do not use wire to clear jets as this will change the size of the holes.

24 Refit needle valve and float, slide in pivot pin to secure. Screw in mixture adjusting needle gently to avoid damage to seat. Turn out 1½ turns for initial setting of mixture.

25 Refit float bowl with large rubber ring seal on the carburettor body and fibre washer and bolt. Fit carburettor throttle control plate remembering to put the 'O' ring back between carburettor and plate.

26 The correct position of governor links and spring are shown.

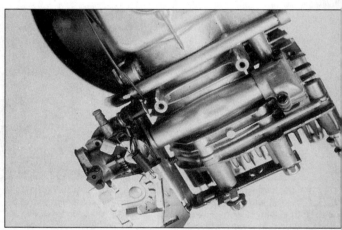

27 Refit carburettor to engine. Wipe inlet pipe end with oil to help it to enter the carburettor. Hook governor link back to plastic lever and slide carburettor on to manifold. Fit remaining cylinder head bolts and tighten in diagonal sequence.

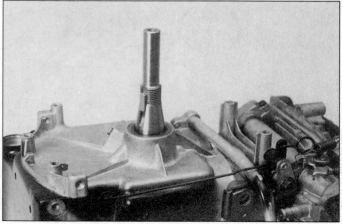

28 Inspect the flywheel key for signs of shear or other damage; if necessary replace the key with the correct replacement. Do not use a steel key. Place the key in the slot in the crankshaft.

29 Fit the flywheel onto the crankshaft taper, making sure that the keyway lines up with the key in the crankshaft.

30 Fit the washer to the crankshaft. If it is a domed washer, fit the dome upwards.

31 Screw on the recoil starter clutch. It will be necessary to jam the flywheel with a large screwdriver placed in the teeth of the flywheel and rested against one of the lugs on the back of the engine. Tighten the starter securely.

32 Fit electric starter to the engine and tighten the two bolts that secure the starter.

33 Fit the mesh screen to the starter clutch and secure with the two bolts.

34 Fit ignition coil and charging coils, remembering the small spacer on the charging coil. Do not tighten the bolts yet.

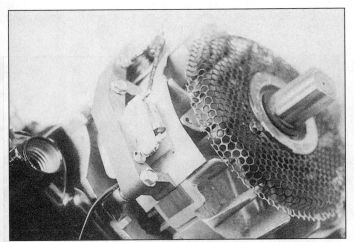

35 Set the air gap on the ignition coil and charging coil. Place a piece of plastic or card of the correct thickness, as given in Technical Data, between the coil and the flywheel magnets. The magnets will attract the coil and hold it against the card. Tighten the bolts and then rotate the flywheel to slide out the card. This process is repeated for the charging coils.

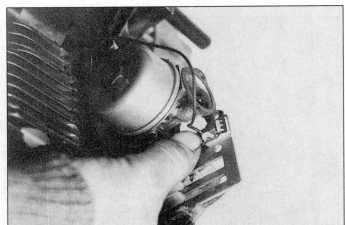

36 Fit the stop wire to throttle control plate. The spring contact should be pushed up towards the plate and the wire is then put through the hole. When the contact is released the wire is held in position.

37 Fit the engine breather with a new gasket. Remember to place the plate under the top bolt.

38 Fit the exhaust silencer. Place the locking strip on the silencer then tighten the bolts and bend over the locking tabs to secure.

39 Fit the exhaust cover with three small screws.

40 Fit the starter cover after checking operation of recoil start, (see the end of this section for full information on renewing the spring or rope). Be careful not to trap spark plug lead or charging lead under the cover. Reconnect charging lead.

41 Check the 'O' ring seal at the base of the dipstick tube for cracks, or other damage and replace where necessary. Fit the dipstick tube to the engine cowl with two bolts.

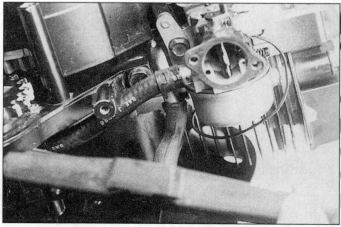

42 Fit the air filter housing, re-connecting the breather pipe at the back when it is in position with the carburettor. Secure with the two bolts.

43 Reconnect the fuel pipe to the fuel tap and fit the fuel tank, securing with three small screws and one larger one.

45 Check the condition of the air filter and if it is dirty or contaminated with oil replace it. Place the air filter in its cover and fit to the engine.

44 Fit the plastic cover over the recoil starter.

46 Refit engine to mower, engaging the power drive belt as you are putting the engine on. Make sure the power drive shaft bearing is the right way up. Insert metal spacers in the plastic bearing carrier. Fit belt retainer and bolt the assembly to the mower deck.

47 Fit the Woodruff key in the crankshaft keyway, tapping it gently home with a soft-faced hammer if necessary.

48 Grease the end of the crankshaft. Slide on the cutter friction disc and twist it gently to line up the keyway with the crankshaft key. Slide it fully home.

49 Check the cutting blade for 'nicks' or cracks. Sharpen and balance the blade as described in Chapter 2, but if it is damaged it is always worthwhile to fit a new blade.

50 Fit blade with special washer; tighten the blade bolt.

51 Hook the end of the throttle cable into its hole in the control lever and secure the outer sheath under the cable clamp. Operate the throttle control to ensure that the choke is fully closed when the control is set to choke.

52 Fit the plastic drive belt cover over the exposed end of the power take-off shaft and secure it with the bolt.

53 Fill the sump with new engine oil to the correct level. Replace the spark plug and reconnect the spark plug cap. Put fresh petrol in the fuel tank.

Electric starter

Dismantling

1 Mark position of end plate to motor body and motor body to gear housing as an aid to reassembly.
2 Remove circlip securing main gear.
3 Pull off gear and engaging spiral, check gear for wear or broken teeth.

4 Undo three bolts to remove gearbox cover.
5 Slide off the large and small gears, noting which way up they are.
6 Undo two screws securing motor back plate and slide motor away from housing. Note there are two washers on each end of the armature, one plastic on the outside then one steel. On the drive end, the steel one is a dished washer.

7 Remove the brush plate carefully and slide out the cable insulator.
8 Remove the armature and check the copper commutator for burning and wear.
9 Check the brushes for free movement and wear. If they are badly worn or burnt they should be replaced.

Reassembly

1 Put a drop of oil on bronze bush in brush plate.

2 Spread brushes and insert armature into bearing. Fit motor body to armature – carefully, as the magnets will pull the armature in. Align brush plate with locating notch and slide in the insulated wire outlet.

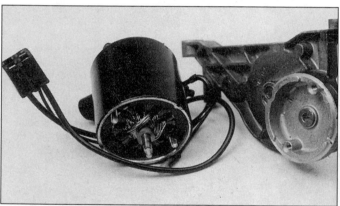

3 Assembled armature and motor body.

4 Fit washers to end of motor shaft, lubricate shaft with oil and refit to gear housing. Make sure the locating notches are aligned.

5 Reassembled motor and greased gears ready for refitting.

6 Refit gears in housing, making sure the small one is located correctly on the motor shaft.

7 Fit cover and gasket and tighten the three screws. Refit starter gear and spiral; this engages in the large gear under the cover. It is fully home when the circlip groove on the shaft is visible.

8 Fit circlip to secure the starter gear to the shaft.

Recoil starter repair

If the recoil starter cord fails to wind back into the rewind housing after being pulled, the most likely cause is a broken recoil spring. The spring is situated on top of the rope pulley. To renew the spring, proceed as follows:

1 Pull the rope fully out and clamp the pulley to hold the spring tension. Keep the knot aligned with the rope outlet hole. Cut off the knot and remove rope.

2 Slacken spring, releasing slowly with a square piece of wood as described. Take a 15 cm (6 in) length of batten, 15 mm (3/4 in) square. Drive a 10 cm (4 in) nail through one end (to enable controlled turning) and insert the other end into the centre of the pulley. Bend tabs up and remove pulley.

3 To fit new spring pass the end of the replacement spring through the hole in the side of the starter and engage in the pulley.

4 Bend down the tabs to secure the pulley. Wind the pulley anti-clockwise to pull the spring in.

5 When fully wound, in the end of the spring will engage in the narrower section in the hole in the cover.

6 Wind the spring up until tight, then back one turn or until the hole lines up with the rope outlet. Lock with self-locking pliers or a clamp and thread rope through.

7 Fit handle to the other end of the rope. Hold the cord and release the self-locking pliers or clamp. Allow the rope to draw back the starter.

Notes

Chapter 4
Briggs & Stratton Intek/Europa OHV 4-stroke engine

Model/spec. number on engine: 121602

Mower application

Every effort has been made to make the list of models that use this engine as comprehensive as possible. Due to model and engine supply changes, you may have a mower that is not listed. Refer to *Engine Identity* on page 6 to identify the engine that you have, or contact an engine supply dealer to assist with identification.

Hayter Harrier 48
IBEA 5361

Mountfield MPR series

TORO Re-cycler
26637/20791/20789/20826/20827

Technical Data

Spark plug gap	0.75 mm (0.030 in)
Spark plug type	NGK B2LM
Cylinder bore ovality limit	0.038 mm (0.0015 in)
Piston ring gap limit	0.8 mm (0.031 in)
Valve clearances:	
Inlet (cold)	0.13 to 0.18 mm (0.005 to 0.007 in)
Exhaust (cold)	0.18 to 0.23 mm (0.007 to 0.009 in)
Armature air gap	0.25 mm (0.010 in)
Oil grade	SAE 30
Oil capacity	0.6 litres

Dismantling

Before starting to dismantle, read Chapter 2. The procedures outlined apply to all engines and if adopted, will ensure an orderly and methodical approach that will make both dismantling and reassembly much easier.

Remove the engine from the mower, and proceed as follows:

1 Unscrew the two bolts and remove the air filter cover.

2 Remove the fuel filler cap and the two bolts securing the plastic engine cover. Lift off the cover. Replace the fuel filler cap.

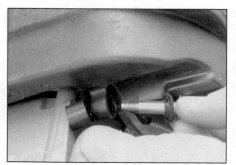

3 Release the clip and pull the supply pipe from the fuel tank. Be prepared for fuel spillage. Unscrew the four bolts securing the fuel tank. Note the position of the spacer fitted to the lower mounting bolt.

4 Using a ⅜" square drive tool, undo the sump plug and drain the engine oil into a suitable container.

5 Unscrew the three bolts and remove the exhaust shield.

6 In order to remove the engine cowling, the oil filler neck must first be removed. Unscrew the one retaining bolt and lift the filler neck away. Note the O-ring at the base of the neck. Unscrew the four bolts and remove the cowling.

7 Unscrew the four retaining bolts, and remove the exhaust system.

8 Disconnect the engine breather pipe from the air filter housing. Unscrew the two retaining bolts and remove the housing.

9 Remove the two carburettor mounting bolts, and unhook the governor linkage as the carburettor is withdrawn.

10 Unscrew the float bowl nut and remove the float bowl. Be prepared for fuel spillage.

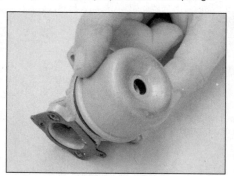

11 Push out the float pivot pin, and carefully lift out the float with the needle valve.

12 Check the condition of the needle valve and seat for any damage or wear (refer to Chapter 2). Examine the float bowl O-ring for any cracks, etc. The float bowl nut incorporates the main jet. Check that the holes are clear. If necessary, clear the holes by blowing or by the use of a thin nylon bristle. Never use a needle or wire to clean a jet. Check the float for damage or leaks.

13 Disconnect the engine stop wire from the ignition magneto, and unscrew the carburettor mounting/linkage plate retaining bolt. Lift the plate away.

14 Remove the engine cowling panel by unscrewing the one retaining bolt, and unhooking the governor linkage.

15 Carefully pull the HT cap from the spark plug. Unscrew the two bolts and remove the ignition magneto.

16 In order to remove the flywheel retaining nut, it is necessary to prevent the flywheel from turning. In the absence of the manufacturer's special tool, this can be done by using a strap wrench around the circumference of the flywheel. Do not be tempted to lever a screwdriver against the flywheel fins; being made of aluminium, they are easily damaged.

17 Remove the plastic cooling fin disc from the flywheel. Note the two locating dowels.

18 With reference to Chapter 2, pull the flywheel from the crankshaft. If you are using the manufacturer's puller, it may be necessary to cut the threads in the flywheel. The puller holes are clearly labelled in the flywheel, and the puller bolts are specially formed to cut the threads. Recover the key from the crankshaft.

19 Unscrew the four bolts and remove the breather chamber cover.

20 Unscrew the two bolts, and remove the breather cover/valve.

21 Undo the four bolts and remove the rocker cover.

22 Remove the rocker arm mounting nuts and hemispherical washers. Carefully remove the rocker arms, pushrods and valve cap pads. Note or label which components are for

the inlet and exhaust valves; it is important that, if re-used, they should be refitted to their original location.

23 Unscrew the four bolts and remove the cylinder head. It may be necessary to gently tap the cylinder head away from the engine block, but avoid levering between the block and cylinder head cooling fins. Note the cylinder head locating dowels.

24 In order to remove a valve, depress the valve collar and push it towards the notch in the rim of the collar. Although a special valve spring compressor is available, due to the size of the spring it is quite possible to compress them sufficiently by hand. The valve collars have two adjoining holes, one of which is larger than the other. This allows the valve stem to slide through the collar. Remove the spring and slide the valve from the cylinder head. It is important to label or arrange the components so that, if re-used, they are refitted to their original locations. Note the seal/spring seat fitted to the inlet valve.

25 Undo the two bolts, and remove the rocker mounting plate. Inspect the valve guides for scoring and excessive wear. Examine the valve seats and renovate as necessary (refer to Chapter 2).

26 Undo the retaining bolt and remove the remaining engine block cowling.

27 Slide the belt drive pulley from the crankshaft, and recover the Woodruff (half moon) key.

28 Remove any dirt or rust from the crankshaft, unscrew the seven retaining bolts and remove the sump. It may be necessary to gently tap the sump with a soft hammer, or piece of wood. Note the two locating dowels.

29 Slide the governor/oil slinger assembly from the end of the camshaft, and lift the camshaft from the crankcase.

30 Remove the cam followers. Note or label each follower as exhaust or inlet, as appropriate.

31 Slide the camshaft drive gear from the crankshaft. If the Woodruff (half moon) key is loose – remove it.

32 Unscrew the retaining bolts and remove the big-end cap.

33 Remove any carbon build-up at the lip of the cylinder bore using a soft tool, and gently push the connecting rod and piston assembly up and out of the cylinder. Take care not to mark the bore with the connecting rod.

34 If required, remove the piston rings from the piston by carefully expanding the rings at their ends and sliding them from the piston. Note the orientation of the rings for reassembly.

35 Remove the circlip and push the gudgeon pin from the piston.

36 Carefully withdraw the crankshaft from the crankcase.

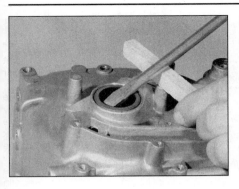

37 The crankshaft oil seals can now be prised out from the crankcase and sump. Note which way round they fit.

38 Prior to removing the governor arm and lever, mark the position of the lever on the shaft. It is essential that the lever is refitted in the original position. Remove the lever pinch-bolt, and pull the lever from the shaft. Prise off the steel 'push-on' clip, and remove the governor arm/shaft from the crankcase.

39 Check the condition of the crankshaft bearing, camshaft bearing and cylinder bore for wear, scores or cracks. If the bore is damaged, worn oval or oversized, then professional skills and special equipment will be necessary to restore it. The same applies to worn or damaged bearings. These can be reamed out to accept bushes obtainable from spares stockists, but special reaming equipment and knowledge are essential. Check all threaded holes for damaged threads, and repair if necessary by fitting a thread insert of the correct size.

Reassembly

1 Fit new oil seals into the crankcase and sump by carefully pushing them into place using an appropriate-sized socket. The seals should be fitted with the sharp rubber edge of the seal towards the inside of the engine.

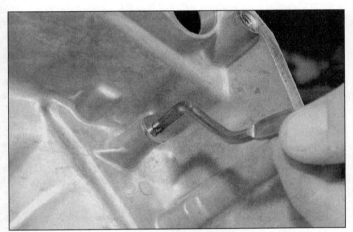

2 Fit the governor arm into the crankcase. Note the washer fitted between the arm and the crankcase on the inside.

3 Fit a new 'push-on' clip on the arm on the outside of the case.

4 Smear the crankcase bearing journal and lip of the oil seal with new engine oil, and fit the crankshaft into the crankcase, tapered end first.

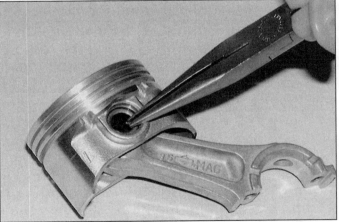

5 If previously removed, fit the gudgeon pin into the piston/connecting rod assembly. The piston is fitted with the arrow on its crown towards the tapered end of the crankshaft, and the 'open' side of the connecting rod towards the camshaft bearing. Always fit a new piston circlip. If the gudgeon pin is reluctant to move, immerse the piston in hot water for a few minutes. This causes the aluminium to expand, and the gudgeon pin to slide easily.

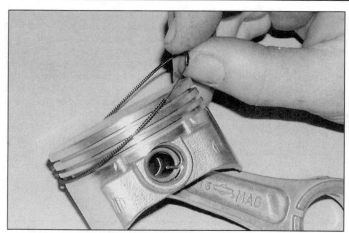

6 Fit the piston rings onto the piston. The oil control (lowest) ring should be fitted first, by carefully expanding the coiled element just enough to slide down over the piston and into its groove.

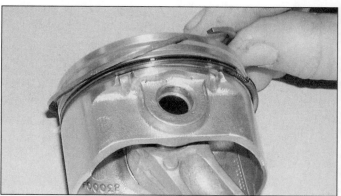

7 Next fit the second element of the oil control ring in the same manner, positioning it so that the coiled element is inside the second element. Next fit the compression ring into the middle groove. This ring must be fitted with the internal chamfer facing down. Finally fit the top compression ring with the internal chamfer facing up. **Beware:** *Piston rings are very brittle. If they are expanded too much, they will break.* Arrange the three ring-end gaps so that they are spaced out around the circumference of the piston at 120° intervals.

8 Smear the piston rings and cylinder bore with oil.

9 Using a piston ring clamp, fit the piston into the cylinder from the top by feeding the connecting rod through first. Make sure that the arrow on the top of the piston points towards the tapered end of the crankshaft, and that the connecting rod does not scratch the cylinder walls. Press the piston firmly into the cylinder, sliding it out of the clamp as the rings enter the bore. If necessary, use a piece of wood or hammer handle and gently tap the piston out of the clamp and into the cylinder; stop and investigate any undue resistance.

10 Smear some oil on the crankshaft journal and engage the big-end onto the journal.

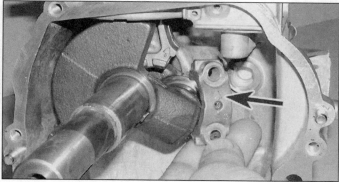

11 Fit the big-end cap, arrow mark pointing towards the piston (arrowed), and secure it with the two bolts. Tighten the bolts securely, as there are no locking devices, but do not over-tighten. Rotate the crankshaft to ensure freedom of movement.

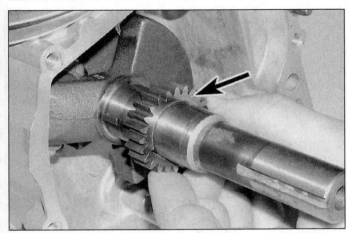

12 If previously removed, fit the Woodruff (half moon) key to the crankshaft, and fit the camshaft drive gear to the crankshaft with the timing mark facing outwards (arrowed).

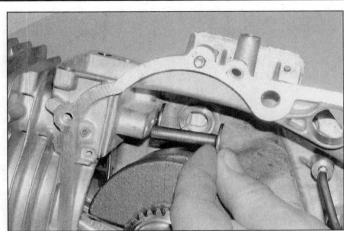

13 Put a drop of oil onto the cam followers, and insert each follower into the same hole from which it was removed.

14 Turn the crankshaft until the timing mark on the gear is pointing at the middle of the camshaft bearing hole in the crankcase (arrowed) Smear some oil on the camshaft bearing journal, and install the camshaft. The timing dimple drilled in the camshaft gear must be aligned exactly with the mark on the crankshaft gear when the gears are meshed. Rotate the crankshaft two revolutions to ensure correct movement.

15 Fit the governor/oil slinger assembly onto the camshaft. Align the head of the bob-weight assembly with the governor arm.

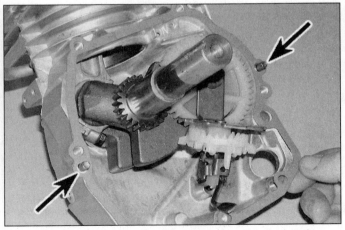

16 Fit a new sump gasket to the crankcase noting the locating dowels (arrowed).

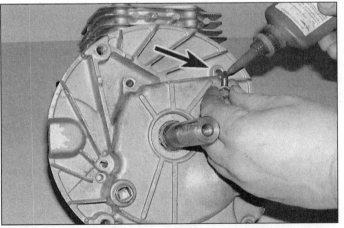

17 Smear some oil onto the crankshaft and camshaft journal. Carefully fit the sump, ensuring that the locating holes engage with the crankcase dowels, and the oil seal lip is not damaged during the process. Tighten the seven bolts securely, using thread locking compound on the bolt that screws into the engine breather chamber (arrowed).

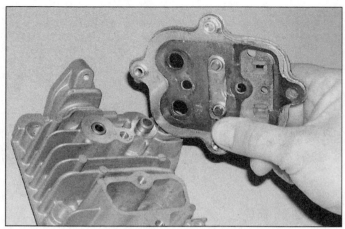

18 With a new gasket in place, fit the rocker mounting plate to the cylinder head.

19 Secure the rocker mounting plate with the two bolts.

20 Refit the valves into the cylinder head, and a new valve seat/seal to the inlet valve.

21 Fit and compress the springs to their respective valves.

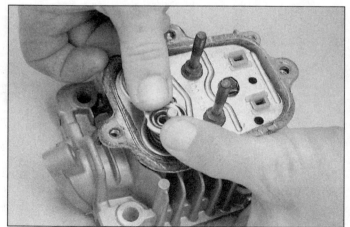

22 Locate the valve collars over the valve stems. Move the collars away from the notch on the rims and slowly release the springs. Ensure that the valve stems have located correctly in their collars.

23 With a new gasket, fit the cylinder head onto the cylinder block. The gasket is not symmetrical, and therefore will only fit one way correctly. Do not use any jointing compound. Ensure that the locating dowels on the underside of the cylinder head engage the gasket and block correctly.

24 Refit the four cylinder head bolts, and tighten securely in a diagonal pattern.

25 Insert the pushrods through the holes in the rocker mounting plate, making sure they locate in the ends of the cam followers. Providing that they are inserted close to vertically, the ends of the pushrods should 'self-locate' in the cam followers. Once the pushrods have been correctly fitted, great care should be taken not to dislodge the protruding ends, as there is a danger of them falling through an oil drain hole and into the crankcase.

26 Fit the contact pads to the valve collars. It is essential that the valve pads and pushrods are refitted to their original locations.

27 Refit the rocker arms, hemispherical washers and mounting nuts to their original locations.

28 Adjust the valve clearances. The clearances are adjusted by turning the rocker arm mounting nut. The exhaust valve clearance should be adjusted when the inlet valve is fully open, and the inlet valve clearance adjusted when the exhaust valve is fully open. Turn the crankshaft to open and close the valves. The clearance dimensions are given in the Technical data.

29 With a new gasket, refit the rocker cover. Tighten the four bolts securely.

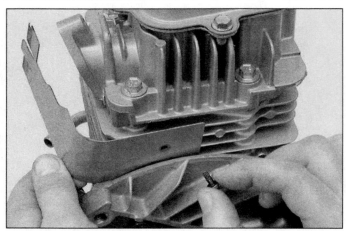

30 Refit the cylinder block cowling. Tighten the bolt securely.

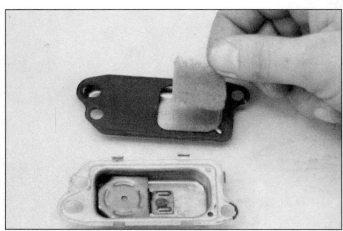

31 Check the fibre disc valve in the engine breather for distortion or cracks. The gap between the disc valve and the body should not exceed 1.1 mm (0.043 in). The valve is held in place by an internal bracket, which will distort if too much pressure is applied to the disc. If the valve is defective, renew the complete breather assembly.

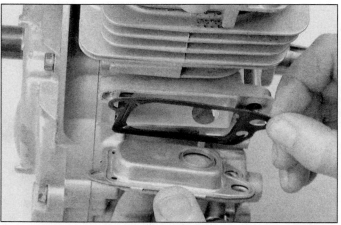

32 Renew the gasket and refit the valve/cover using the two bolts. Tighten securely.

33 With a new gasket, refit the breather chamber cover. Tighten the four bolts securely.

34 Refit the Woodruff (half moon) key to the crankshaft, and slide on the belt drive pulley.

35 Fit and tighten the oil drain plug to the sump, using a ⅜" square drive tool.

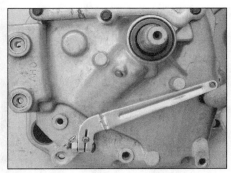

36 Refit the governor lever to the arm, aligning the previously made marks. Tighten the pinch-bolt securely. If the aligning marks have been lost, turn the governor shaft until the arm inside the crankshaft comes into contact with the bob-weight assembly. Then push the lever against its stop and tighten the pinch-bolt.

37 Slide the flywheel over the tapered end of the crankshaft and insert the key.

38 Fit the plastic cooling fin disc to the flywheel, ensuring that the locating pins have engaged correctly.

39 Fit the starter flange over the end of the crankshaft and fit the retaining nut. Tighten the nut very securely, preventing the flywheel from turning by means of a strap wrench around the circumference of the flywheel.

40 Refit the ignition magneto. The magneto body is marked 'Cylinder side' on one side, and 'This side out' on the other. Before tightening the two mounting bolts, turn the flywheel so that the magnets are on the opposite side to the magneto, and use a feeler gauge to measure the air gap between the two legs of the magneto's armature and the flywheel. The correct air gap is 0.254 mm (0.010 in). The mounting holes in the armature legs are slotted. Move the armature until the correct gap is achieved. Tighten the bolts securely.

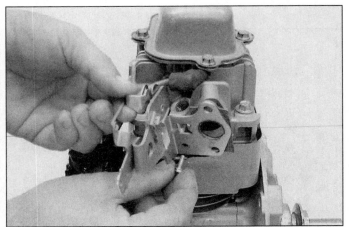

41 Connect the governor linkage to the governor lever, and refit the crankcase cowling – secured with a single bolt.

42 Place a new gasket around the inlet port, and refit the carburettor mounting/linkage plate securing the single bolt. Reconnect the magneto earthing wire from the linkage plate to the ignition magneto.

43 Reassemble the carburettor by refitting the needle valve into its holder in the float, and carefully lowering the assembly into place.

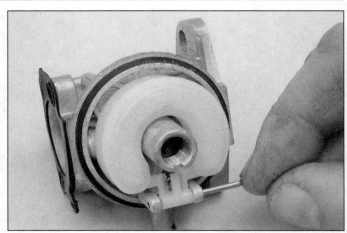

44 Insert the float pivot pin. There is no provision for adjusting the float height.

45 Refit the float bowl and secure with the nut. Do not overtighten. Note the fibre washer between the nut and float chamber (arrowed).

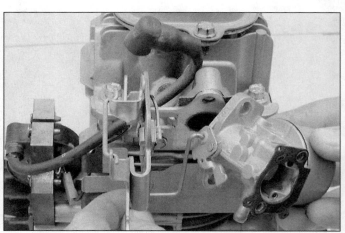

46 Engage the end of the governor linkage with the relevant hole in the carburettor throttle arm.

47 Holding the heat shield in place, fit the carburettor using a new gasket. Tighten the two bolts securely.

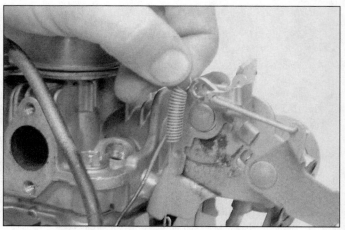

48 Reconnect the end of the governor linkage spring to the relevant hole in the linkage plate.

49 Fit the air filter housing to the carburettor using a new gasket. Note the locating pins on the housing gasket face. Tighten the two bolts.

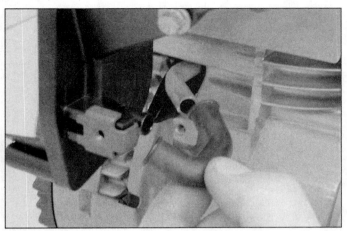

50 Connect the crankcase breather pipe to the air filter housing.

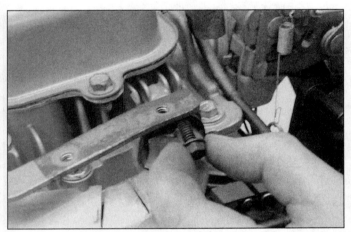

51 Using a new gasket, refit the exhaust system. The two self-tapping bolts fit into the crankcase and the side of the cylinder head, whilst the remaining two bolts secure the system to the exhaust port.

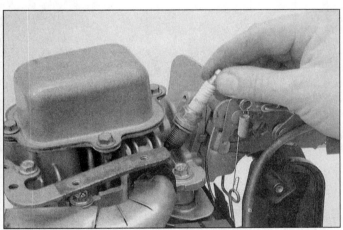

52 Fit the spark plug to the cylinder head, and reconnect the HT lead.

53 Refit the engine cowling, and secure with the four bolts. Ensure that the edge of the cowling interlocks with the crankcase cowling already fitted.

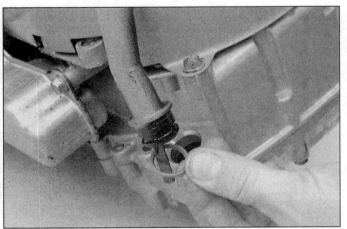

54 Fit a new O-ring to the base of the oil filler spout, and secure the spout in place with the bolt.

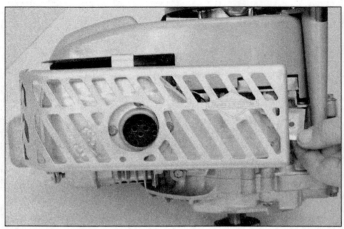

55 Refit the exhaust heat shield. Tighten the three bolts securely.

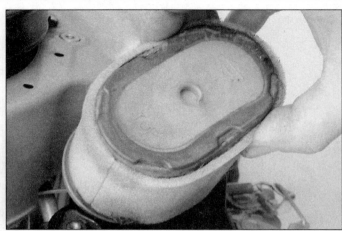

56 Fit the air filter element. One side is marked 'Top'.

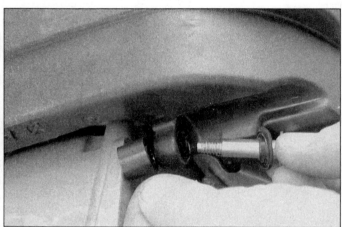

57 The fuel tank is secured by four bolts. Three on the topside, and one longer bolt, on the underside. Note the spacer that locates between the bottom mounting bracket and the crankcase.

58 Fit the fuel pipe between the fuel tank and the carburettor. Secure the ends of the pipe with the two clips.

59 Remove the fuel tank cap, and fit the plastic engine cover. Tighten the two bolts, and refit the fuel tank cap.

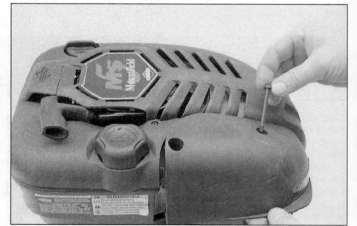

60 Refit the air filter cover, and tighten the two bolts.

61 Remember to fill the engine sump with the correct grade and quantity of oil.

Starter repair

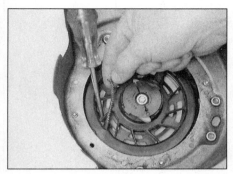

1 With the starter/engine cowling removed, pull the starter rope to its full extension. Lock the rope pulley in this position by inserting a screwdriver (or similar) through the spokes of the pulley and the slots of the engine cowling.

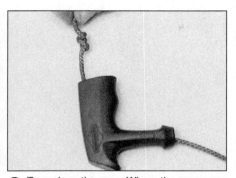

2 To replace the rope: Where the rope goes through the pulley, cut off the knot and pull the rope from the starter. Feed the new rope through the outer hole in the cowling and the hole in the pulley. Tie the knot. Feed the other end of the rope through the hole in the starter handle, again tie the knot. Tension the rope and remove the screwdriver from the pulley spokes. Be prepared for the spring to violently rewind the starter rope. Refit the starter/engine cowling.

3 To replace the recoil spring: Where the rope goes through the pulley, untie the knot and pull the rope from the starter. Pull the screwdriver from the pulley. Unscrew the central bolt from the pawl mechanism, and lift off the guide plate. Note the position of the pawls, and remove them.

4 Carefully lift out the pulley, noting the locating slot for the end of the spring. Lift out the spring.

5 Insert the new spring, locating the inner end around the lug on the cowling.

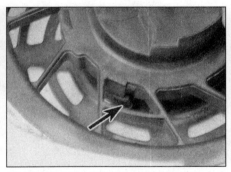

6 Fit the pulley, locating the outer end of the spring in the slot on the pulley (arrowed).

7 Check the starter pawls for damage or excessive wear, and refit them to the pulley. Refit the guide plate onto the pawls, ensuring that the pawl locating pins engage with the slots on the underside of the guide plate. Tighten the central bolt.

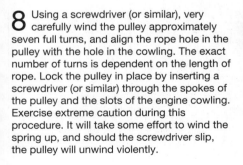

8 Using a screwdriver (or similar), very carefully wind the pulley approximately seven full turns, and align the rope hole in the pulley with the hole in the cowling. The exact number of turns is dependent on the length of rope. Lock the pulley in place by inserting a screwdriver (or similar) through the spokes of the pulley and the slots of the engine cowling. Exercise extreme caution during this procedure. It will take some effort to wind the spring up, and should the screwdriver slip, the pulley will unwind violently.

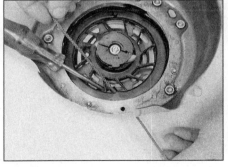

9 Feed the rope through the outer hole in the cowling and the hole in the pulley. Tie a knot in the end of the rope. Tension the rope and remove the screwdriver from the pulley spokes. Be prepared for the spring to violently rewind the starter rope. Refit the starter/engine cowling.

Notes

Chapter 5
Briggs & Stratton Quantum 55 'L' Head 4-stroke engine

Model/spec. number on engines: 128802, 127702, 12H802, 12F802

Mower application

Every effort has been made to make the list of models that use this engine as comprehensive as possible. Due to model and engine supply changes, you may have a mower that is not listed. Refer to *Engine Identity* on page 6 to identify the engine that you have, or contact an engine supply dealer to assist with identification.

Ariens LM series
Atco Admiral
Atco Viscount
Bearcat BC series
BRILL Hattrick
Efco LR/MR series
Harry 302/C48/322/C49C50/424
Hayter Harrier 41
Hayter Hayterette
Hayter Jubilee
Hayter Ranger

IBEA
4221/4237/4238/4204/4704/4721
Lawn-Boy 400
Lawnflite by MTD 384
Lawnflite by MTD 991 SP6
Lawnflite by MTD GES 45 C
Lawnflite by MTD GES 53
Lawn-King PA/NP/T484 series
McCulloch ML857
Mountfield Emperor
Mountfield Empress 16

Mountfield Empress 18
Oleomac G47
Oleomac MAX 53
Rally 21/MR series
Rover 100/200/260
Stiga Turbo 48/55
Suffolk Punch P19
Suffolk Punch P19S
TORO Re-cycler 20776
Viva PB seies
Yardman by MTD YM series

Technical Data

Spark plug type	NGK B2LM
Spark plug gap	0.75 mm (0.030 in)
Valve clearances (cold):	
Inlet	0.12 to 0.17 mm (0.005 to 0.007 in)
Exhaust	0.17 to 0.22 mm (0.007 to 0.009 in)
Armature air gap	0.15 to 0.25 mm (0.006 to 0.010 in)
Oil grade	SAE 30
Oil capacity	0.6 litres
Torque wrench settings:	
Flywheel nut	74 Nm
Big-end bolts	11 Nm
Cylinder head	16 Nm

Dismantling

Before starting to dismantle, read Chapter 2. The procedures outlined apply to all engines and if adopted, will ensure an orderly and methodical approach that will make both dismantling and reassembly much easier.

Remove the engine from the mower, and proceed as follows:

1 Refer to Chapter 2 for dismantling hints and tips.

2 Remove the two bolts and the carburettor shielding.

3 Unscrew the retaining bolt and remove the air filter cover. Withdraw the element.

4 Remove the air filter housing and primer assembly. Note the use of thread locking compound on the three bolts. Disconnect the engine breather tube from the housing.

5 Remove the top plastic mesh from the engine by squeezing at the thumb shaped recess, and lifting the retaining lug clear.

6 Disconnect the fuel pipe from the carburettor to the fuel tank. Be prepared for fuel spillage.

7 In order to remove the fuel tank, unscrew the three retaining bolts at the top, and the bolt under the side securing the tank to the crankcase. Note the position of the spacer and washer.

8 Unscrew the bolt and remove the oil filler tube. Note the O-ring fitted to the base of the tube.

9 Remove the four retaining bolts, and lift the engine cowling/starter away.

10 Unscrew the two retaining bolts, disconnect the magneto earthing wire, and remove the flywheel brake assembly.

11 Remove the two bolts retaining the exhaust heat shield.

12 The two exhaust system mounting bolts are locked using a tab washer. Bend back the washer tabs, unscrew the bolts, and remove the exhaust system.

13 Undo the bolts securing the carburettor. As the carburettor is withdrawn, disengage the linkage rod and spring from the governor arm.

14 Unscrew the float bowl bolt and remove the float bowl. Be prepared for fuel spillage.

15 Push out the float pivot pin, and carefully lift out the float with the needle valve.

16 Check the condition of the needle valve and seat for any damage or wear (*refer to Chapter 2*). Examine the float bowl O-ring for any cracks, etc. The float bowl nut incorporates the main jet. Check that the holes are clear. If necessary, clear the holes by blowing or by the use of a thin nylon bristle. Never use a needle or wire to clean a jet. Check the float for damage or leaks.

17 Disconnect the earthing wire from the magneto, unscrew the two bolts, and remove the carburettor mounting/linkage plate. Note the locations of the fibre washers.

18 Remove the cylinder block cowling.

19 Remove the crankcase cowling.

20 Disengage the linkage rod from the governor lever.

21 Pull the HT cap from the spark plug, unscrew the two bolts, and remove the magneto.

22 The nut retaining the flywheel to the crankshaft can be extremely tight. To prevent the flywheel from turning, in the absence of the manufacturer's special tool, use a strap wrench around the circumference of the flywheel, and undo the nut. The help of an assistant to steady the engine may be necessary.

23 Remove the starter flange. With reference to Chapter 2, pull the flywheel from the crankshaft. If you are using the manufacturer's puller, it may be necessary to cut the threads in the flywheel. The puller holes are clearly labelled in the flywheel, and the puller bolts are specially formed to cut the threads. Recover the key from the crankshaft.

24 Remove the inlet manifold.

25 Undo the two retaining bolts, and prise away the engine breather valve/tappet cover.

26 Remove the breather chamber cover – four bolts.

27 Remove the spark plug.

28 Using a ⅜" square drive tool, unscrew the sump plug and drain the engine oil into a suitable container.

29 Unscrew the eight cylinder head bolts, and with the assistance of a light tap from a soft hammer if necessary, lift away the cylinder head.

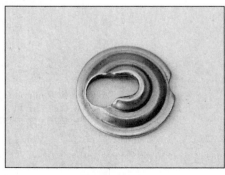

30 Turn the exhaust valve spring collar until the notch in its rim faces out. The valve collars

have two adjoining holes, one of which is larger than the other. This allows the valve stem to slide through the collar. Using a pair of thin-nosed pliers (or similar) compress the spring, move the collar away from the cylinder, slide the collar off the end of the valve stem, and remove the valve. Repeat for the inlet valve. It is important to label or arrange the components so that, if re-used, they are refitted to their original locations.

31 Inspect the valve guides for scoring and excessive wear. Examine the valve seats and renovate as necessary (*refer to Chapter 2*).

32 Unscrew the seven retaining bolts, and remove the sump. A light tap from a soft hammer may be necessary as the sump locates over two dowels in the crankcase gasket face. Note the shim fitted to the end of the camshaft.

33 In order to remove the power take off (PTO) shaft, undo the Allen screw from the outside of the sump. Using a suitable punch through the hole left by the screw, drive the roll-pin from the gear on the PTO shaft. Remove the retaining screw and lock plate, slide the shaft from the sump.

34 Pull the camshaft and governor assembly from the crankcase. Recover the shims fitted to both ends of the shaft. No further dismantling of this assembly is possible.

35 Slide out the cam followers. It is important to label or arrange the followers so that, if re-used, they are refitted to their original locations.

36 The camshaft drive gear should slide easily from the crankshaft. Note, and if loose recover, the Woodruff (half moon) key.

37 Unscrew the big-end bolts and withdraw the bearing cap.

38 Remove any carbon build-up at the lip of the cylinder bore using a soft tool, and gently push the connecting rod and piston assembly up and out of the cylinder. Take care not to mark the bore with the connecting rod.

39 Carefully withdraw the crankshaft from the crankcase.

40 The crankshaft oil seals can now be prised out from the crankcase and sump. Note which way round they fit.

41 Prior to removing the governor arm and

lever, mark the position of the lever on the shaft. It is essential that the lever is refitted in the original position. Remove the lever pinch-bolt, and pull the lever from the shaft. Prise off the steel 'push-on' clip, and remove the governor arm/shaft from the crankcase.

43 Check the condition of the crankshaft bearing, camshaft bearing and cylinder bore

for wear, scores or cracks. If the bore is damaged, worn oval or oversized, then professional skills and special equipment will be necessary to restore it. The same applies to worn or damaged bearings. These can be reamed out to accept bushes obtainable from spares stockists, but special reaming equipment and knowledge are essential. Check all threaded holes for damaged

threads, and repair if necessary by fitting a thread insert of the correct size.

44 If required, remove the piston rings from the piston by carefully expanding the rings at their ends and sliding them from the piston. Note the orientation of the rings for reassembly.

45 Remove the circlip and push the gudgeon pin from the piston.

Reassembly

1 Fit new oil seals into the crankcase and sump by carefully pushing them into place using an appropriate sized socket. The seals should be fitted with the sharp rubber edge of the seal towards the inside of the engine.

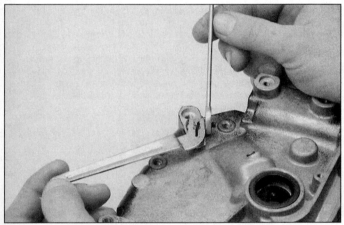

2 Fit the governor arm into the crankcase. Note the washer fitted between the arm and the crankcase on the inside. Fit a new 'push-on' clip on the arm on the outside of the case. Align the previously made mark, and refit the governor lever. Tighten the pinch-bolt.

3 Smear the lip of the crankcase oil seal with new engine oil, and fit the crankshaft into the crankcase, tapered end first.

4 If previously removed, fit the gudgeon pin into the piston/connecting rod assembly. The piston is fitted with the notch on its crown towards the tapered end of the crankshaft, and the 'open' side of the connecting rod towards the camshaft bearing. If the gudgeon pin is reluctant to move, immerse the piston in hot water for a few minutes. This causes the aluminium to expand, and the gudgeon pin to slide easily.

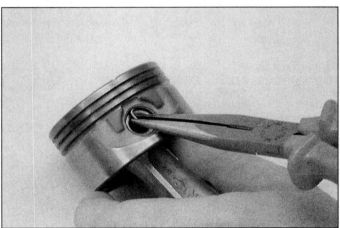

5 Always fit a new piston circlip.

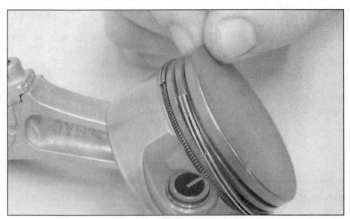

6 Fit the piston rings onto the piston. The oil control (lowest) ring should be fitted first, by carefully expanding the coiled element just enough to slide down over the piston and into its groove.

7 Fit the second element of the oil control ring in the same manner, positioning it so that the coiled element is inside the second element. Next fit the compression ring into the middle groove. This ring must be fitted with the step in its circumference facing down. The top compression ring is symmetrical in profile. However, if the rings are marked with a dot, fit the ring with the dot facing up. **Beware:** *Piston rings are very brittle. If the are expanded too much, they will break.* Arrange the three ring-end gaps so that they are spaced out around the circumference of the piston at 120° intervals.

8 Smear the piston rings and cylinder bore with oil. Using a piston ring clamp, fit the piston into the cylinder from the top by feeding the connecting rod through first. Make sure that the notch on the top of the piston points towards the tapered end of the crankshaft, and that the connecting rod does not scratch the cylinder walls. Press the piston firmly into the cylinder, sliding it out of the clamp as the rings enter the bore. If necessary, using a piece of wood or hammer handle, gently tap the piston out of the clamp and into the cylinder, but stop and investigate any undue resistance.

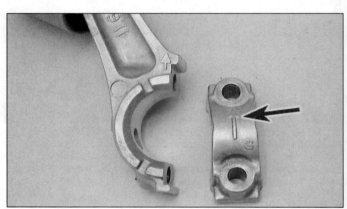

9 Smear some oil on the crankshaft journal and engage the big-end onto the journal. Fit the big-end cap with the arrow pointing towards the piston (arrowed).

10 If you have a suitable torque wrench, tighten the bolts to the torque given in Technical Data. If not, tighten the bolts securely, but do not over-tighten. Rotate the crankshaft to ensure freedom of movement.

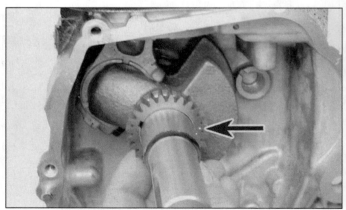

11 If previously removed, fit the Woodruff (half moon) key to the crankshaft, and fit the camshaft drive gear to the crankshaft with the timing mark facing outwards (arrowed).

12 Put a drop of oil onto the cam followers, and insert each follower into the same hole from which it was removed.

13 Turn the crankshaft until the timing mark on the gear is pointing at the middle of the camshaft bearing hole in the crankcase. Smear some oil on the camshaft bearing journal, and install the camshaft with relevant shims fitted to each end. The timing dimple drilled in the camshaft gear must be aligned exactly with the mark on the crankshaft gear when the gears are meshed. Rotate the crankshaft two revolutions to ensure correct movement. Align the head of the governor with the arm.

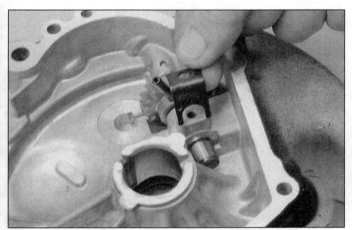

14 If removed, slide the power take off (PTO) shaft gear onto the shaft as it is inserted into the sump. Fit the locking plate and tighten the retaining bolt securely.

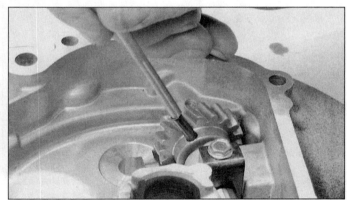

15 Align the holes in the PTO gear and shaft, and drive a new roll-pin into the gear until its end is flush. Fit the Allen screw into the hole in the sump.

16 Fit a new gasket over the locating dowels in to the crankcase gasket face. Refit the sump, and tighten the seven retaining bolts securely. Use thread-locking compound on the bolt that enters the engine breather chamber (arrowed). Refit the sump plug.

17 Prior to fitting the valve springs, turn the crankshaft until the piston is at top dead centre on the compression stroke. Slowly continue to turn the crankshaft until the piston has moved down the bore approximately 6 mm. Insert the valves into their respective guides and, with reference to Chapter 2, check both valve clearances. The dimensions are given in Technical Data. Once the correct clearances have been achieved, remove the valves.

18 Fit the exhaust valve spring and collar into place in the tappet chest. Ensure that the notch in the rim of the collar is facing out.

19 Fit the valve.

20 Using a pair of thin-nosed pliers (or similar), compress the valve spring, slide the collar over the end of the valve stem, and move the collar in towards the cylinder. Slowly allow the spring to uncompress, and check that the collar has located correctly on the end of the valve stem. Repeat this procedure for the inlet valve.

21 Place the new head gasket in the correct position. The gasket will only align with the bolt holes one way round. Do not use any jointing compound.

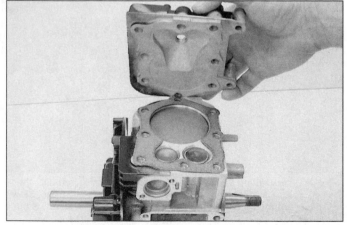

22 Refit the cylinder head, and tighten the eight retaining bolts evenly, in a diagonal sequence, to the torque given in Technical Data.

23 Refit the spark plug.

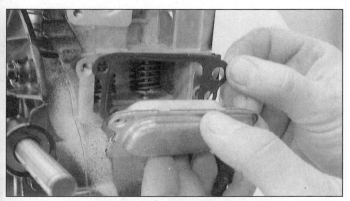

24 Check the fibre disc valve in the engine breather for distortion or cracks. The gap between the disc valve and the body should not exceed 1.1 mm (0.43 in). The valve is held in place by an internal bracket, which will distort if too much pressure is applied to the disc. If the valve is defective, renew the complete breather assembly. Renew the gasket and refit the valve/cover using the two bolts. Tighten securely.

25 With a new gasket, refit the breather chamber cover. Tighten the four bolts securely.

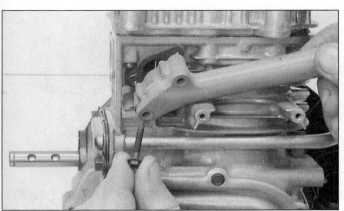

26 Renew the gasket, and refit the inlet manifold.

27 Slide the flywheel over the tapered end of the crankshaft and insert the key.

28 Fit the starter flange over the end of the crankshaft and fit the retaining nut. Tighten the nut to the torque given in Technical Data, preventing the flywheel from turning by means of a strap wrench around the circumference of the flywheel. The help of an assistant may be required to steady the engine.

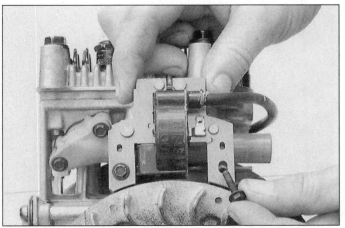

29 Refit the ignition magneto. The magneto body is marked 'Cylinder side' on one side, and 'This side out' on the other.

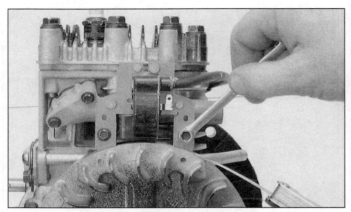

30 Before tightening the two mounting bolts, turn the flywheel so that the magnets are on the opposite side to the magneto, and use a feeler gauge to measure the air gap between the two legs of the magneto's armature and the flywheel. The correct air gap is given in Technical Data. The mounting holes in the armature legs are slotted. Move the armature until the correct gap is achieved. Tighten the bolts securely. Refit the HT cap to the spark plug.

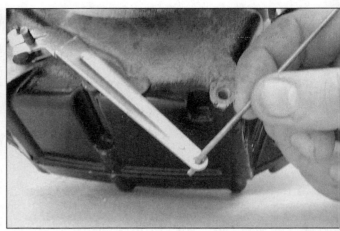

31 Connect the governor linkage to the governor lever.

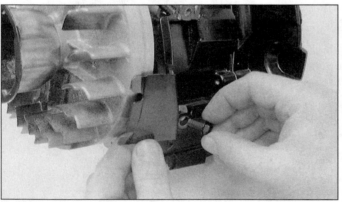

32 Refit the crankcase cowling – secured with a single bolt.

33 Refit the cylinder block cowling – also secured with a single bolt.

34 With the fibre washers in their correct locations, refit the carburettor mounting/linkage plate. Make sure that the HT lead is routed under the plate. Reconnect the earthing wire to the magneto. Feed the other wire behind the magneto, under the breather pipe to the flywheel brake mounting location.

35 Reassemble the carburettor by refitting the needle valve into its holder in the float, and carefully lowering the assembly into place.

36 Insert the float pivot pin. There is no provision for adjusting the float height.

37 Refit the float bowl and secure with the bolt. Do not overtighten.

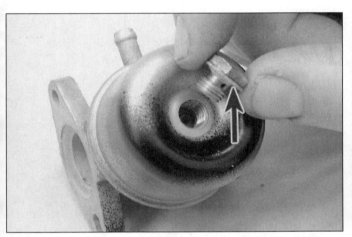

38 Note the fibre washer between the bolt and float chamber (arrowed).

39 Use a new O-ring (arrowed).

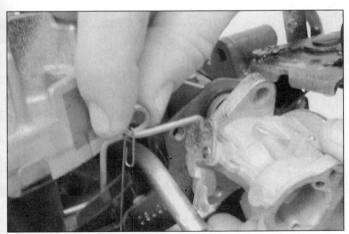

40 Engage the end of the governor linkage with the throttle arm, and refit the carburettor. Tighten the two bolts securely.

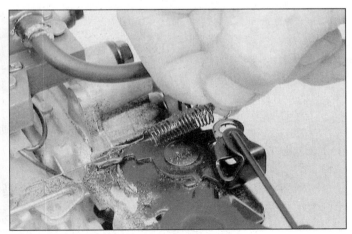

41 Reconnect the governor linkage spring.

42 Refit the exhaust system, and tighten the two mounting bolts.

43 Bend the tabs of the locking washer to secure the bolts.

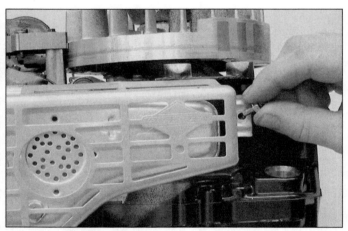

44 Refit the exhaust shield. Tighten the two retaining bolts securely.

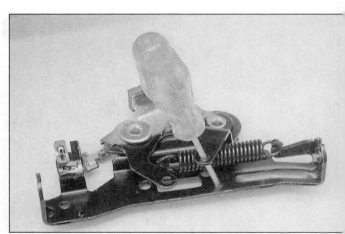

45 In order to fit the flywheel brake, it is necessary to expand the brake spring. Pull the brake levers apart and insert a screwdriver through the brackets.

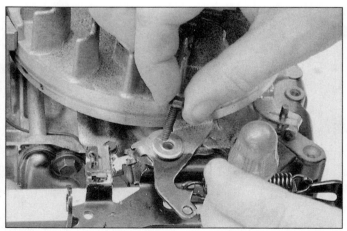

46 Locate the assembly and tighten the two retaining bolts. Remove the screwdriver.

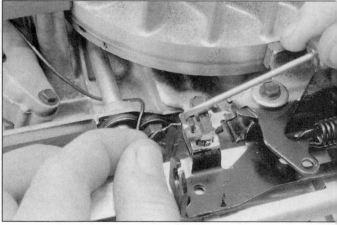

47 Reconnect the magneto earthing wire.

48 Refit the engine cowling/starter. Before tightening the four retaining bolts, ensure that the cowling edge is correctly interlocked with the crankcase cowling already fitted.

49 Refit the oil filler tube. Note the O-ring at its base (arrowed).

50 The fuel tank is secured by four bolts. Three on the topside, and one longer bolt, on the underside.

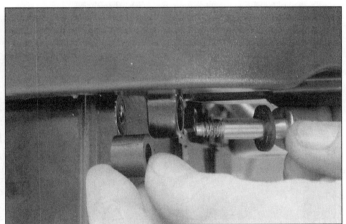

51 Note the spacer that locates between the bottom mounting bracket and the crankcase, and the washer under the head of the bolt.

52 Reconnect the fuel pipe between the fuel tank and the carburettor. Secure the ends of the pipe with the two clips.

53 Refit the top plastic cover.

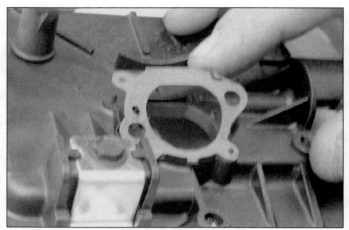

54 Using a new gasket, and locking compound on the three retaining bolts, refit the housing to the carburettor...

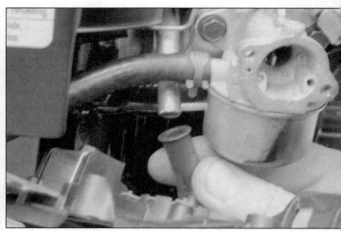

55 ...connecting the air filter housing/primer to the engine breather pipe.

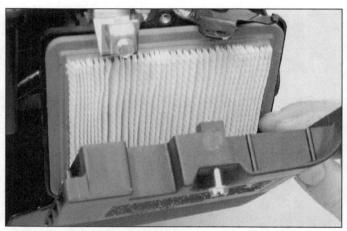

56 Refit the air filter element and cover. Tighten the retaining bolt securely.

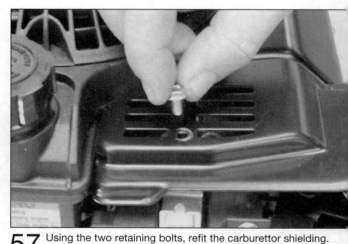

57 Using the two retaining bolts, refit the carburettor shielding.

58 Remember to fill the sump with the correct grade and quantity of oil.

Starter repair

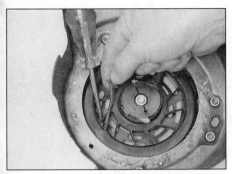

1 With the starter/engine cowling removed, pull the starter rope to its full extension. Lock the rope pulley in this position by inserting a screwdriver (or similar) through the spokes of the pulley and the slots of the engine cowling.

2 To replace the rope: Where the rope goes through the pulley, cut off the knot and pull the rope from the starter. Feed the new rope through the outer hole in the cowling and the inner hole in the pulley. Tie the knot. Then feed the other end of the rope through the hole in the starter handle, again tie the knot. Tension the rope and remove the screwdriver from the pulley spokes. Be prepared for the spring to violently rewind the starter rope. Refit the starter/engine cowling.

3 To replace the recoil spring: Where the rope goes through the pulley, untie the knot and pull the rope from the starter. Pull the screwdriver from the pulley. Unscrew the central bolt from the pawl mechanism, and lift off the guide plate. Note the position of the pawls, and remove them.

4 Carefully lift out the pulley, noting the locating slot for the end of the spring. Lift out the spring.

5 Insert the new spring, locating the inner end around the lug on the cowling.

6 Fit the pulley, locating the outer end of the spring in the slot on the pulley (arrowed).

7 Check the starter pawls for damage or excessive wear, and refit them to the pulley. Refit the guide plate onto the pawls, ensuring that the pawl locating pins engage with the slots on the underside of the guide plate. Tighten the central bolt.

8 Using a screwdriver (or similar), very carefully wind the pulley approximately seven full turns, and align the rope hole in the pulley with the hole in the cowling. The exact number of turns is dependent on the length of rope. Lock the pulley in place by inserting a screwdriver (or similar) through the spokes of the pulley and the slots of the engine cowling. Exercise extreme caution during this procedure. It will take some effort to wind the spring up, and should the screwdriver slip, the pulley will unwind violently.

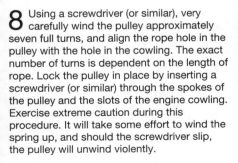

9 Feed the rope through the outer hole in the cowling and the hole in the pulley. Tie a knot in the end of the rope. Tension the rope and remove the screwdriver from the pulley spokes. Be prepared for the spring to violently rewind the starter rope. Refit the starter/engine cowling.

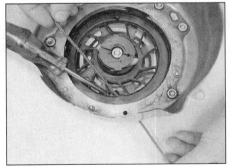

Notes

Chapter 6
Briggs & Stratton I/C horizontal crank 'L' Head 5 hp 4-stroke engine

Model/spec. number on engine: 135232

Mower application

Every effort has been made to make the list of models that use this engine as comprehensive as possible. Due to model and engine supply changes, you may have a mower that is not listed. Refer to *Engine Identity* on page 6 to identify the engine that you have, or contact an engine supply dealer to assist with identification.

Atco Club   Atco Royale   Kompact 90S

Technical Data

Valve clearances (cold):	
Inlet	0.13 to 0.18 mm (0.005 to 0.007 in)
Exhaust	0.23 to 0.28 mm (0.009 to 0.011 in)
Spark plug type	NGK B2LM
Spark plug gap	0.75 mm (0.030 in)
Crankshaft end float	0.05 to 0.20 mm (0.002 to 0.008 in)
Magneto armature air gap	0.254 to 0.355 mm (0.010 to 0.014 in)
Piston ring gap:	
Compression rings	0.80 mm (0.031 in) max
Oil control ring	1.14 mm (0.045 in) max
Oil grade	SAE 30, SAE 10W–30
Oil capacity	0.62 litres
Torque wrench settings	
Big-end bolts	11 Nm
Cylinder head bolts	16 Nm
Flywheel nut	88 Nm
Crankcase end plate bolts	10 Nm

Dismantling

Before starting to dismantle, read Chapter 2. The procedures outlined apply to all engines and if adopted, will ensure an orderly and methodical approach that will make both dismantling and reassembly much easier.

1 Unscrew the two bolts, and remove the air filter cover. Lift out the filter element.

2 Remove the air filter housing.

3 The engine cowling/starter is secured by four bolts. Two on the top, and one on each side at the crankcase base. Remove the cowling.

4 Bend back the tab washers, and undo the exhaust system mounting bolts. Remove the system.

5 Loosen the Torx screw securing the carburettor to the fuel tank sufficiently to allow the engine breather pipe to be disconnected and removed.

6 Unscrew the two Torx screws, and remove the remote control panel. Disconnect the linkage and the magneto earthing wire as the panel is removed.

7 Disconnect the magneto earthing wire under the fuel tank, by unscrewing the retaining nut.

8 Remove the carburettor and fuel tank together. Two bolts secure the carburettor to the cylinder head, and one, under the fuel tank, secures the tank to the crankcase. As the assembly is withdrawn, recover the heat shield, disconnect the governor arm-to-throttle butterfly linkage, and the spring between the governor arm and pivot plate.

9 To separate the carburettor from the fuel tank, undo the Torx screws, and disengage the throttle linkage. Lift the carburettor from the tank. Be prepared for fuel spillage.

10 Remove the wire gauze over the main jet, and clean if required. To gain access to the pilot jet for cleaning, undo the brass cover screw.

11 Inspect the screen in the base of the fuel pick-up pipe for damage and cleanliness. Do not brush or rub the screen, as it is very delicate.

12 The fuel pump is integral with the carburettor. Remove the four Torx screws, withdraw the cover, diaphragm, cup and spring. Check for cleanliness and diaphragm damage.

13 Unscrew the two magneto retaining bolts, disconnect the HT cap from the spark plug, and remove the magneto. Note how the deflector plate slots under the armature post.

14 The nut retaining the flywheel to the crankshaft can be extremely tight. To prevent the flywheel from turning, in the absence of the manufacturer's special tool, use a strap wrench around the circumference of the flywheel, and undo the nut. The help of an assistant to steady the engine may be necessary.

15 Remove the starter flange and mesh.

16 To remove the flywheel, tap the back of the flywheel with a soft hammer, whilst pulling the flywheel away from the crankcase. Do not tap

the aluminium element or the magnets of the flywheel. Recover the key from the crankshaft.

17 Unscrew the two retaining bolts, and remove the crankcase cowling.

18 In order to remove the cylinder block cowling, unscrew the three cylinder head bolts, and the bolt on the side of the cylinder block.

19 Remove the remaining five bolts, and lift away the cylinder head. Note that the three bolts around the exhaust valve are slightly longer than the others.

20 Unscrew the two retaining bolts, and prise away the tappet cover/breather valve.

21 Turn the exhaust valve spring collar until the notch in its rim faces out. The valve collars have two adjoining holes, one of which is larger than the other. This allows the valve stem to slide through the collar. Using a pair of thin-nosed pliers (or similar) compress the spring, move the collar away from the cylinder, slide the collar off the end of the valve stem, and remove the valve. Repeat for the inlet valve. It is important to label or arrange the components so that, if re-used, they are refitted to their original locations.

22 Inspect the valve guides for scoring and excessive wear. Examine the valve seats and renovate as necessary (*refer to Chapter 2*).

23 Using a ³⁄₈" square drive tool, undo the sump plug and drain the engine oil into a suitable container.

24 Remove all rust and dirt from the crankshaft. Unscrew the six retaining bolts, and remove the crankcase end plate.

25 If required, the governor cup assembly can be removed from the end plate by pulling.

26 Unscrew the big-end bolts. Recover the oil dipper and the bearing cap.

27 Remove any carbon build-up at the lip of the cylinder bore using a soft tool, and gently push the connecting rod and piston assembly up and out of the cylinder. Take care not to mark the bore with the connecting rod. If required, remove the piston rings from the piston by carefully expanding the rings at their ends and sliding them from the piston. Note the orientation of the rings for reassembly. Remove the circlip and push the gudgeon pin from the piston.

28 Align the timing mark on the crankshaft counterweight with the drilling on the

camshaft gear, and withdraw the crankshaft and camshaft together.

29 Slide out the cam followers. It is important to label or arrange the followers so that, if re-used, they are refitted to their original locations.

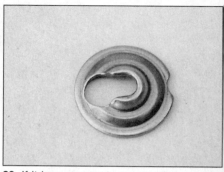

30 If it is necessary to remove the governor lever from the shaft, mark the position of the lever on the shaft before undoing the pinch-bolt. Pull out the 'R-clip', and withdraw the governor shaft from the crankcase.

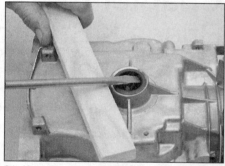

31 If required, prise out the crankcase and end plate oil seals. Note which way round they are fitted.

32 Check the condition of the crankshaft bearing, camshaft bearing and cylinder bore for wear, scores or cracks. If the bore is damaged, worn oval or oversized, then professional skills and special equipment will be necessary to restore it. The same applies to worn or damaged bearings. It may be possible to have these reamed out to accept bushes obtainable from spares stockists, but special reaming equipment and knowledge are essential. Check all threaded holes for damaged threads, and repair if necessary by fitting a thread insert of the correct size.

33 If the output side crankshaft main ball-bearing requires replacement, a bearing press will be needed, as the bearing is a press fit on the shaft. To install a new bearing, suspend the bearing in hot oil at 120°C. Take all necessary safety measures to protect the skin from hot oil splashes. With the crankshaft clamp in a soft-jawed vice, slide the bearing onto the shaft with the shield side inwards. As the bearing cools, it will tighten on the journal. Do not quench the bearing.

Reassembly

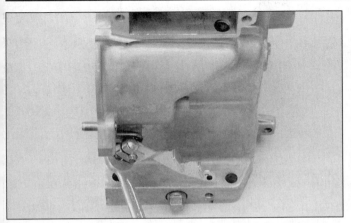

1 If removed, refit the governor arm into the crankcase, and secure with the 'R-clip'. Refit the governor lever to the arm, aligning the previously made marks. Tighten the pinch-bolt.

2 Fit new oil seals into the crankcase and sump by carefully pushing them into place using an appropriate sized socket. The seals should be fitted with the sharp rubber edge of the seal towards the inside of the engine.

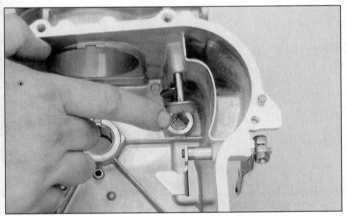

3 Refit the cam followers to their respective holes. A smear of grease can be useful to hold the followers in place.

4 Oil the crankshaft and camshaft bearing journals. The crankshaft and camshaft must be inserted together. Prior to fitting the shafts into the crankcase, mesh the drive gear on the crankshaft with the camshaft gear, and align the timing marks. Fit the shafts into the crankcase.

5 If previously removed, fit the gudgeon pin into the piston/ connecting rod assembly. If the gudgeon pin is reluctant to move, immerse the piston in hot water for a few minutes. This causes the aluminium to expand, and the gudgeon pin to slide easily.

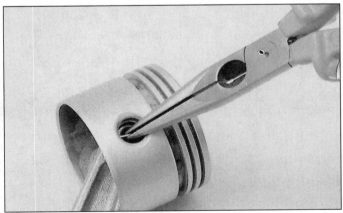

6 Always fit a new piston circlip.

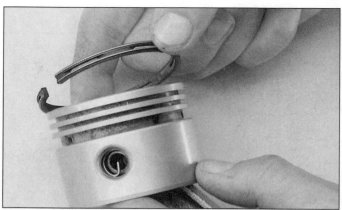

7 Fit the piston rings onto the piston. The oil control (lowest) ring should be fitted first, by carefully expanding the ring just enough to slide down over the piston and into its groove. The oil control ring is symmetrical in profile.

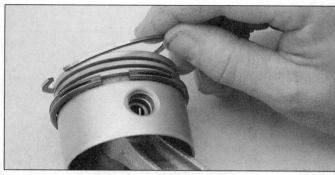

8 Next fit the compression ring into the middle groove. This ring must be fitted with the step in its circumference facing down. The top compression ring is symmetrical in profile. However, if the rings are marked with a dot, fit the ring with the dot facing up. **Beware:** *Piston rings are very brittle. If they are expanded too much, they will break.* Arrange the three ring-end gaps so that they are spaced out around the circumference of the piston at 120° intervals.

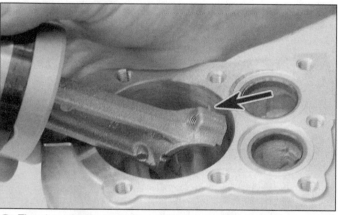

9 The piston is fitted with the circlip groove towards the tapered end of the crankshaft, and the connecting rod with the cast lug (arrowed) at the big-end journal towards the camshaft bearing.

10 Smear the piston rings and cylinder bore with oil. Using a piston ring clamp, fit the piston into the cylinder from the top by feeding the connecting rod through first. Make sure that the connecting rod does not scratch the cylinder walls. Press the piston firmly into the cylinder, sliding it out of the clamp as the rings enter the bore. If necessary, using a piece of wood or hammer handle, gently tap the piston out of the clamp and into the cylinder, but stop and investigate any undue resistance.

11 Smear some oil on the crankshaft journal and engage the big-end onto the journal. Fit the big-end cap with the cast lug (arrowed) towards the camshaft.

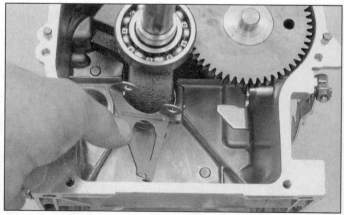

12 Fit the oil dipper, and, if you have a suitable torque wrench, tighten the bolts to the torque given in Technical Data. If not, tighten the bolts securely, but do not over-tighten. Rotate the crankshaft to ensure freedom of movement.

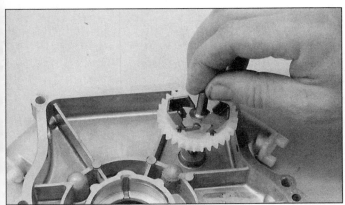

13 If removed, push the washer and governor cup assembly onto its mounting shaft on the inside of the crankcase end plate.

14 Liberally grease the main bearing ball race. Place a new gasket over the locating dowels, and refit the crankcase end plate. As the cover engages on the locating dowels, it may be necessary to rotate the governor cup gear, in order for it to mesh with the camshaft gear.

15 Tighten the crankcase end plate bolts, evenly in a diagonal sequence, to the torque given in Technical Data. Check the crankshaft end float is within the limits given in the Specifications. If it is less than the lower limit, an additional paper gasket must be fitted under the crankcase end plate. If it is more than the upper limit, a thrust washer is available, and must be fitted on the crankshaft between the camshaft drive gear and the main bearing.

16 Prior to fitting the valve springs, turn the crankshaft until the piston is at TDC on the compression stroke. Slowly continue to turn the crankshaft until the piston has moved down the bore approximately 6 mm. Insert the valves into their respective guides and, with reference to Chapter 2, check both valve clearances. The dimensions are given in the Technical Data. Once the correct clearances have been achieved, remove the valves.

17 Fit the exhaust valve spring and collar into place in the tappet chest. Ensure that the notch in the rim of the collar is facing out. Note that the exhaust valve spring has a seal fitted to its top end.

18 Using a pair of thin-nosed pliers (or similar), compress the valve spring, slide the collar over the end of the valve stem, and move the collar in towards the cylinder. Slowly allow the spring to uncompress, and check that the collar has located correctly on the end of the valve stem. Repeat this procedure for the inlet valve.

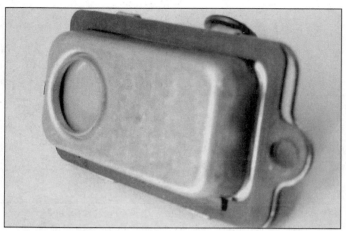

19 Check the fibre disc valve in the engine breather for distortion or cracks. The gap between the disc valve and the body should not exceed 1.1 mm (0.043 in). The valve is held in place by an internal bracket, which will distort if too much pressure is applied to the disc. If the valve is defective, renew the complete breather assembly. Renew the gasket and refit the valve/cover using the two bolts. Tighten securely.

20 Place the new head gasket in the correct position. The gasket will only align with the bolt holes one way round. Do not use any jointing compound.

21 Fit the cylinder head and cowling.

22 The three long bolts (arrowed) fit into the holes around the exhaust valve. The bolt with the stud extension is located as shown. Tighten the cylinder head bolts evenly, in a diagonal sequence, to the torque given in Technical Data.

23 Tighten the bolt retaining the cylinder block cowling.

24 Refit the crankcase cowling using the two retaining bolts.

25 Fit the flywheel over the tapered end of the crankshaft, and insert the square section key into the keyway.

26 After fitting the flywheel mesh and starter flange, tighten the flywheel nut to the torque given in Technical Data. Use a strap wrench around the circumference of the flywheel to prevent it from turning. The help of an assistant will be necessary.

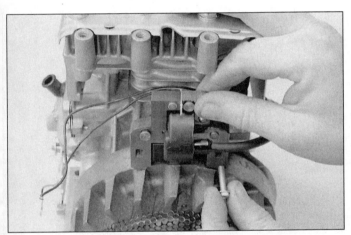

27 Refit the ignition magneto. The magneto body is marked 'Cylinder side' on one side, and 'This side out' on the other.

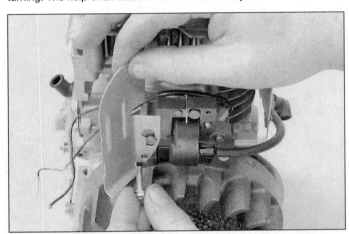

28 Fit the deflector plate over its locating post on the armature.

29 Before tightening the two mounting bolts, turn the flywheel so that the magnets are on the opposite side to the magneto, and use a feeler gauge to measure the air gap between the two legs of the magneto's armature and the flywheel. The correct air gap is given in Technical Data. The mounting holes in the armature legs are slotted. Move the armature until the correct gap is achieved. Tighten the bolts securely. Refit the HT cap to the spark plug.

30 Refit the fuel pump spring, cup and diaphragm to the carburettor. Secure the cover with the four Torx screws.

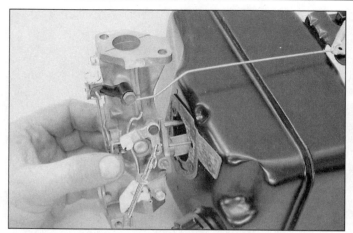

31 Using a new gasket, refit the carburettor to the fuel tank. The carburettor is secured to the tank by two Torx screws – one long one down through the body of the carburettor, and one short Torx screw through the mounting flange.

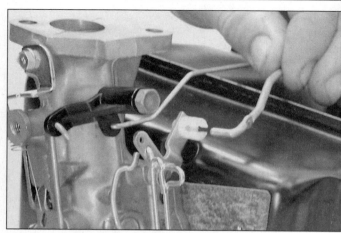

32 Reconnect the throttle linkage.

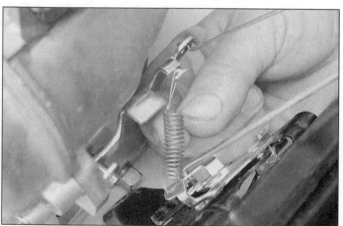

33 Refit the carburettor and fuel tank assembly. As the assembly is fitted, reconnect the governor linkage and spring.

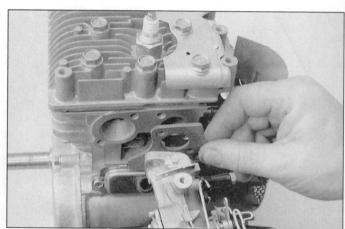

34 Fit the heat shield between the carburettor and cylinder head. Secure with the two retaining bolts. The fuel tank is secured with one bolt to the crankcase base.

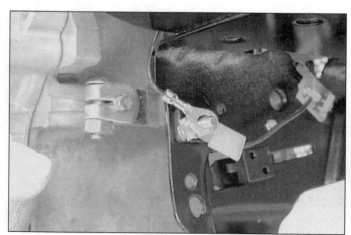

35 Reconnect the magneto earthing wire under the fuel tank.

36 Refit the remote control panel to the carburettor/fuel tank assembly. As the panel is fitted, reconnect the choke linkage, and ensure that the throttle lever pin engages with the sliding linkage. Secure the panel with the two Torx screws.

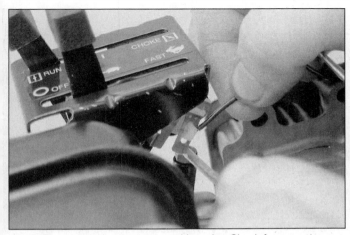

37 Reconnect the magneto earthing wire. Check for correct operation.

38 Install the engine breather pipe between the breather valve cover and air intake. The pipe is retained by a clamp under a carburettor-to-fuel tank mounting Torx screw.

39 Fit the exhaust system. Tighten the retaining bolts, and secure them by bending the tabs of the locking washer.

40 The engine cowling/starter is retained by four bolts. Two on the top, and one on each side secures the cowling to the crankcase. Before tightening the bolts, ensure that it interlocks correctly with the cylinder block cowling already fitted, and that the HT lead has not been trapped.

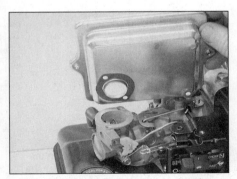

41 Refit the air filter housing using the four bolts with integral shake-proof washers.

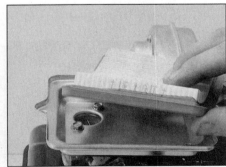

42 Refit the air filter element. One side is marked 'UP'.

43 Secure the air filter cover with two bolts.

44 Remember to fill the sump with the correct grade and quantity of oil.

Starter repair

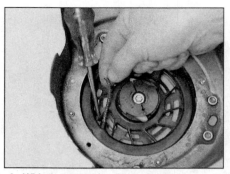

1 With the starter/engine cowling removed, pull the starter rope to its full extension. Lock the rope pulley in this position by inserting a screwdriver (or similar) through the spokes of the pulley and the slots of the engine cowling.

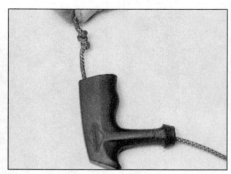

2 To replace the rope: Where the rope goes through the pulley, cut off the knot and pull the rope from the starter. Feed the new rope through the outer hole in the cowling and the inner hole in the pulley. Tie the knot. Then feed the other end of the rope through the hole in the starter handle, again tie the knot. Tension the rope and remove the screwdriver from the pulley spokes. Be prepared for the spring to violently rewind the starter rope. Refit the starter/engine cowling.

3 To replace the recoil spring: Where the rope goes through the pulley, untie the knot and pull the rope from the starter. Pull the screwdriver from the pulley. Unscrew the central bolt from the pawl mechanism, and lift off the guide plate. Note the position of the pawls, and remove them.

4 Carefully lift out the pulley, noting the locating slot for the end of the spring. Lift out the spring.

5 Insert the new spring, locating the inner end around the lug on the cowling.

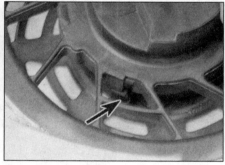

6 Fit the pulley, locating the outer end of the spring in the slot on the pulley (arrowed).

7 Check the starter pawls for damage or excessive wear, and refit them to the pulley. Refit the guide plate onto the pawls, ensuring that the pawl locating pins engage with the slots on the underside of the guide plate. Tighten the central bolt.

8 Using a screwdriver (or similar), very carefully wind the pulley approximately seven full turns, and align the rope hole in the pulley with the hole in the cowling. The exact number of turns is dependent on the length of rope. Lock the pulley in place by inserting a screwdriver (or similar) through the spokes of the pulley and the slots of the engine cowling. Exercise extreme caution during this procedure. It will take some effort to wind the spring up, and should the screwdriver slip, the pulley will unwind violently.

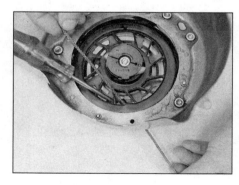

9 Feed the rope through the outer hole in the cowling and the hole in the pulley. Tie a knot in the end of the rope. Tension the rope and remove the screwdriver from the pulley spokes. Be prepared for the spring to violently rewind the starter rope. Refit the starter/engine cowling.

Chapter 7
Briggs & Stratton 35 Sprint/Classic 2.6 kW 4-stroke engine

Model/spec. number on engines: 9D902, 10D902, 98902

Mower application

Every effort has been made to make the list of models that use this engine as comprehensive as possible. Due to model and engine supply changes, you may have a mower that is not listed. Refer to *Engine Identity* on page 6 to identify the engine that you have, or contact an engine supply dealer to assist with identification.

Efco LR series
Harry 313
Lawnflite by MTD 383
Lawnflite by MTD GE40

Lawn-King NG series
Mountfield Emblem 15
Mountfield Laser Delta 42/46
Oleomac G43

Partner 431
Rover 100
Stiga Multiclip Pro 48
Suffolk Punch P16

Technical Data

Spark plug gap	0.76 mm (0.030 in)
Spark plug type	NGK B2LM
Valve clearances (cold):	
Inlet	0.13 to 0.18 mm (0.005 to 0.007 in)
Exhaust	0.18 to 0.23 mm (0.007 to 0.009 in)
Armature air gap	0.15 to 0.25 mm (0.006 to 0.010 in)
Oil grade	SAE 30
Oil capacity	0.6 litres
Torque wrench settings:	
Flywheel nut	74 Nm
Big-end bolts	11 Nm
Cylinder head bolts	16 Nm

Dismantling

Before starting to dismantle, read Chapter 2. The procedures outlined apply to all engines and if adopted, will ensure an orderly and methodical approach that will make both dismantling and reassembly much easier.

1 Undo the retaining bolt, and remove the cutting blade.

2 Slide the blade mounting flange from the shaft, and remove the Woodruff (half moon) key.

3 Disconnect the engine stop cable from the flywheel brake assembly, by squeezing the retaining tabs of the cable ferrule, and pulling it from the bracket. Disengage the cable end fitting from the arm.

4 Unscrew and remove the three engine mounting nuts and bolts.

5 Lift the engine away from the mower body. Recover the three washers between the engine and body.

6 Using a $\frac{3}{8}$" square drive tool, remove the sump plug and drain the oil into a suitable container.

7 Undo the retaining bolt, and remove the air filter/cover assembly. Recover the sealing washer.

8 Remove the flywheel brake cover.

9 Unscrew the two retaining bolts, and remove the exhaust shield.

10 The engine cowling/starter is secured by two bolts. One into the cylinder head, and the other into the crankcase at the side. Unscrew the bolts and remove the cowling/starter.

11 Note their location, and disconnect the two throttle springs from the throttle linkage.

12 Undo the two mounting bolts and remove the carburettor and fuel tank together. As the assembly is withdrawn, disengage the throttle linkage from the engine governor.

13 To separate the carburettor from the fuel tank, undo the six mounting screws, and very carefully prise the carburettor from the fuel tank. As the carburettor is removed, take care not to lose the spring that fits between the carburettor body and the mounting gasket/diaphragm. Be prepared for fuel spillage.

14 Remove the wire gauze over the main jet, and clean if required. Carefully clean the wire gauze in the end of the fuel pick-up pipe. Clean any obscured jets, or air/fuel passages by blowing only.

15 The carburettor has fixed main and pilot jets, and no further dismantling is possible.

16 Remove the crankcase cowling between the fuel tank and crankcase.

17 Carefully pull the HT cap from the spark plug.

18 Undo the two retaining bolts, and remove the ignition magneto together with the governor arm. As the magneto is removed, disconnect the earthing wire.

19 In order to remove the flywheel brake assembly, use a screwdriver to wedge the brake in the 'OFF' position. Unscrew the two retaining bolts and remove the brake. Disconnect and remove the magneto earthing wire.

20 Bend back the two tab washers, undo the bolts, and remove the exhaust system.

21 The nut retaining the flywheel to the crankshaft can be extremely tight. To prevent the flywheel from turning, in the absence of the manufacturer's special tool, use a strap wrench around the circumference of the flywheel, and undo the nut. The help of an assistant to steady the engine may be necessary.

22 Remove the starter flange. With reference to Chapter 2, pull the flywheel from the crankshaft. If you are using the manufacturer's puller, it may be necessary to cut the threads in the flywheel. The puller holes are clearly labelled in the flywheel, and the puller bolts are specially formed to cut the threads. Recover the key from the crankshaft.

23 Remove the inlet manifold.

24 Undo the two retaining bolts, and prise away the engine breather valve/tappet cover.

25 Remove the spark plug.

26 Unscrew the eight cylinder head bolts, and lift away the head with the cowling.

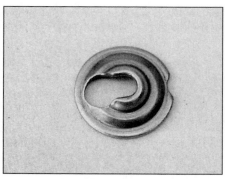

27 Turn the exhaust valve spring collar until the notch in its rim faces out. The valve collars have two adjoining holes, one of which is larger than the other. This allows the valve stem to slide through the collar. Using a pair of thin-nosed pliers (or similar) compress the spring, move the collar away from the cylinder, slide the collar off the end of the valve stem, and remove the valve. Repeat for the inlet valve. It is important to label or arrange the components so that, if re-used, they are refitted to their original locations.

28 Inspect the valve guides for scoring and excessive wear. Examine the valve seats and renovate as necessary (*refer to Chapter 2*).

29 Unscrew the engine breather pipe from the crankcase.

30 Ensure that the crankshaft is free of dirt and rust. Unscrew the six retaining bolts, and remove the sump. A light tap from a soft hammer may be necessary as the sump locates over two dowels in the crankcase gasket face.

31 Remove the oil slinger from the end of the camshaft.

32 Align the timing mark on the camshaft gear with the mark on the camshaft drive gear fitted to the crankshaft. Carefully remove the camshaft.

33 Slide out the cam followers. It is important to label or arrange the followers so that, if re-used, they are refitted to their original locations.

34 The camshaft drive gear should slide easily from the crankshaft.

35 Unscrew the big-end bolts and withdraw the bearing cap.

36 Remove any carbon build-up at the lip of the cylinder bore using a soft tool, and gently push the connecting rod and piston assembly up and out of the cylinder. Take care not to mark the bore with the connecting rod.

37 If required, remove the piston rings from the piston by carefully expanding the rings at their ends and sliding them from the piston. Note the orientation of the rings for reassembly. Remove the circlip and push the gudgeon pin from the piston.

38 Prise the oil seals from the crankcase and sump.

39 Check the condition of the crankshaft bearing, camshaft bearing and cylinder bore for wear, scores or cracks. If the bore is damaged, worn oval or oversized, then professional skills and special equipment will be necessary to restore it. The same applies to worn or damaged bearings. It may be possible to have these reamed out to accept bushes obtainable from spares stockists, but special reaming equipment and knowledge are essential. Check all threaded holes for damaged threads, and repair if necessary by fitting a thread insert of the correct size.

Reassembly

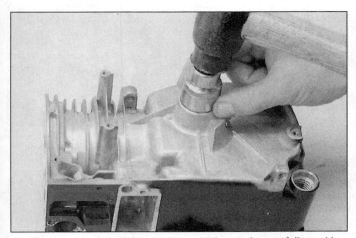

1 Fit new oil seals into the crankcase and sump by carefully pushing them into place using an appropriate sized socket. The seals should be fitted with the sharp rubber edge of the seal towards the inside of the engine.

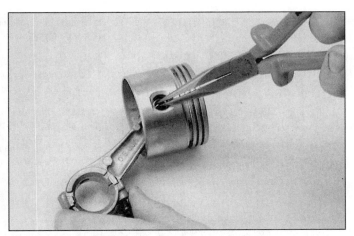

2 Oil the main bearing journal in the crankcase, and insert the crankshaft tapered end first.

3 If previously removed, fit the gudgeon pin into the piston/connecting rod assembly. The piston is fitted with the circlip groove towards the non-tapered end of the crankshaft, and the 'open' side of the connecting rod towards the camshaft bearing. If the gudgeon pin is reluctant to move, immerse the piston in hot water for a few minutes. This causes the aluminium to expand, and the gudgeon pin to slide easily.

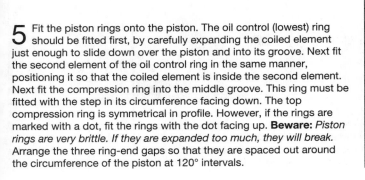

4 Always fit a new piston circlip.

5 Fit the piston rings onto the piston. The oil control (lowest) ring should be fitted first, by carefully expanding the coiled element just enough to slide down over the piston and into its groove. Next fit the second element of the oil control ring in the same manner, positioning it so that the coiled element is inside the second element. Next fit the compression ring into the middle groove. This ring must be fitted with the step in its circumference facing down. The top compression ring is symmetrical in profile. However, if the rings are marked with a dot, fit the rings with the dot facing up. **Beware:** *Piston rings are very brittle. If they are expanded too much, they will break.* Arrange the three ring-end gaps so that they are spaced out around the circumference of the piston at 120° intervals.

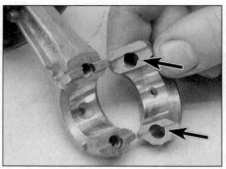

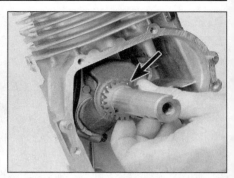

6 Smear the piston rings and cylinder bore with oil. Using a piston ring clamp, fit the piston into the cylinder from the top by feeding the connecting rod through first. Make sure that the connecting rod does not scratch the cylinder walls. Press the piston firmly into the cylinder, sliding it out of the clamp as the rings enter the bore. If necessary, using a piece of wood or hammer handle, gently tap the piston out of the clamp and into the cylinder, but stop and investigate any undue resistance.

7 Oil the crankshaft journal and engage the big-end onto the journal. Fit the big-end cap. Due to the stepped shape of the cap, it will only fit one way round (arrowed). If you have a suitable torque wrench, tighten the bolts to the torque given in Technical Data. If not, tighten the bolts securely, but do not over-tighten. Rotate the crankshaft to ensure freedom of movement.

8 Slide the camshaft drive gear over the end of the crankshaft with the timing mark facing outwards (arrowed). The gear locates over a pin in the crankshaft.

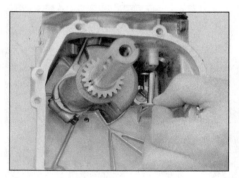

9 Oil the cam followers, and refit them to their original locations.

10 Turn the crankshaft until the timing mark on the gear is pointing at the middle of the camshaft bearing hole in the crankcase. Smear some oil on the camshaft bearing journal, and install the camshaft. The timing dimple cast in the camshaft gear must be aligned exactly with the mark on the crankshaft gear when the gears are meshed (arrowed). Rotate the crankshaft two revolutions to ensure correct movement.

11 Refit the oil slinger assembly to the end of the camshaft.

12 Fit a new gasket over the locating dowels in the crankcase gasket face, and carefully refit the sump. Take care not to damage the lip of the oil seal. Secure the sump with the six bolts, using thread sealer on the bolt that enters the engine breather chamber (arrowed). Refit the sump plug and filler/dipstick.

13 Prior to fitting the valve springs, turn the crankshaft until the piston is at top dead centre on the compression stroke. Slowly continue to turn the crankshaft until the piston has moved down the bore approximately 6 mm. Insert the valves into their respective guides and, with reference to Chapter 2, check both valve clearances. The dimensions are given in the Technical Data. Once the correct clearances have been achieved, remove the valves.

14 Fit the exhaust valve spring and collar into place in the tappet chest, with the close-coiled end of the spring towards the valve head. Ensure that the notch in the rim of the collar is facing out. Insert the exhaust valve. Using a pair of thin-nosed pliers (or similar), compress the valve spring, slide the collar over the end of the valve stem, and move the collar in towards the cylinder. Slowly allow the spring to uncompress, and check that the collar has located correctly on the end of the valve stem. Repeat this procedure for the inlet valve

15 Check the fibre disc valve in the engine breather for distortion or cracks. The gap between the disc valve and the body should not exceed 1.1 mm. The valve is held in place by an internal bracket, which will distort if too much pressure is applied to the disc. If the valve is defective, renew the complete breather assembly. Renew the gasket.

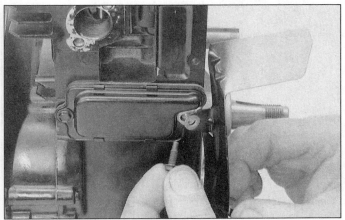

16 Refit the valve/cover and crankcase cowling using the two bolts. Tighten securely.

17 Grease the threads of the engine breather pipe, and screw it into the breather chamber.

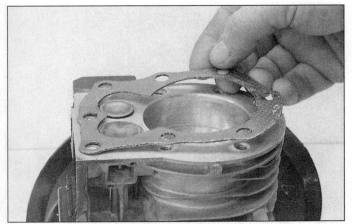

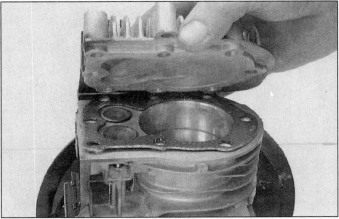

18 Place the new head gasket in the correct position. The gasket will only align with the bolt holes one way round. Do not use any jointing compound.

19 Refit the cylinder head and cowling.

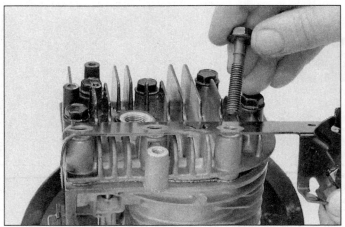

20 Tighten the eight retaining bolts evenly, in a diagonal sequence, to the torque given in Technical Data. Refit the spark plug.

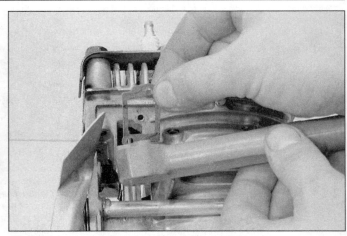

21 Using a new gasket, refit the inlet manifold.

22 Fit the flywheel over the tapered end of the crankshaft, align the keyway, and slide the square sectioned key into place.

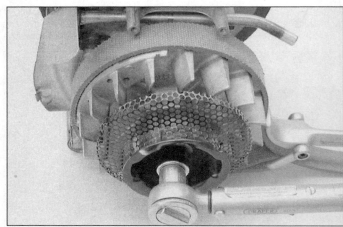

23 Refit the screen mesh, starter flange, and retaining nut to the crankshaft. Using a strap wrench to prevent the flywheel from turning, tighten the retaining nut to the torque given in Technical Data. The help of an assistant will be required to steady the engine during this procedure.

24 Check the condition of the gasket, and refit the exhaust system. The two retaining bolts are locked in place by bending the tabs of the locking washer.

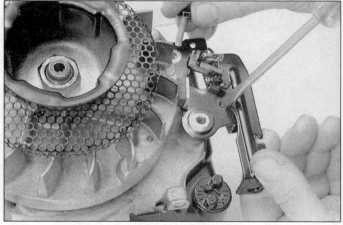

25 Using a screwdriver, wedge the flywheel brake assembly in the 'OFF' position, and refit it to the crankcase using the two retaining bolts. Remove the screwdriver.

26 Route the magneto earthing wire under the engine breather pipe, through the retaining clip, and reconnect it to the engine stop element of the flywheel brake assembly.

27 Refit the magneto and engine governor using the two retaining bolts. The magneto body is marked 'Cylinder side' on one side, and 'This side out' on the other. Before tightening the two mounting bolts, turn the flywheel so that the magnets are on the opposite side to the magneto, and use a feeler gauge to measure the air gap between the two legs of the magneto's armature and the flywheel. The correct air gap is given in Technical Data. The mounting holes in the armature legs are slotted. Move the armature until the correct gap is achieved. Tighten the bolts securely. Reconnect the magneto earthing wire. Refit the HT cap to the spark plug.

28 Refit the carburettor to the fuel tank using a new gasket. As the carburettor is fitted, ensure that the spring is correctly located in the carburettor body (arrowed). Tighten the six retaining bolts securely.

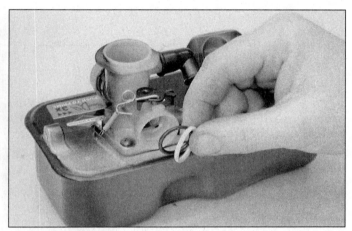

29 The carburettor-to-inlet manifold joint is sealed by an O-ring, retained by a collar in the carburettor outlet. Carefully prise out the collar and check the O-ring for and signs of damage or wear. Fit a new O-ring if in any doubt. Refit the collar by pushing it into place.

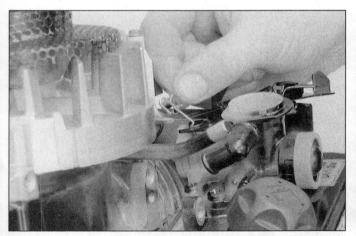

30 As the carburettor and fuel tank assembly is fitted, reconnect the throttle arm-to-governor linkage and reconnect the engine breather pipe. Retain the assembly with the end mounting bolt, but do not tighten.

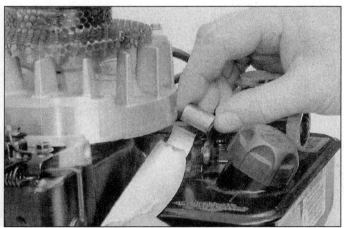

31 Fit the crankcase cowling and spacer, insert the fuel tank-retaining bolt, and tighten both mounting bolts.

32 Reconnect the governor return spring ...

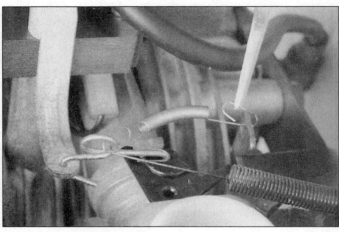

33 ... and the throttle spring.

34 Refit the engine cowling/starter using two retaining bolts. One into the top of the cylinder head, and one into the crankcase which also retains the crankcase cowling.

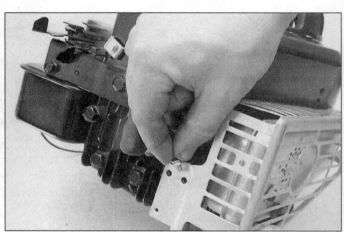

35 Fit the exhaust shield using the two retaining bolts. One into the cylinder head, and the other into the crankcase which also secures the engine cowling.

36 Note the locating peg (arrowed), and fit the flywheel brake cover.

37 Refit the air filter assembly, not forgetting the sealing washer between the housing and carburettor.

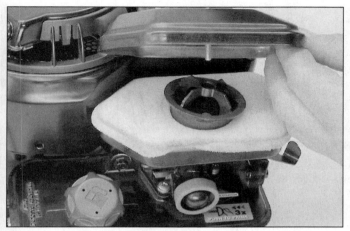

38 If the air filter element is dirty, clean it with fresh petrol, and soak it in clean engine oil. Squeeze the excess oil from the foam and refit it into the housing.

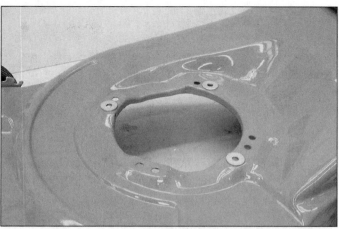

39 Position the three washers around the relevant body mounting holes, and refit the engine to the body. Tighten the nuts and bolts securely.

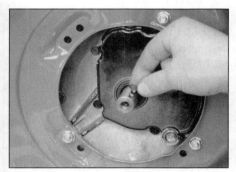

40 Refit the Woodruff (half moon) key to the keyway nearest the end of the shaft, and fit the blade mounting flange.

41 Mount the blade on the flange using the locating lugs, and tighten the retaining bolt securely.

42 Reconnect the flywheel brake/engine stop cable by engaging the inner cable in the hole in the lever, and pushing the outer cable ferrule into the locating hole in the bracket.

43 Remember to add the correct quantity and grade of engine oil.

Starter repair

1 With the starter/engine cowling removed, pull the starter rope to its full extension. Lock the rope pulley in this position by inserting a square sectioned piece of wood through the cowling next to the lug on the pulley rim. The lug jams against the wood, and the pulley is held.

2 To replace the rope: Where the rope goes through the pulley, cut off the knot and pull the rope from the starter. Feed the new rope through the outer hole in the cowling and the inner hole in the pulley. Tie the knot. Then feed the other end of the rope through the hole in the starter handle, again tie the knot. Tension the rope and remove the piece of wood. Be prepared for the spring to violently rewind the starter rope. Refit the starter/engine cowling.

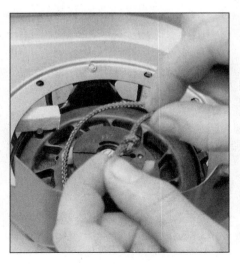

3 To replace the recoil spring: Where the rope goes through the pulley, untie the knot and pull the rope from the starter. Unscrew the central bolt from the pawl mechanism, and lift off the guide plate. Note the position of the pawls, and remove them.

4 Carefully lift out the pulley, noting the locating slot for the end of the spring. Lift out the spring.

5 Insert the new spring, locating the inner end around the lug on the cowling.

6 Fit the pulley, locating the outer end of the spring in the slot on the pulley (arrowed).

7 Check the starter pawls for damage or excessive wear, and refit them to the pulley. Refit the guide plate onto the pawls, ensuring that the pawl locating pins engage with the slots on the underside of the guide plate. Tighten the central bolt.

8 Using a screwdriver (or similar), very carefully wind the pulley approximately seven full turns, and align the rope hole in the pulley with the hole in the cowling. The exact number of turns is dependent on the length of rope. Lock the pulley in place by inserting a piece of square sectioned wood through the cowling, jamming the lug on the pulley rim. Exercise extreme caution during this procedure. It will take some effort to wind the spring up, and should the piece of wood slip, the pulley will spin violently.

9 Feed the rope through the outer hole in the cowling and the hole in the pulley. Tie a knot in the end of the rope. Tension the rope and remove the piece of wood from the cowling. Be prepared for the spring to violently rewind the starter rope. Check for correct operation. Refit the starter/engine cowling.

Chapter 8
Honda GV100 4-stroke engine

Model/spec. number on engine: GV100

Mower application

Every effort has been made to make the list of models that use this engine as comprehensive as possible. Due to model and engine supply changes, you may have a mower that is not listed. Refer to *Engine Identity* on page 7 to identify the engine that you have, or contact an engine supply dealer to assist with identification.

Honda HR17   Honda HRB423   Rover 00
Honda HR173   Mountfield Laser Delta 42

Technical Data

Spark plug gap	0.6 to 0.7 mm (0.024 to 0.028 in)
Points gap	0.3 to 0.4 mm (0.012 to 0.016 in)
Valve clearances:	
Inlet and exhaust (standard)	0.04 to 0.10 mm (0.002 to 0.004 in)
Piston ring gap:	
Standard	0.15 to 0.35 mm (0.006 to 0.014 in)
Wear limit	1.0 mm (0.04 in)
Piston ring side clearance:	
Top Ring:	
Standard	0.025 to 0.055 mm (0.0010 to 0.0022 in)
Service limit	0.10 mm (0.004 in)
Second and Oil rings:	
Standard	0.010 to 0.040 mm (0.0004 to 0.0016 in)
Service limit	0.10 mm (0.004 in)
Oil	SAE 10W-30 or 10W-40 all temps.
Oil capacity	0.6 litres

Dismantling

Before starting to dismantle, read Chapter 2. The procedures outlined apply to all engines and if adopted, will ensure an orderly and methodical approach that will make both dismantling and reassembly much easier.

1 Disconnect the plug lead. Drain the oil from the engine.

2 Remove the recoil starter from the fan shroud.

3 Remove the air cleaner.

4 Remove the fan shroud, disconnecting the fuel pipe before lifting the shroud away.

5 Lift the collars from the studs on which the shroud was mounted.

6 Remove the cutter. Be prepared to take the spring pressure as the central bolt is loosened.

7 Remove the exhaust muffler cover, bottom plate, deflector pipe and gasket.

8 Remove the roto-stop link and spring.

9 Disconnect the ignition cut-off lever from the handle bar lead.

10 Remove the engine holding nuts and bolts and lift the engine from the deck.

11 Pull the breather tube off the connection on the air cleaner housing.

12 Disconnect the automatic choke link.

13 Disconnect the governor link and spring, noting which holes the link and spring connect into.

14 Disconnect the petrol pipe from the carburettor.

15 Remove the carburettor.

16 Remove the carburettor joint plate with the studs in it, the two gaskets and the plastic insulator from the cylinder inlet port.

17 Remove the automatic choke bimetallic strip.

18 Remove the tappet cover complete with the fuel pipe supported by it, the gasket and the separator box.

19 Remove the flywheel nut.

20 Remove the recoil starter drive dish, the screen grid and the plastic impeller.

21 Remove the flywheel from the crankshaft taper and remove the key from the groove in the taper. To free the flywheel, replace the flywheel nut until it is flush with the end of the crankshaft threads. Hold the weight of the engine by the flywheel. Using a soft hammer or a normal hammer and a block of soft metal, strike the nut flush on the face. This should break the grip of the taper. The nut and flywheel can then be removed. Some assistance will be needed for this operation. This method is a useful alternative when a proper flywheel puller is not available, but take great care not to damage the threads. If the hammer or block are not held square while striking the nut, the crankshaft can be bent or the end broken off.

22 Remove the cover from the contact breaker assembly and remove the assembly.

23 Remove the coil assembly.

24 Remove the cylinder head.

25 Remove the crankcase flange bolts and split the oil pan from the crankcase.

26 With the crankshaft on Top Dead Centre of the compression stroke to relieve the camshaft load, withdraw the camshaft and the two thrust washers. Note that the larger washer is at the outer end.

27 Mark the cam followers for reassembly in the same holes then remove them.

28 Remove the valves

29 Remove the big end cap, separate the connecting rod from the crankpin and withdraw the crankshaft.

30 Remove the piston and connecting rod through the bottom of the bore and into the crankcase. This avoids the risk of scratching the cylinder bore with the connecting rod. Remove the piston from the connecting rod, noting carefully which way round it fitted, and which way round the gudgeon pin fitted.

31 Withdraw the crankshaft complete with the main ball bearing.

Reassembly

1 The correct assembly relationship of the piston and connecting rod is shown in the photo.

2 If the original piston rings are being refitted they must be placed in the same grooves and the same way up as originally fitted. The step on the middle ring must be uppermost. After fitting the piston rings, assemble the piston to the connecting rod. The gudgeon pin must be the same way round as when removed. Secure it with the circlip.

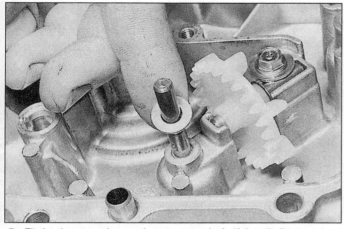

3 Fit the thrust washer on the governor shaft. If the oil slinger or governor weight holder wheel are worn or damaged, renew them.

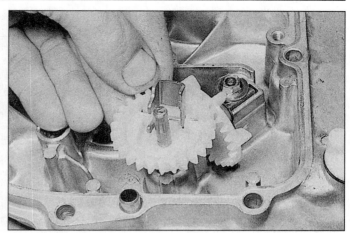

4 Fit the governor wheel on the stub shaft with one of the weights fitted.

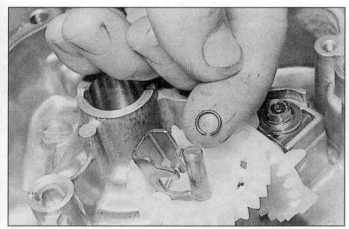

5 Secure the wheel with a C-clip. Ensure that the C-clip is properly seated in the groove on the shaft.

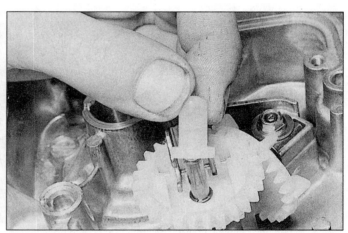

6 Fit the slider onto the shaft with the flange located between the prongs of the weight.

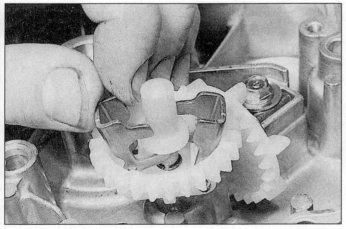

7 Position the other weight on the wheel with its two prongs located either side of the slider flange.

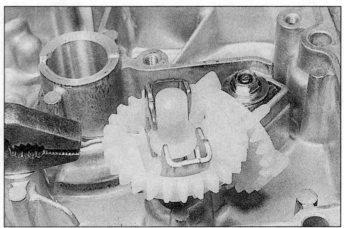

8 Secure the weight with the split pin.

9 Renew the oil seal in the flywheel bearing of the crankcase if necessary. The part numbers and slots in the face of the seal should face outwards. Prise out the old seal with a screwdriver. Smear the new seal with oil and tap gently into place.

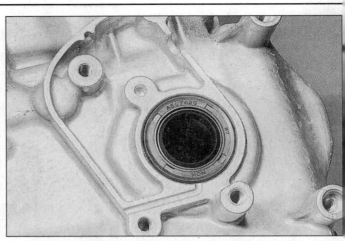

10 Renew the oil seal in the oil pan if necessary, in the same manner as for the flywheel bearing.

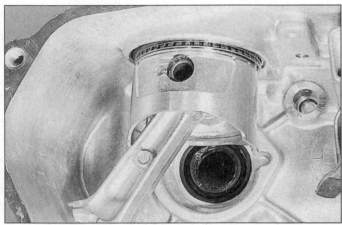

11 Smear the piston with oil then carefully enter it into the bore of the cylinder from the crankcase end. The lead-in chamfer of the bore will guide the piston rings into the cylinder. The offset big end should be facing away from the governor side of the crankcase.

12 Smear the crankshaft with oil to ease it through the seal. Insert it into the crankcase, complete with the flywheel ball bearing. Tap it gently home with a soft hammer until the bearing seats against the shoulder in the crankcase housing. Smear the crankpin with oil.

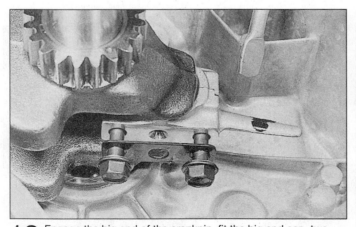

13 Engage the big end of the crankpin, fit the big end cap, two bolts, two lock washers and the flat washer.

14 Tighten the bolts firmly. Turn the crankshaft to ensure free rotation.

15 Smear the cam followers with oil and insert them into the same holes from which they were removed.

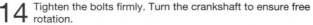

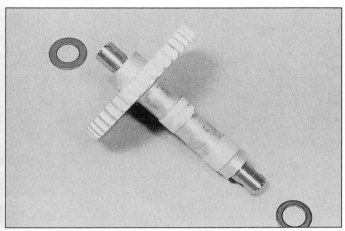

16 The small thrust washer fits at the lower end of the camshaft and the larger one to the upper end. Position the smaller one on the camshaft bearing in the crankcase.

17 Turn the crankshaft until the timing mark on the cam gear will coincide with the mark on the camshaft. Fit the camshaft and mesh the gear with the timing mark aligned with the crankshaft cam gear mark.

18 The correct position of the two timing marks is shown in the photo.

19 Fit the large thrust washer to the top of the camshaft.

20 Fit the thrust washer onto the crankshaft.

21 Fit the two hollow dowels into the crankcase.

22 Fit a new crankcase gasket. Do not use jointing compound.

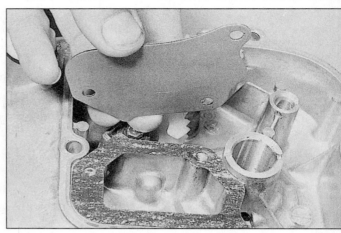

23 Fit the oil chamber gasket and cover plate.

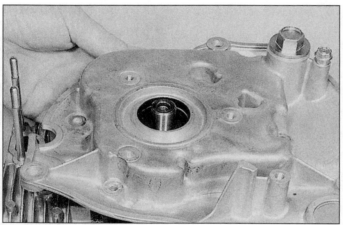

24 Oil the crankshaft and fit the oil pan onto it. Slide the oil pan down the crankshaft, locate it on the hollow dowels then mate it onto the crankcase face

25 Fit the six crankcase flange bolts and tighten a little at a time diagonally to avoid cracking or distorting the oil pan.

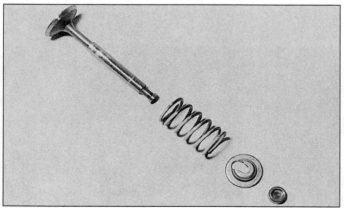

26 The valve components are shown in the photo. The large end of the oval hole in the collar allows the full width of the valve stem through. The collar can then be slid sideways so that the narrow end of the oval fits under the shoulder on the valve stem, thus locking the valve and spring together. The adjuster cap is fitted onto the tip of the valve stem after reassembly of the valve. Note that the inlet valve is larger than the exhaust valve.

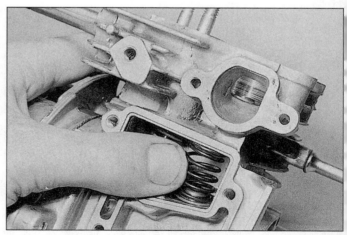

27 To fit the valves, place the coil spring in the valve chest with the collar under, and the dished side of the collar upward.

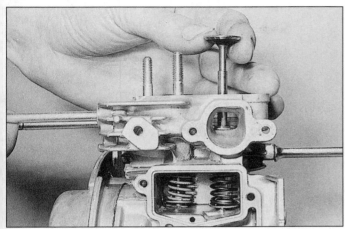

28 Oil the valve stem and slide it down through the guide and the collar. Lever the collar up with a screwdriver while pressing the valve down, slide the collar sideways until it engages under the shoulder of the valve stem, then release the leverage.

29 To fit the valve clearance adjuster cap, lever the valve up with the screwdriver again until the head of the valve is well clear of the seat. Slide an open spanner under the head to hold the valve open.

30 Fit the cap onto the valve stem and withdraw the spanner gently, so as not to damage the valve seat or cylinder head face.

31 Check the valve clearance with a feeler gauge. Both valves should have clearances as given in Technical Data. An adjuster cap of the approximate length is obtainable to achieve this clearance. Failing this, the head of the cap can be lapped to achieve the required clearance. The cap must be held square while lapping. If the valves need grinding in, the clearances will also need attention.

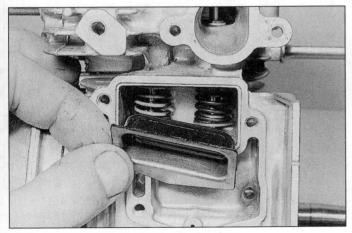

32 Fit the separator box into the valve chest.

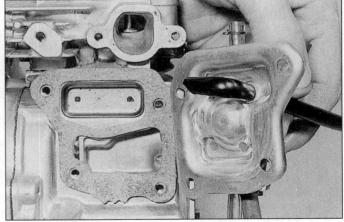

33 Fit the gasket and tappet cover, complete with the fuel pipe which is supported on it.

34 Using a new cylinder head gasket, fit the cylinder head.

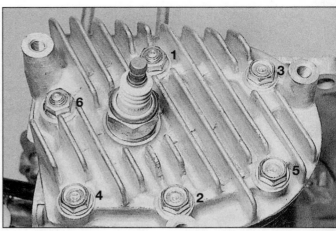

35 Tighten the two nuts and four bolts a little at a time in rotation, to the pattern shown in the photo. Even tightening is essential to avoid cylinder head distortion.

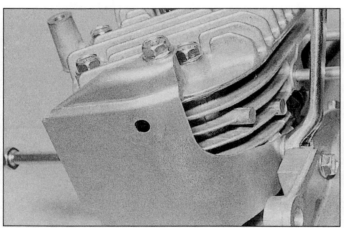

36 Fit the shroud.

37 Place the coil assembly in position on the two mounting bosses, with the small electrical lead grommet pressed into the slot in the crankcase web.

38 Fit the condenser with its mounting plate hole on the coil assembly hole, and secure the condenser and coil assembly with the two set screws. Press the condenser lead into the slot in the grommet containing the coil assembly lead.

39 Fit the contact breaker assembly with the peg on the base plate in the plain hole near the crankshaft oil seal.

40 Tighten the cross-head screw when the adjustment is correct. Connect the two leads (one from the condenser, the other from the coil unit) to the nut and bolt on the contact breaker base plate. The tags are to be on the outside of the insulating washer.

41 Impregnate the breaker oil pad with light grease. Fit a gasket on the breaker housing.

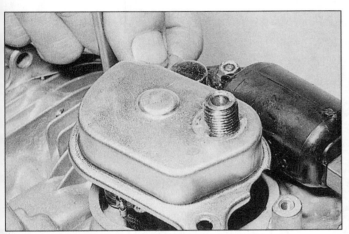

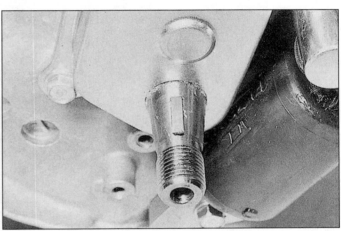

42 Fit the cover over the contact breaker assembly.

43 Place the Woodruff key in the slot in the crankshaft.

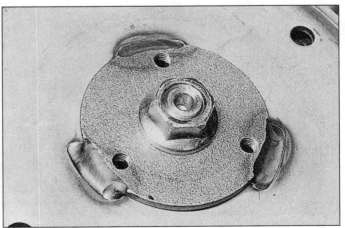

44 Fit the flywheel. Ensure that it engages properly with the key in the crankshaft.

45 Fit and tighten the flywheel nut.

46 Place the plastic impeller on the flywheel. Make sure that the three pegs in the underside locates in the matching holes in the flywheel,

47 Place the screen grid on the impeller with the locating hole over the peg on the impeller.

48 Position the recoil starter drive dish on the screen grid. Fit and tighten the three bolts.

49 Thoroughly clean the main jet (the smallest of the components shown in the picture) by rinsing in petrol and blowing through it. Do not use a pin in the jet or the metered orifice will be damaged. Similarly clean the main nozzle (shown next to the main jet). Again, do not poke pins into the metering holes. Insert the main nozzle into the carburettor body, then secure the main jet into the same hole and tighten gently.

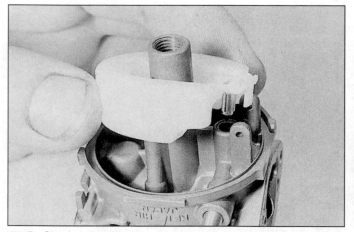

50 Check the needle valve for wear and ridging. Check the spring (which pushes the head onto the valve seat) for weakness. Replace the whole valve if defects are found. The valve slides into a slot in the float and is easily removable. Place the float and valve assembly on the carburettor body.

51 Insert the float hinge pin.

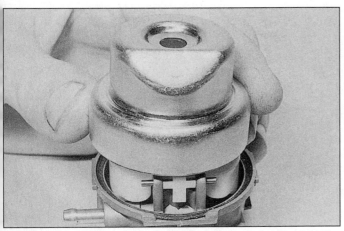

52 Check that the float chamber gasket is correctly seated and is not damaged or distorted. Renew if necessary. Fit the float chamber.

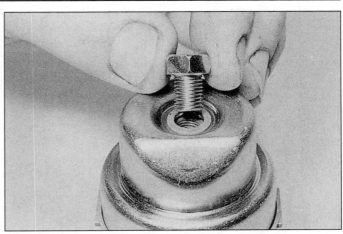

53 Secure the float chamber with the set bolt and washer.

54 Check the pilot jet screw for a damaged or bent needle tip. Screw it in gently until it seats, then unscrew 1½ turns. This setting can be fine tuned later when the engine is started.

55 Prise off the lid of the automatic choke housing. Move the choke lever gently away from its stop and check that it returns freely to the stop under spring pressure. The spring can be replaced by undoing the choke butterfly and withdrawing the spindle from the choke housing. Press the snap fit cover back onto the housing.

56 Fit the gasket to the inlet port. Install the plastic insulator on the port, with the tongue inside the port.

57 Place the triangular gasket on the insulator. Fit the carburettor joint plate and secure it with the two cross-head screws.

58 Place the gasket on the joint plate.

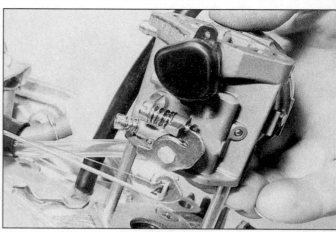

59 Pass the governor link through the coils of the throttle return spring and connect the link and the spring to the hole in the tip of the governor lever. The coils of the spring must be at the governor lever end of the link. Slide the carburettor onto the studs of the joint plate and connect the other end of the link, and the throttle return spring, into the throttle butterfly lever. Do not secure the carburettor at this stage.

60 Ease the carburettor up the studs sufficiently to fit the bimetal strip and its bolt. Tighten the bimetal strip in place.

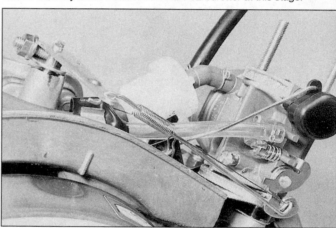

61 Hook one end of the choke rod into the choke housing. Connect the other, sharply hooked, end into the bimetallic strip and secure it with the lock pin.

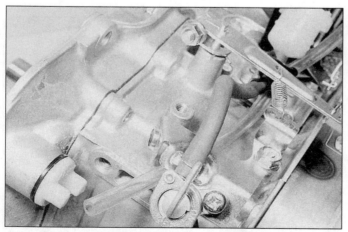

62 Fit the fuel pipe assembly, with the filter situated near the carburettor. Secure the fuel tap with the cross-head screw. Fit the governor lever return spring.

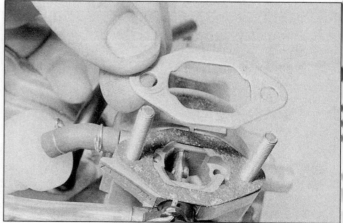

63 Fit the air cleaner gasket and the packing to the carburettor inlet.

64 Attach the air cleaner housing to the carburettor joint plate studs and push the breather pipe on to the housing connector.

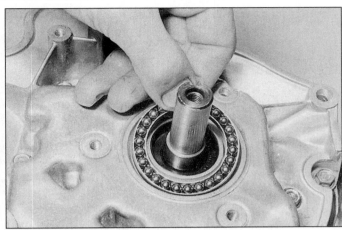

65 Press the ball track into the recess in the oil pan.

66 Place the muffler gasket on the engine deck.

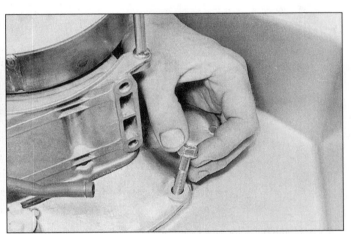

67 Position the engine on the deck, entering the exhaust port studs down through the muffler gasket. Fit the three engine bolts and screw the nuts onto them from under the deck.

68 Tighten the engine mounting nuts and bolts firmly.

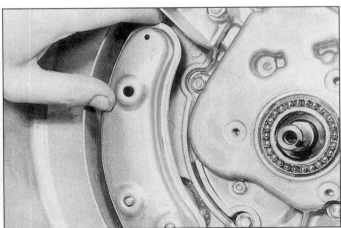

69 Position the muffler on the two studs under the deck.

70 Fit the muffler bottom plate.

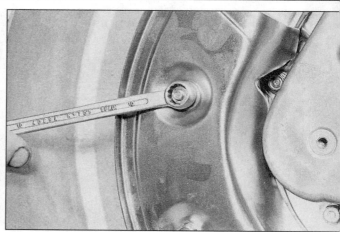

71 Fit the muffler cover onto the bottom plate, fit the two nuts onto the studs and tighten them.

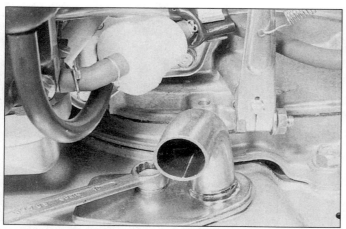

72 Fit the deflector pipe over the muffler exit hole in the deck, pass the long flange bolt down through the deflector pipe and muffler assembly, fit the nut and tighten it.

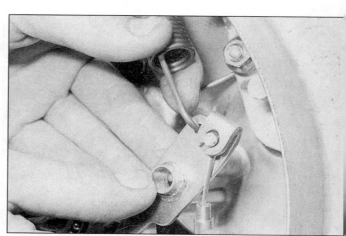

73 Engage the Roto-stop cable nipple in the lever, then hook the Roto-stop spring to the lever.

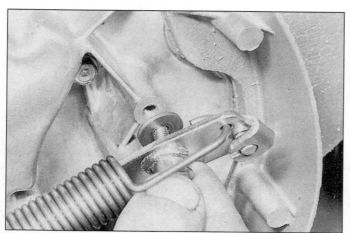

74 Line the lever up with the threaded hole, fit the bolt through it, place the flat washer on the bolt then screw the bolt into the threaded hole and tighten it.

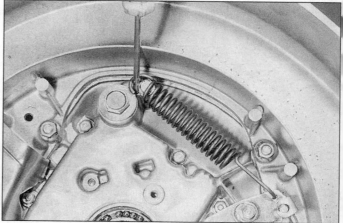

75 Lever the other end of the spring over the head of the bolt in the crankcase.

76 Fit the ball control plate with the gap in its rim engaged with the roto-stop lever.

77 Place the ball retainer on the ball control plate.

78 Place the Roto-stop disc on the ball control plate.

79 Secure it with the three bolts.

80 Insert the key into the slot in the crankshaft.

81 Fit the drive disc onto the crankshaft.

82 Place the driven disc on the drive disc. And the clutch spring on the driven disc.

83 Insert the bolt into the blade holder and locate the boss of the blade holder in the clutch spring.

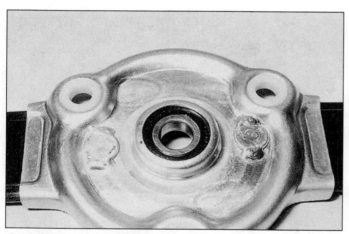

84 Press the blade holder against the clutch spring, locate the three bushes in the blade holder on the three pegs of the driven disc and screw the bolt into the crankshaft.

85 Tighten the bolt firmly.

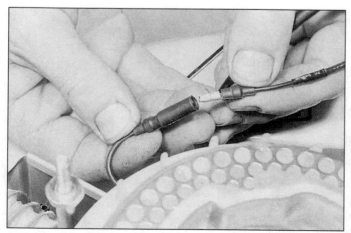

86 Connect the ignition shorting lead from the engine to the lead on the handle bar. Connect the HT lead on the sparking plug.

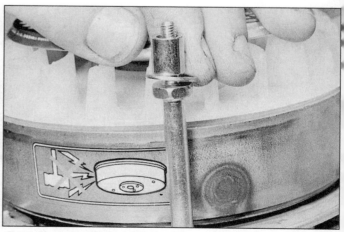

87 Place the flat washer and collar on each shroud mounting stud.

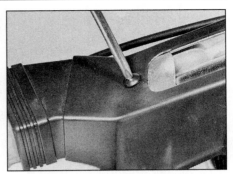

88 Install the shroud complete with the fuel tank on the studs. Secure it with the long bolt through the fuel tank. Connect the fuel pipe to the tank with the spring clip.

89 If the recoil starter requires no attention, position it on the mounting studs and fit and tighten the cap nuts. If repair is necessary, do not install the starter at this stage but refer to Starter repair at the end of this chapter.

90 Replace the handle column cover.

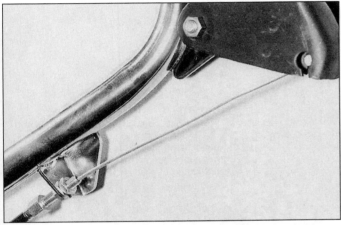

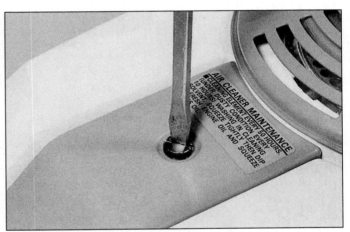

91 Adjust the rotor-stop brake cable as necessary to brake the cutter blade when the handle is released. Free play at the tip of the lever should be 5 to10 mm (0.2 to 0.4 in).

92 Clean the air cleaner foam element by rinsing in solvent, not petrol, and squeeze it dry. Do not wring it as this crushes and tears the foam. Saturate the element in clean oil, squeeze out the excess and install the element in the house. Fit cover.

Starter repair

To fit a new cord or recoil spring, the starter housing must be removed from the shroud, and dismantled. With the housing removed, proceed as follows:

1 To release pulley tension, pull out the starting handle 3 turns of the pulley, trap the cord in the pulley notch, then let the pulley unwind 3 turns, taking the cord with it.

2 Remove the central bolt and lift off the friction plate complete with friction spring.

3 Check the ratchet and ratchet spring for unobstructed movement and positive return of the ratchet. Renew the ratchet spring if necessary.

4 Lift off the pulley. Remove the recoil spring if broken. Fit a new cord to the pulley if necessary.

5 To fit a new spring, hook the outer edge end into the slot in the housing, then wind the spring anti-clockwise into the housing, working from outside in towards the centre. Apply grease to the spring coils.

6 Replace the pulley onto the centre stub shaft. Turn it anti-clockwise until it seats right down and engages with the hook on the inner end of the spring.

7 Fit the friction plate and spring onto the pulley with the two legs of the spring on either side of the lug on the ratchet.

8 Fit the central bolt.

9 Trap the cord in the pulley notch, wind the pulley and cord 3 turns anti-clockwise. Hold the pulley, free the cord from the notch and release the pulley.

10 Pull the cord and release it to ensure full movement and a positive return action.

11 Install the housing on the studs and secure it with the cap nuts. Pull the handle and check that engagement of the ratchet feels right and that the ratchet does not jump out.

Chapter 9
Honda GXV120 4-stroke engine

Model/spec. number on engine: GXV120

Mower application

Every effort has been made to make the list of models that use this engine as comprehensive as possible. Due to model and engine supply changes, you may have a mower that is not listed. Refer to *Engine Identity* on page 7 to identify the engine that you have, or contact an engine supply dealer to assist with identification.

Hayter (various)
Honda HR194
Honda HRA214

Honda HR214
IPU 400 series

Rover (various)
Tracmaster Camon

Technical Data

Spark plug gap	0.7 to 0.8 mm (0.028 to 0.031 in)
Valve clearances:	
Inlet	0.08 to 0.13 mm (0.003 to 0.005 in)
Exhaust	0.13 to 0.18 mm (0.005 to 0.007 in)
Armature air gap	0.25 mm (0.010 in)
Piston ring gap (standard)	0.23 to 0.525 mm (0.009 to 0.021 in)
Roto-stop brake cable adjustment (free play at tip of lever)	5 to 10 mm (0.20 to 0.39 in)
Drive clutch cable (free play at handle bar)	5 to 10 mm (0.20 to 0.39 in)
Speed change cable (free play at tip of lever)	1 to 3 mm (0.04 to 0.12 in)
Oil	SAE 10W-40
Oil capacity	0.6 litres

Dismantling

Before starting to dismantle, read Chapter 2. The procedures outlined apply to all engines and if adopted, will ensure an orderly and methodical approach that will make both dismantling and reassembly much easier.

1 Disconnect the plug lead. Drain the oil from the engine.

2 Remove the handle bars. Be careful not to damage or kink the control cables.

3 Loosen the handle bar locknuts of the Roto-stop cable and unscrew the adjuster to release tension in the cable.

4 Free the throttle cable from the carburettor.

5 Remove the cutter blade.

6 Remove the cover panel from the transmission. Remove the plastic cover from the drive shaft.

7 Remove the engine mounting bolts.

8 Slide the engine forward so that the transmission drive shaft slides off the serrations on the final drive unit shaft.

9 Undo the two nuts securing the air cleaner duct to the carburettor. Remove the bolt securing the air cleaner to the engine. Remove the air cleaner complete with the engine breather pipe.

10 Remove the fuel filler cap.

11 Remove the engine cover.

12 Remove the petrol tank from the engine. Disconnect the fuel pipe from the tank, withdrawing the filter from the tank connector as the pipe is removed. Handle the filter with great care as it is very fragile.

13 Remove the clutch central bolt. Withdraw the cover plate, spring, clutch plate and pressure plate.

14 Make a careful note of the positions of all springs and links to assist reassembly in the same holes.

15 Remove the linkage mounting plate from the engine.

16 Remove the carburettor and the plastic insulator plate. Remove the float chamber, float and needle valve for inspection. Dismantle the fuel tap.

17 Remove the ignition unit.

18 Remove the exhaust muffler assembly (consisting of a shield, muffler box and gasket).

19 Remove the central bolt holding the brake assembly together and lift off the Roto stop brake components.

20 Remove the Woodruff key from the crankshaft.

21 Unscrew the three flange bolts and springs from the brake housing and lift off the housing.

22 Lift the ball retainer from the ball control plate.

23 Remove the Roto-stop return springs and lift off the ball control plate.

24 Remove the circular spacer from the crankshaft.

25 As a precaution, make a permanent mark on the governor lever and the shaft. If the lever ever becomes loose it is then easy to set it to the original datum.

26 Remove the flywheel nut from the crankshaft and lift off the rotating screen/starter hub, and the flywheel and impeller. Remove the key from the crankshaft taper.

27 Remove the overhead valve cover and gasket.

28 Remove the cylinder head complete with valves.

29 Remove the crankcase cover. Make a careful note of where the bolts of differing lengths fit to assist reassembly.

30 Mark the big end of the connecting rod and the cap before removing the latter, as the cap will fit both ways. It must be reassembled the same way round as originally fitted.

31 Withdraw the piston and connecting rod through the top of the cylinder, taking care not to scratch the bore.

32 Withdraw the camshaft and then the crankshaft. Pull the R-shaped clip off the drive shaft. Withdraw the drive shaft from the crankcase cover. To remove and dismantle the final drive unit, remove the right hand rear wheel.

33 Remove the height adjusting plate pivot bolts from both back wheels.

34 Remove the torque reacting bracket.

35 Lift the back axle clear.

36 Disconnect the speed change cable and the drive engage cable.

37 Remove the protector plate from the axle.

38 Remove the final drive case bolts, split the two halves of the casing and remove the internal components.

Note: *If any difficulty is experienced in carrying out these instructions, refer to the photographs in the reassembly instructions that follow, Used in the reverse sequence, these photographs indicate the steps in dismantling and will help to identify the components mentioned above.*

Reassembly

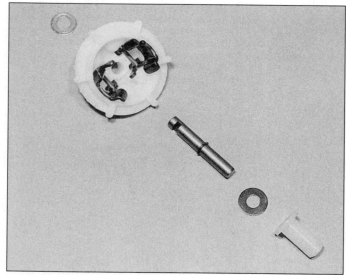

1 The governor components are shown in the photo. Fit the C-clip into the groove in the shaft; it is easier to do this at this stage.

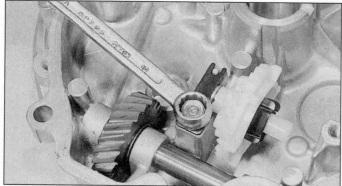

2 Slide the carrier wheel onto the governor shaft from the end with the slot in it. The weights on the wheel must be facing away from the slot. Fit the smaller washer onto the shaft after the wheel, With the wheel and washer as far onto the shaft as they will go, fit the shaft into the crankcase cover. The slot in the shaft mates onto a key machined in the cover casting. Fit the shaft clamp with the fork in the end engaged on the peg on the cover. (The gear seen in the photo will not have been fitted at this stage). Place the larger washer in the shaft, then fit the slider onto the shaft with its flange engaged between the weights.

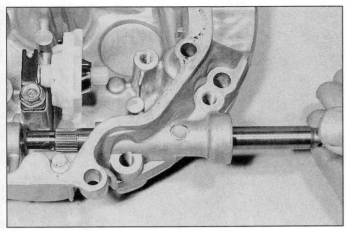

3 Insert the drive shaft into the crankcase cover.

4 The gear and its fixing components are shown in the photo.

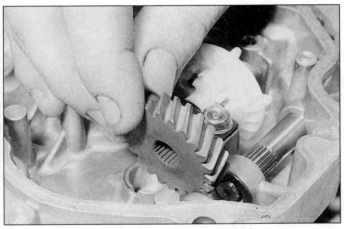

5 Fit the washer with the smaller hole onto the shaft, so that it will be between the first bearing and the gear. Slide the shaft into the gear.

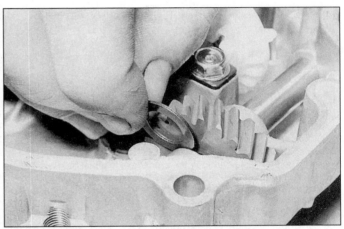

6 Fit the washer with the larger hole onto the end of the shaft then push the shaft into the second bearing.

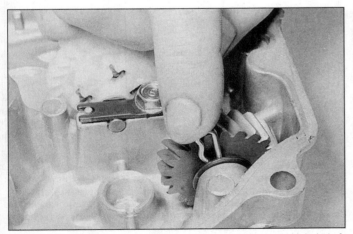

7 Insert the clip between the gear and the washer. Fit the straight leg of the clip into the hole in the shaft and press until it clicks fully home.

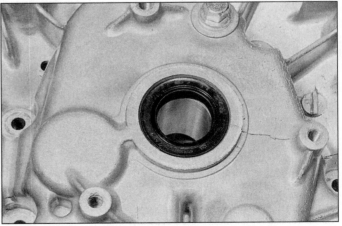

8 Fit a new oil seal to the crankcase cover bearing if necessary.

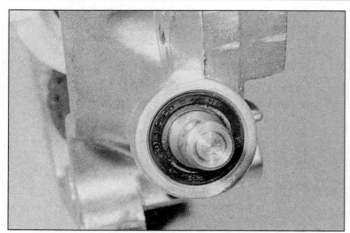

9 The drive shaft is also fitted with an oil seal, If necessary, renew the seal before fitting the drive shaft.

10 Fit a new oil seal to the crankcase flywheel bearing if necessary.

11 The flywheel bearing in the crankcase is a ball bearing. To renew it, remove the oil seal and drive the old bearing in towards the crankcase interior. Fit the new bearing from the interior. Drive it into the housing with a piece of tube that bears on the outer race only. If the ball cage or the inner race are struck, the bearing will be damaged. Keep the bearing square as it is driven into the casting.

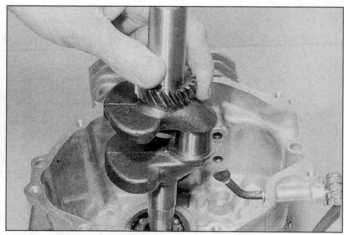

12 Smear a little oil on the crankshaft parallel portion at the tapered end. Insert the crankshaft into the crankcase bearing.

13 Assemble the connecting rod to the piston the same way round as when removed i.e. the oil hole on the same side as the arrow on the piston crown. If the gudgeon pin has been removed, fit it in the conventional manner, the same way round as when it was removed, and replace the circlips securely.

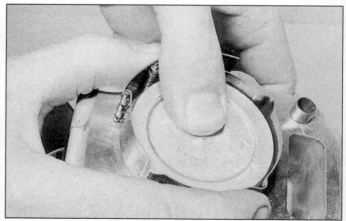

14 Fit a piston ring clamp to the piston. Oil the bore of the cylinder and insert the piston into it, taking care not to scratch the bore with the connecting rod. Press the piston out of the clamp and into the bore. Tap it gently with a piece of wood if necessary, but stop and investigate any obstruction or the piston rings may break. The arrow on the piston crown must be pointing towards the ohv push rod hole in the casting.

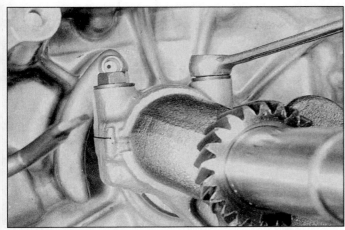

15 Invert the engine and oil the crank pin, engage the big end on it and fit the big end cap the same way round as marked when dismantling. Note that the cap will fit the wrong way round. Tighten the bolts firmly.

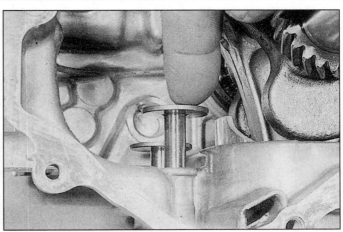

16 Oil the cam followers and fit them into the holes in which they were originally fitted (marked during dismantling).

17 Check the action of the decompressor on the camshaft gear. Ensure that the spring is undamaged, not stretched, and imparts a positive return action.

18 Check that the toe of the decompressor lever and the two prongs on the weight lever are not worn, and that they remain engaged throughout full travel of the weight lever.

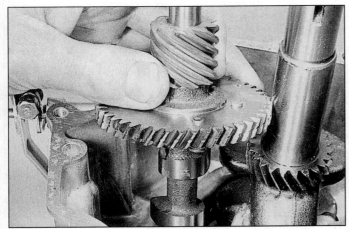

19 Lay the engine on its side and oil the camshaft bearing and insert the camshaft into the crankcase.

20 Mesh the cam gear with the crankshaft gear, with the timing marks aligned.

21 Place a new gasket on the crankcase. Oil the camshaft bearing and the crankshaft bearing. Fit the dowel into the crankcase.

22 Fit the oil return pipe into the elongated hole in the crankcase.

23 Fit the crankcase cover, ensuring that the governor slider and washer do not fall off. Guide the internal governor lever into the space between the governor slider and the side of the crankcase. Engage the cover on the dowel and seat the cover onto the crankcase.

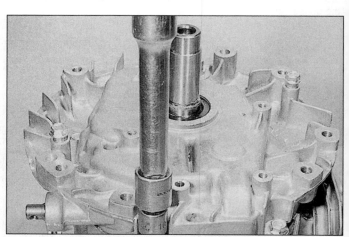

24 Secure the crankcase cover with the six bolts. Tighten diagonally opposite bolts a little at a time to avoid distorting or cracking the cover.

25 Insert the valves into the cylinder head. The exhaust valve has the smaller head of the two.

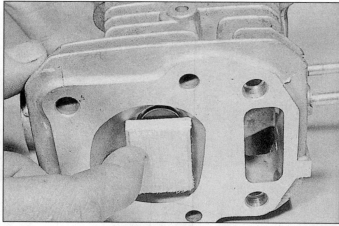

26 Place a small block of wood in the cylinder head to hold the valves on the seats while the springs are fitted. Turn the cylinder head on to its face with the wooden block in position.

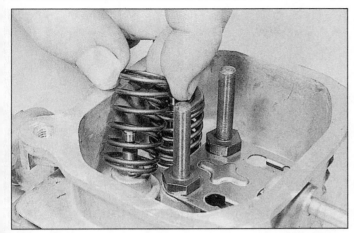

27 Fit the push rod guide plate onto the two studs in the cylinder head and secure with the two nuts. Place the valve spring over the valve stem.

28 Press the collar down onto the spring, slightly off to one side so that the larger, offset hole in the collar can pass down onto the valve stem, then centralise the collar with a sideways movement so that the smaller hole fits under the shoulder near the tip of the valve stem.

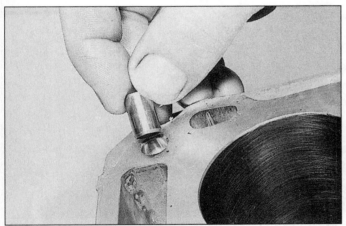

29 Place the two dowels in the top of the cylinder.

30 Place a new gasket on the cylinder.

31 Fit the assembled cylinder head onto the cylinder.

32 Secure the cylinder head with the four bolts, tightening them diagonally to avoid distortion or cracking.

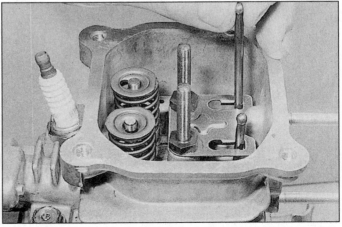

33 Insert the push rods through the retainer plate and locate them in the concave holes in the followers.

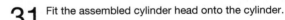

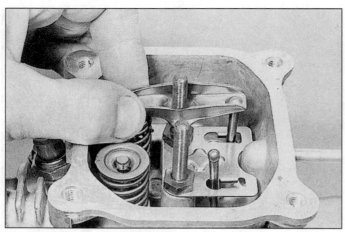

34 Place the rocker arms onto the studs with the smaller dimple seated on the top of the pushrod.

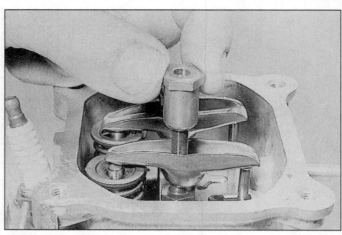

35 Screw the shouldered nuts onto the studs.

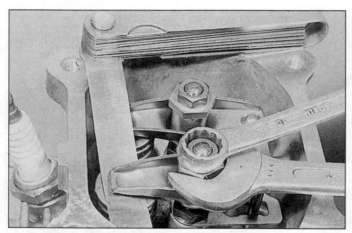

36 Fit the locknuts and set the valve clearances as given in Technical Data. Lock the locknuts. This operation must be carried out at Top Dead Centre of the firing stroke.

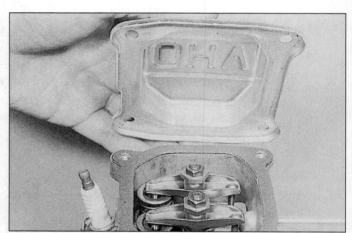

37 Fit a new valve cover gasket, then fit the valve cover but do not tighten down as two of the four bolts are used later to install the cowl.

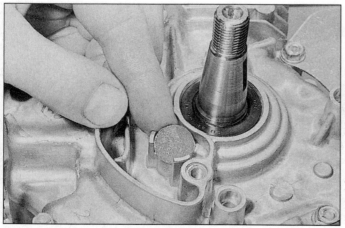

38 Inspect the breather disc valve for damage or distortion. Renew if necessary.

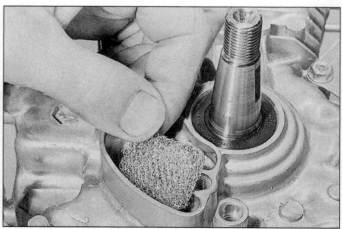

39 Rinse the gauze in solvent, dry thoroughly and insert it into the cavity in the breather housing.

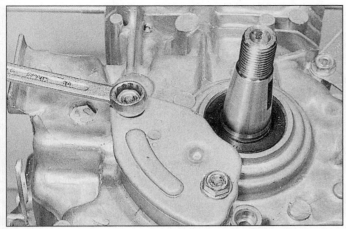

40 Fit a new gasket to the breather cover and secure the cover in position.

41 Place the Woodruff key in the slot in the crankshaft taper. If there are any shear marks or serious burrs, use a new key.

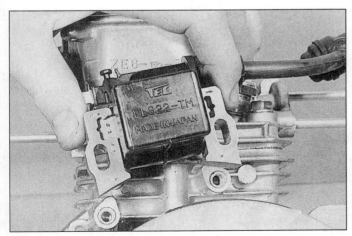

42 Install the flywheel and the impeller on the crankshaft, aligned with the key. The impeller has four locating pegs which fit into four holes in the flywheel.

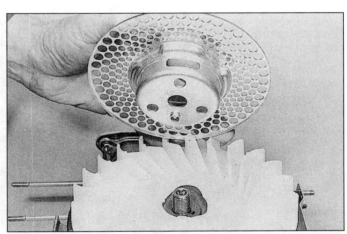

43 Fit the rotary screen and starter hub onto the impeller, with the screen located in the hole in the impeller. The three holes in the hub fit onto three pegs on the impeller. Fit the flywheel nut.

44 Install the ignition unit.

45 Using a non-ferrous feeler gauge, set an air gap as given in Technical Data between the armature legs and the flywheel.

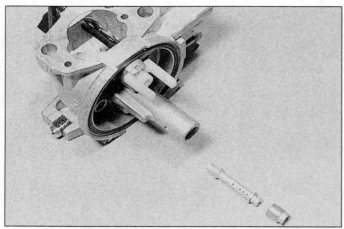

46 Remove the main jet and metering tube and examine them for dirt or gummy deposits. Clean by rinsing and blowing them. Do not poke the openings with a pin or wire, as they may be damaged and the accurate metering lost. Replace the metering tube and the main jet in the carburettor body.

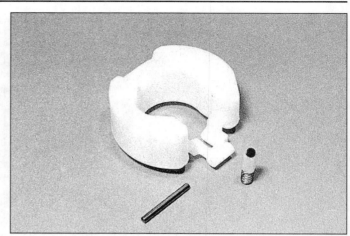

47 To remove the float, pull out the hinge pin. Remove the needle valve by pushing against the coil spring and sliding it out of the slot in the float. Examine the needle head for ridging or wear and renew if necessary.

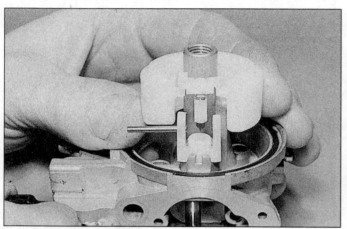

48 Fit the needle valve back into the slot in the float. Place the float hinge in position between the carburettor hinge posts, with the needle in the hole between the posts. Press the hinge pin through the holes and check it for free movement.

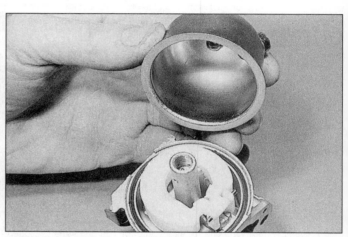

49 Examine the float chamber gasket for distortion or other damage. Renew it if necessary. Ensure that it is properly seated in the groove. Fit the float chamber with the drain plug towards the choke butterfly. Secure it with the bolt and fibre washer.

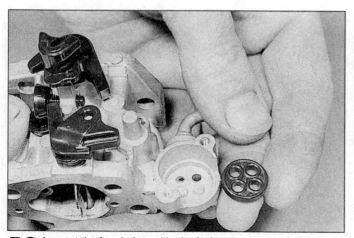

50 Inspect the four hole seal in the fuel tap and renew it if torn, distorted or hardened. Place it on the two shallow studs.

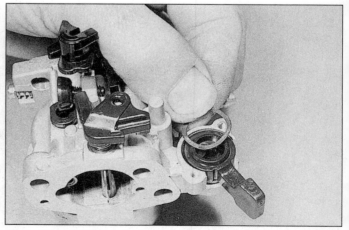

51 Place the lever valve body in the housing. Fit the wave washer on top of the body.

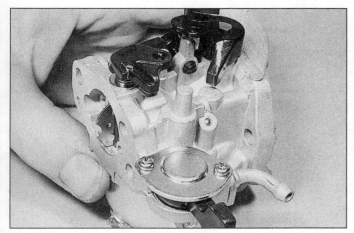

52 Fit the cover plate onto the housing.

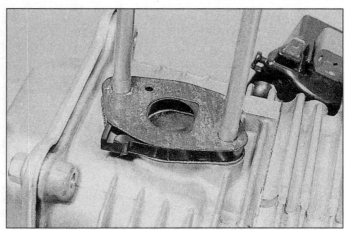

53 Fit a new gasket on the inlet port, place the plastic insulator block on top of it, then fit another new gasket on the insulator block – the small hole in the insulator block must be pointing towards the bottom of the engine.

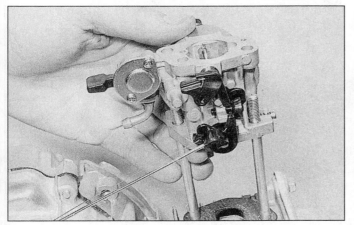

54 Position the carburettor near the studs and connect the governor link to the larger hole in the throttle butterfly lever. Connect the governor spring to the smaller hole in the lever. Slide the carburettor onto the studs.

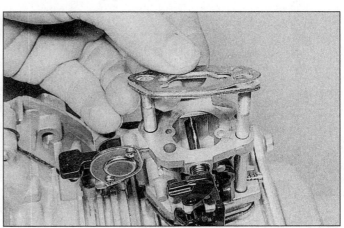

55 Fit the gasket, spacer and second gasket to the carburettor intake.

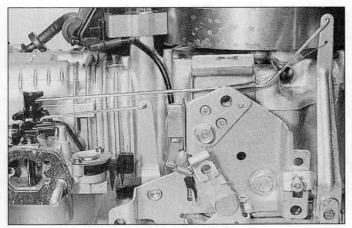

56 Fit the linkage plate to the engine. Connect the short link from the choke butterfly to the lever on the plate. Connect the coil spring from the hole marked STD in the control lever to the small lever at the bottom of the governor lever.

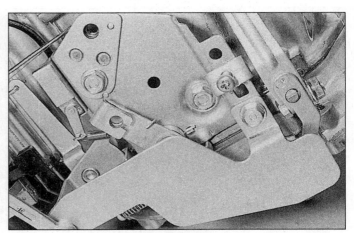

57 Fit the guard over the linkage plate.

58 Place the heat shield gasket on the exhaust port studs with the slanted edge positioned as shown above.

59 Place the muffler on the studs.

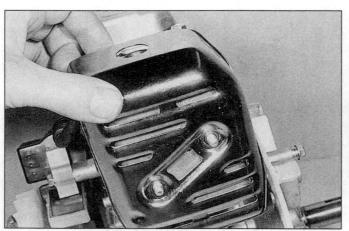

60 Finally, fit the heat shield. Secure with the two nuts.

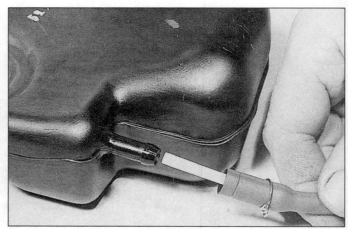

61 Gently rinse the fuel pipe filter mesh in clean petrol. Blow down the pipe from the other end to remove any particles left on the filter. Do not brush or rub it or the mesh will be damaged. Connect the pipe to the tank and secure with the clip.

62 The fuel tank attaching parts are shown in the photo.

63 Place the washer on the bolt, then the spacer tube. Fit a rubber grip on the tube. Insert the tube and bolt through the hole in the fuel tank, through the other rubber grip and screw the bolt into the mounting bracket on the crankcase.

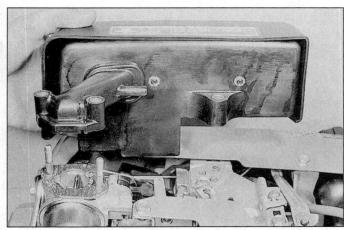

64 Pass the fuel pipe behind the linkage plate and press the pipe support clip into the hole in the linkage plate. Connect the pipe to the carburettor and secure it with the spring clip. Fit the cowl to the engine with the five bolts.

65 Position the air cleaner duct on the carburettor mounting studs.

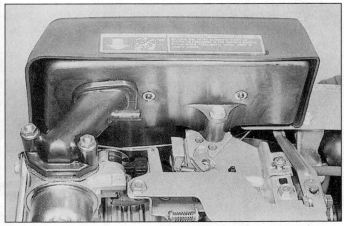

66 Secure the air cleaner to the studs with the two nuts. Bolt the air cleaner mounting lug to the linkage plate.

67 Place the spacer on the crankshaft.

68 Fit the Roto-stop ball control plate onto the crankshaft.

69 Connect the two Roto-stop return springs to the two levers and to the anchor bolts.

70 Place the ball retainer on the ball control plate with the balls located in the three concave pressings.

71 Place the brake housing in position with its blisters located on the balls.

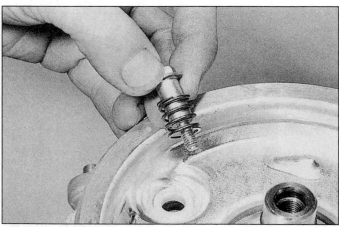

72 Place the brake springs on the flange bolts.

73 Line the brake housing up with its three bolt holes in line with the threaded holes in the crankcase cover. Fit the flange bolts.

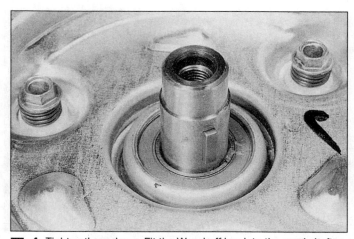

74 Tighten them down. Fit the Woodruff key into the crankshaft slot.

75 Fit the drive disc onto the crankshaft, aligned with the key.

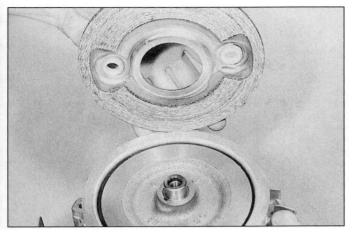

76 Place the brake lining plate on the drive disc.

77 Place the clutch spring on the brake lining plate. Fit the driven disc on the brake lining plate with the two pegs in the holes in the brake lining plate. The driven disc has a ball bearing and an oil seal in its centre. Renewal of these is straightforward and the same as for the crankcase bearings described previously.

78 Fit and tighten the central bolt.

79 Examine the seal in the final drive case for damage or distortion. Ensure that it is properly seated in the groove.

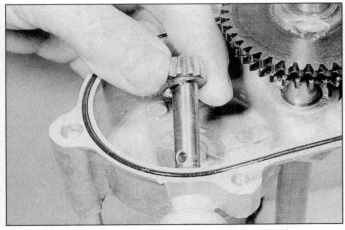

80 Renew the oil seal at the bevel drive shaft bearing if necessary. Insert the bevel drive shaft.

81 Place the thrust washer in the casing.

82 Install the bevel gear.

83 Insert the drive selector fork into the bearing in the case.

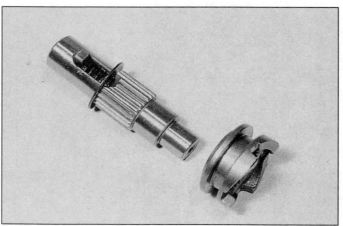

84 The drive gear shaft and clutch ratchet hub are shown in the photo. The internal coil spring can be renewed by withdrawing the cross key from the slots.

85 Slide the ratchet hub onto the gear shaft splines. Oil the end of the gear shaft and insert it through the bevel gear into the bearing in the case. Engage the hub in the selector fork as the shaft is inserted.

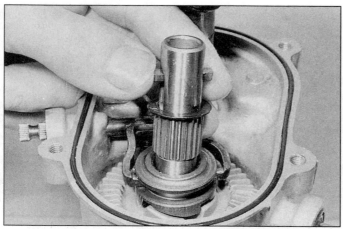

86 Engage the hub ratchet with the bevel gear ratchets.

87 Fit the larger gear flange upwards onto the gear shaft.

88 Fit the smaller gear onto the shaft.

89 Fit the thrust washer. The cross key in the shaft fits into the cross of the small gear.

90 Insert the drive actuating plunger into the gear shaft.

91 Insert the hollow dowel in the case lip. Fill the case with a light transmission oil.

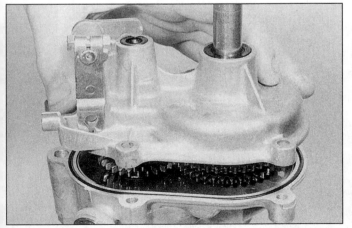

92 Slide the other half of the case onto the axle, engage it on the dowel and mate the two halves together. Secure with the five bolts. Two are longer and are fitted one over the extended torque reactor bolt, and the other at the opposite end of the case.

93 Clamp the speed selector lever to the selector fork shaft. The index mark on the end of the shaft must coincide with the centre pop mark on the lever.

94 Fit the washer into the hub of the ratchet drive rear wheel.

95 Fit the ratchet freewheel unit into the wheel hub.

96 Place the cover over the hub with the lip pointing outwards.

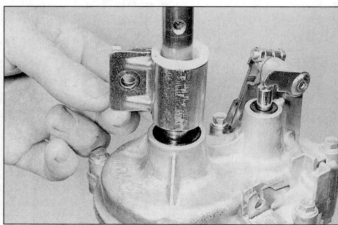

97 Slide the clamp bracket for the protector plate onto the axle.

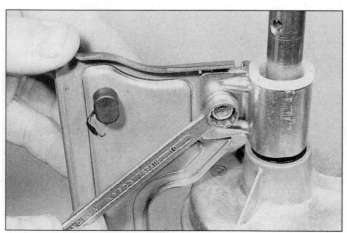

98 Bolt the protector plate to the bracket. The tabs on the clamp bracket must be entered in the matching holes in the protector plate.

99 Fit the universal joint onto the drive shaft and secure it by pushing the shear pin through the hole in the shaft.

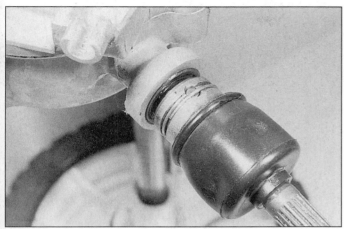

100 Spring the clip into the groove to retain the pin.

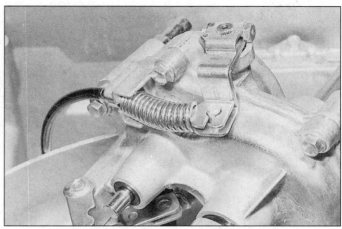

101 Turn the mower frame upside down and lift the axle assembly into position. Connect the speed selector cable to the selector fork lever.

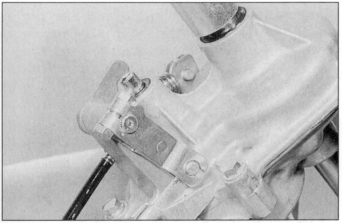

102 Connect the drive engage cable to the plunger actuating lever.

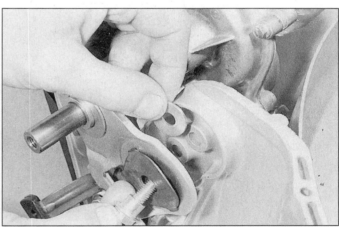

103 Remove the left-hand back wheel to improve access. Fit the shouldered bolt through the curved end plate of the height adjusting lever. Pass the bolt through the height pivoting plate. Fit a washer onto the bolt between the pivoting plate and the boss on the mower frame. Insert the bolt into the higher of the two bosses on the frame and secure it with the nut.

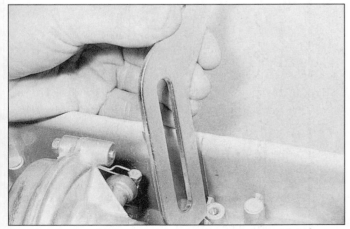

104 Locate the slot in the torque plate on the extended torque reactor bolt on the drive case.

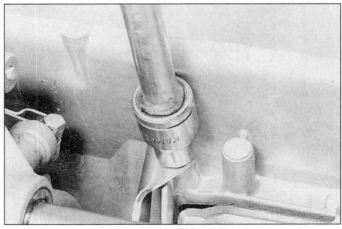

105 Secure the torque plate with the two bolts.

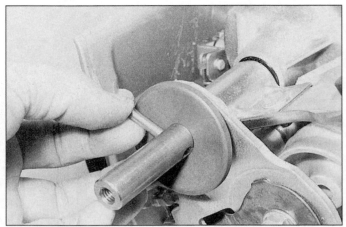

106 Fit the wheel cup onto the axle with the flange lip inward. Insert the drive pin into the axle hole.

107 Fit the wheel onto the axle so that the drive pin engages the slots in the hub.

108 Secure the wheel with the central bolt and fit the hub cap.

109 To fit the Roto-stop operating cable to the bottom of the engine, connect the nipple in the slot first.

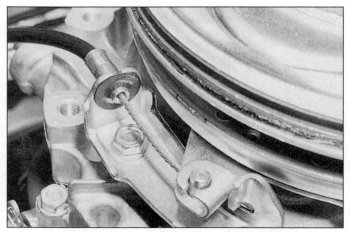

110 Then pull the bracket into position and secure it with the two screws. Do not remove the cable sheath retaining spring disc unless a spare is available, as these discs can only be used once. Note that it is not possible to assemble this bracket after the engine has been mounted on the chassis.

111 Mount the engine and secure it with the four bolts.

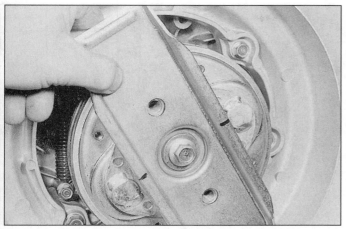

112 Mount the blade holder on the crankshaft with the blade attachment holes aligned with the holes in the driven disc.

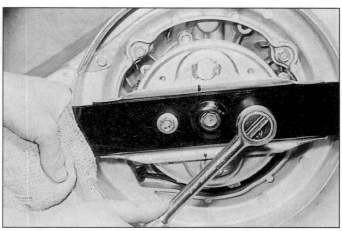

113 Fit the cutter blade. Hold it with a piece of rag to avoid injury from the cutting edge.

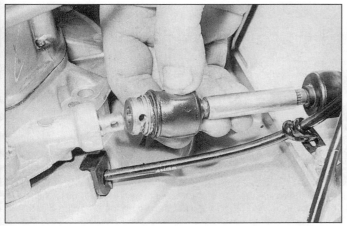

114 Place the spring clip in position next to the groove on the drive shaft. Slide the drive shaft onto the serrations on the drive bevel shaft.

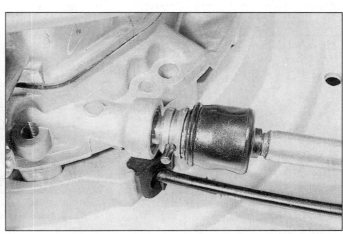

115 Connect the forward universal joint of the drive shaft onto the engine output shaft, align the drive pin hole and insert the pin.

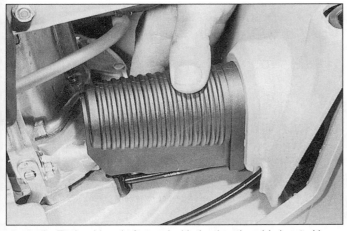

116 Fit the drive shaft guard with the throttle cable located in the slot.

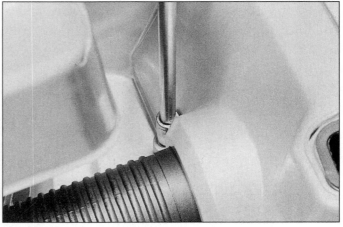

117 Secure it with the screw.

118 Connect the throttle cable to the lever on the link plate. Clamp the cable sheath in the clip in a position that gives full range of movement. Push the engine breather pipe onto the air cleaner duct and secure it with the spring clip. Push the other end of the breather pipe into the hole in the crankcase.

119 Adjust the cables as necessary to give correct operation (see Technical Data). The cables in the photo above on the underside of the control quadrant are, from left to right, the Roto-stop, self-propel drive, throttle and speed change.

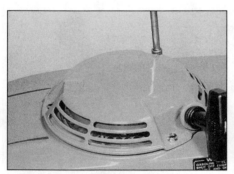

120 Fit the recoil starter onto the engine cowl.

121 Place the element in the air cleaner housing and fit the cover.

122 Fill the engine with oil to the level shown on the filler plug dipstick.

Starter repair

To fit a new recoil spring or starter cord, proceed as follows:

1 Remove the recoil starter from the engine cowl.

2 Bend the tab near the cord exit hole up to allow the rope to be unwound.

3 Release pulley tension by pulling the cord out about 60 cm (2 ft), holding the pulley and unwinding the cord. Gently release the pulley.

4 Remove the central bolt and lift off the cover. There is no need to lift the pawls or their spring out unless they need renewing

5 Lift the pulley from the shaft. Remove the recoil spring.

6 Hook the outer end of the new spring into the slot in the housing. Wind the spring anti-clockwise into the housing, working in towards the middle. Put a blob of grease in the coils. Attach a new cord to the pulley if necessary and wind it anti-clockwise round the pulley. Place the pulley on the stub shaft and turn it gently anti-clockwise until it engages with the hook on the inner end of the recoil spring.

7 If a new cord was fitted, thread the end through the exit hole and knot the handle in place. Inspect the pawls and their spring, renew if damaged. To tension the pulley, wind it about three turns anti-clockwise, hold it and wind the slack in the cord anti-clockwise onto the pulley, then release the pulley.

8 Fit the cover with the two legs of the clip on either side of the peg on the pawl.

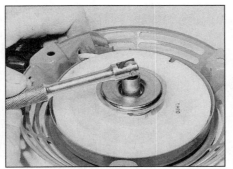

9 Then fit and tighten the bolt.

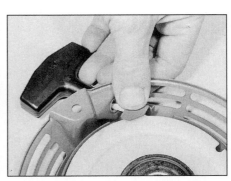

10 Bend the tab down over the cord. Pull the starter handle and check for freedom of movement and a positive return action. Install the starter on the engine cowl with the handle facing the left side of the mower.

Notes

Chapter 10
Honda OHC GCV135 4.5 hp (3.3 kW) 4-stroke engine

Model/spec. number on engine: GJAF

Mower application

Every effort has been made to make the list of models that use this engine as comprehensive as possible. Due to model and engine supply changes, you may have a mower that is not listed. Refer to *Engine Identity* on page 7 to identify the engine that you have, or contact an engine supply dealer to assist with identification.

AL-KO 42/48	Honda HRG415C	Rover 200 18"
AL-KO Euroline 4200/4700	Honda HRG465C	SARP 484
Honda HRB425C	Oleomac G47	Stiga Multiclip Pro 48

Technical Data

Spark plug type	NGK BPR6ES
Spark plug gap	0.7 to 0.8 mm (0.028 to 0.031 in)
Valve clearances (cold):	
Inlet	0.15 mm ± 0.04 mm (0.006 ± 0.016 in)
Exhaust	0.20 mm ± 0.04 mm (0.008 ± 0.016 in)
Ignition armature air gap	0.254 to 0.355 mm (0.010 to 0.014 in)
Engine oil grade	10W-40
Engine oil capacity	0.55 litres
Torque wrench settings:	
Big-end bolts	12 Nm
Flywheel nut	52 Nm

Dismantling

Before starting to dismantle, read Chapter 2. The procedures outlined apply to all engines and if adopted, will ensure an orderly and methodical approach that will make both dismantling and reassembly much easier.

1 Squeeze together the tabs of the outer cable ferrule, and pull the engine stop/flywheel brake outer cable from the supporting bracket. Disengage the inner cable from the lever.

2 Loosen the clamp retaining screw, and pull the throttle outer cable free. Disengage the inner cable end.

3 Working underneath the mower, remove the blade retaining bolt, dished washer, mounting flange and Woodruff (half moon) key from the shaft.

4 Unscrew and remove the three engine mounting bolts. Lift the engine clear of the body.

5 Undo the three retaining nuts, and remove the starter assembly. Note the three spacers in the assembly mounting holes.

6 Disconnect the fuel pipe from the fuel tank to the fuel tap. Be prepared for fuel spillage.

7 Remove the oil filler cap/dipstick and drain the engine oil into a suitable container.

8 Unscrew the three retaining bolts, and remove the exhaust shield.

9 Remove the exhaust system.

10 Press down the retaining clips, and remove the air filter cover. Lift out the element.

11 The air filter housing is secured by three bolts. Two silver-coloured bolts, which also retain the carburettor, and one-gold coloured bolt which secures the housing to the linkage plate. Remove the bolts and, as the housing is lifted away, disconnect the engine breather pipe.

12 Disconnect the governor arm-to-linkage plate spring.

13 Undo the mounting screw, disconnect the fuel pipe, and remove the fuel tap.

14 Unscrew the linkage plate mounting bolt. As the plate is lifted away, disengage the choke linkage, and the throttle spring and linkage.

15 Remove the carburettor, heat shield and insulator block.

16 Undo the retaining bolt, and remove the carburettor float bowl. Recover the gasket

17 Push out the pivot pin, and carefully lift away the float with the needle valve attached.

18 Unscrew the main jet, and slide out the emulsion tube.

19 Counting the number of turns required, unscrew the mixture adjustment screw, and the throttle stop screw.

20 Remove the air jet screw.

21 No further dismantling of the carburettor is advised. Clean any fuel/air passages by blowing only.

22 Carefully pull the HT cap from the spark plug.

23 Unscrew the two mounting bolts, disconnect the earthing wire, and remove the ignition magneto.

24 The flywheel retaining nut can be extremely tight. In order to prevent the flywheel from turning, use a strap wrench around the circumference of the flywheel. Disconnect the flywheel brake spring, so that the brake arm can be pushed away from the flywheel, which will give sufficient clearance to fit the strap wrench. The help of an assistant will be needed to steady the engine. Loosen the nut.

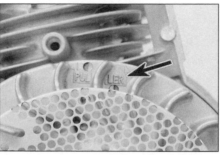

25 Leaving the retaining nut flush with the end of the crankshaft, use a two-legged puller to remove the flywheel. The correct location for the puller legs is cast into the rim of the flywheel (arrowed). Whilst the puller exerts pressure on the crankshaft, a gentle tap with a soft hammer on the end of the puller may help to free the flywheel. Recover the Woodruff (half moon) key from the shaft.

26 Unscrew the two retaining bolts, and remove the flywheel brake assembly.

27 Remove the engine breather valve cover, complete with breather pipe.

28 Bend back the tab washer, and unscrew the oil filler spout from the crankcase.

29 Make aligning marks between the governor lever and shaft. Undo the pinch-bolt and remove the lever.

30 Remove the spark plug.

31 Undo the four retaining bolts, and gently prise the cam box cover from the cylinder head.

32 Align the timing marks moulded in to the outside face of the camshaft pulley with gasket face of the cylinder head (arrowed). This should correspond to top dead centre on the compression stroke.

33 Pull out the rocker arm pivot shafts, and lift the rocker arms away. It is important to label or arrange the components so that, if re-used, they are refitted to their original locations.

34 Slip the belt from the camshaft pulley, pull out the pulley spindle, and remove the camshaft/pulley. Note the O-ring fitted to the pulley spindle.

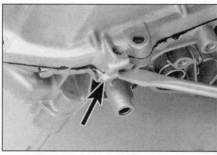

35 Unscrew the eight retaining bolts, and carefully prise the crankcase halves apart. Leverage points are cast into the casings at the locating dowel points (arrowed).

36 Recover the bevelled washer fitted between the crankshaft and crankcase.

37 Undo the retaining bolt and remove the oil slinger/governor assembly.

38 Pull the 'R-clip' from the governor arm, and withdraw the arm and washer from the crankcase.

39 If it is to be re-used, note the direction of rotation, and remove the camshaft drive belt.

40 Undo the retaining bolts, and remove the big-end bearing cap. Gently push the connecting rod up into the cylinder.

41 Carefully lift the crankshaft from the crankcase.

42 Pull the connecting rod down and withdraw the piston from the cylinder.

43 If required, remove the piston rings from the piston by carefully expanding the rings at their ends and sliding them from the piston. Note the orientation of the rings for reassembly.

44 Remove the circlips and push the gudgeon pin from the piston.

45 In order to remove a valve, depress the valve collar and push it towards the flat in the rim of the collar. Due to the size of the spring, it is quite possible to compress them sufficiently by hand. The valve collars have two adjoining holes, one of which is larger than the other. This allows the valve stem to slide through the collar. Remove the spring and slide the valve from the cylinder head. It is important to label or arrange the components so that, if re-used, they are refitted to their original locations.

46 Inspect the valve guides for scoring and excessive wear. Examine the valve seats and renovate as necessary (*refer to Chapter 2*).

47 If required, prise the oil seals from the crankcase halves, noting which way round they are fitted.

48 Check the condition of the crankshaft bearing, camshaft bearing and cylinder bore for wear, scores or cracks. If the bore is damaged, worn oval or oversized, then professional skills and special equipment will be necessary to restore it. The same applies to worn or damaged bearings. Check all threaded holes for damaged threads, and repair if necessary by fitting a thread insert of the correct size.

Reassembly

1 If required, fit new oil seals to the crankcase halves using appropriate sized sockets.

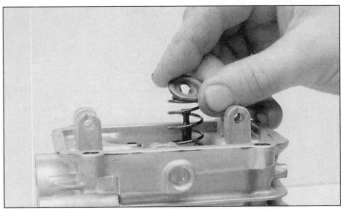

2 Smear the valve stem with oil and refit the exhaust valve into the cylinder head. Fit the exhaust valve spring and collar over the valve stem. As the spring is compressed, slide the valve stem through the larger end of the slot in the collar. Centralise the collar and slowly release the spring. Check that the collar is correctly located. Repeat this procedure for the inlet valve.

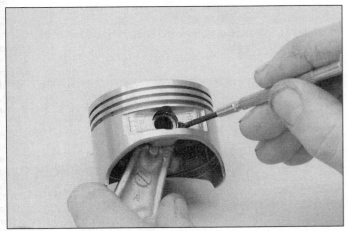

3 If previously removed, fit the gudgeon pin into the piston/ connecting rod small end. The piston should be fitted with the valve cut-outs in its crown on the timing belt side, and the connecting rod with the cast lug at the big-end towards the inlet port. Always refit the gudgeon pin using new circlips. If the gudgeon pin is reluctant to fit, immerse the piston in hot water for a few minutes. This causes the aluminium to expand, and the gudgeon pin to slide easily.

4 Fit the piston rings to the piston. All of the rings have a small letter 'T' stamped into the face that should be fitted towards the piston crown. The oil control ring should be fitted first, by carefully expanding the ring just enough to slide it down over the piston and into its groove. Although a special tool is available to fit piston rings, with care the task is easily accomplished without. However, piston rings are very brittle. If they are expanded too much, they will break. Fit the middle and top compression rings in the same manner. The top ring is identified by its grey-coloured coating on the outside edge. Arrange the three ring-end gaps so that they are spaced out at 120° intervals.

5 Smear the piston rings and cylinder bore with oil. Ensure that the valve cut-outs in the piston crown are on the timing belt side. Insert the piston crown into the cylinder bore. Slowly push the piston into the bore, feeding the piston rings into the lead-in at the lip of the bore. Take great care during this procedure, as the rings are easily broken. Stop and investigate any undue resistance. With the rings successfully engaged in the bore, push the piston/connecting rod assembly to the top of the cylinder.

6 Oil the crankcase bearing journals and insert the crankshaft, tapered end first, into the crankcase. Take care not to damage the oil seal lip.

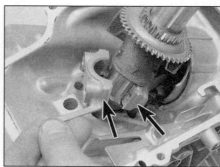

7 Smear the big-end journal with oil, and pull the connecting rod down to engage with the bearing journal of the crankshaft. Fit the bearing cap with the cast lug towards the inlet port side (arrowed). If you have a suitable torque wrench, tighten the bearing cap retaining bolts to the torque given in Technical Data. If not, tighten the bolts securely.

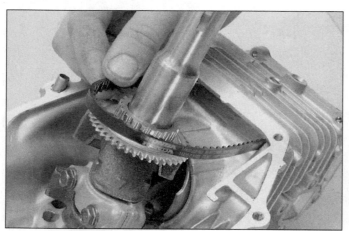

8 Fit the camshaft drive belt over the end of the crankshaft, and up through the tunnel. Engage the belt with the drive pulley teeth. If re-using a belt, ensure that it is refitted in it original direction of rotation.

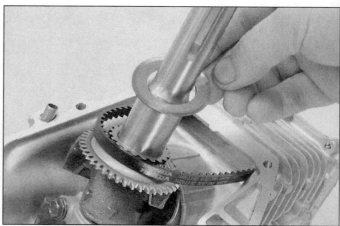

9 Refit the bevelled washer over the end of the crankshaft, concave side facing outwards.

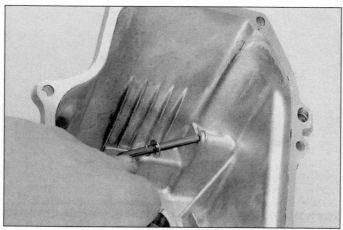

10 Insert the governor arm and washer through the hole in the crankcase.

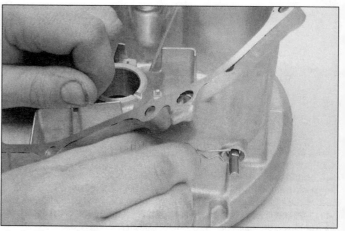

11 The arm is secured with an 'R-clip', which fits into its locating groove in the arm on the outside of the case.

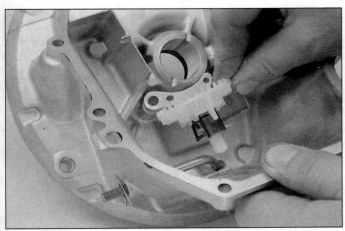

12 Mount the governor/oil slinger assembly over the two locating lugs in the crankcase. Tighten the retaining bolt securely. Ensure that the governor head aligns with the arm.

13 Check that the two crankcase locating dowels are in place (arrowed).

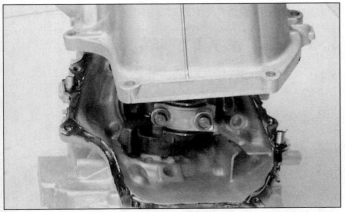

14 Smear the gasket face with non-hardening RTV-type sealant. Oil the main bearing journal, and carefully lower the other crankcase half into place. It may be necessary to turn the crankshaft a little, as the crankcase is fitted, to ensure that the governor gear teeth mesh with the corresponding teeth on the crankshaft. Take care not to damage the oil seal lip. Tighten the eight bolts evenly in a diagonal sequence. Rotate the crankshaft to check for freedom of movement.

15 Turn the crankshaft to Top Dead Centre (TDC). In this position the piston, viewed through the spark plug hole, will be at its highest point, and both crankshaft keyways at the twelve o'clock position (arrowed).

16 Gently push the camshaft drive belt towards the valves, and place the camshaft in position. Check the condition of the O-ring, and insert the pulley spindle so that the flat in the end of the spindle faces up towards, and is parallel with the cam box cover gasket face.

17 Rotate the camshaft pulley until the timing marks align with the cam box gasket face (arrowed).

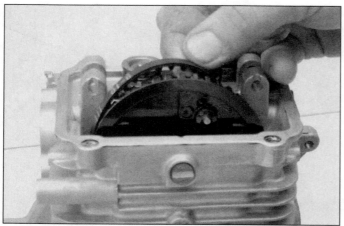

18 Check to ensure that the crankshaft is still at TDC, and slide the belt onto the pulley without turning the camshaft or crankshaft. With the belt fitted, check that the timing marks align and that the crankshaft is at TDC. Rotate the crankshaft two full revolutions, and check again. There is no provision for tensioning the belt.

19 Refit the rocker arms to their original locations. The rocker arm pivot shafts must be inserted from the spark plug side.

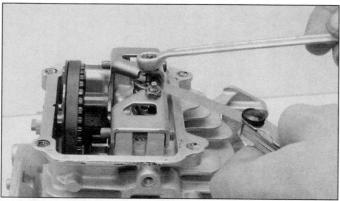

20 Both valve clearances should be checked with the crankshaft and camshaft at TDC on the compression stroke, as previously set. The clearances are given in Technical Data. If the clearances require adjustment, loosen the relevant tappet locknut, turn the tappet until the correct clearance is obtained, and tighten the locknut. Re-check the clearance.

21 Oil the camshaft and followers. Smear some non-hardening RTV-type sealant onto the cam box cover gasket face, and refit the cover. Tighten the four bolts securely. Refit the spark plug.

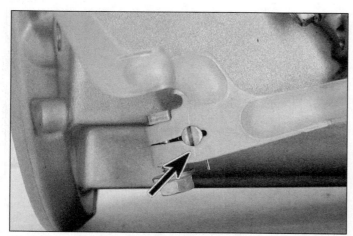

22 Refit the governor lever to the arm, aligning the previously made marks (arrowed). Tighten the pinch-bolt.

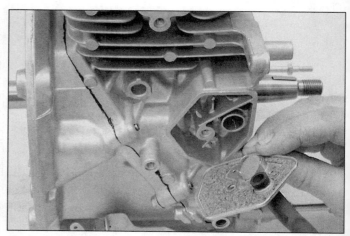

23 Check the condition of the engine breather valve, cover and pipe. Refit the cover. Tighten the retaining bolt.

24 Refit the flywheel brake assembly, and tighten the two retaining bolts securely. Do not reconnect the spring at this stage.

25 Refit the Woodruff (half moon) key and slide the flywheel over the tapered end of the crankshaft.

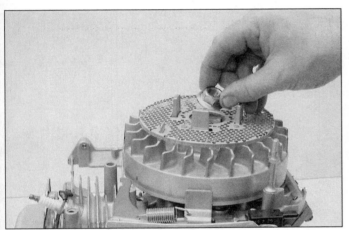

26 Refit the retaining nut.

27 Use a strap wrench to prevent the flywheel from turning. Tighten the retaining nut to the torque given in Technical Data. The help of an assistant may be necessary to steady the engine.

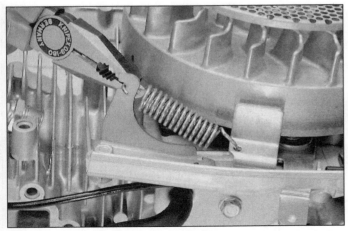

28 Reconnect the flywheel brake spring.

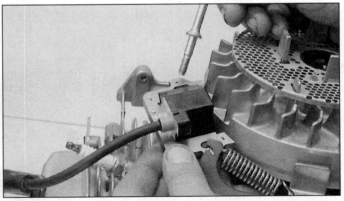

29 Refit the ignition magneto, with the elongated mounting bolt screwed into the hole in the centre of the cylinder, and the earthing wire terminal facing out. Before tightening both mounting bolts, turn the flywheel so that the magnets are on the opposite side to the magneto. Using feeler gauges, check the air gap between the two magneto armature legs, and the flywheel. The correct air gap is given in Technical Data. The mounting holes in the magneto legs are slotted. Move the magneto until the correct air gap is obtained. Tighten the bolts securely, and reconnect the earthing wire. Refit the HT cap to the spark plug.

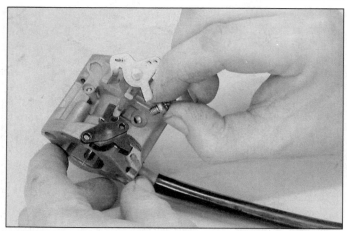

30 Refit the air jet screw to the carburettor body.

31 Referring to the notes made during their removal, refit the throttle stop and mixture adjustment screws. The base setting for the mixture is to turn the screw in until it seats, then one full turn out.

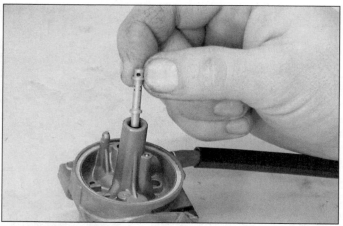

32 Refit the emulsion tube, small holes nearest the carburettor venturi.

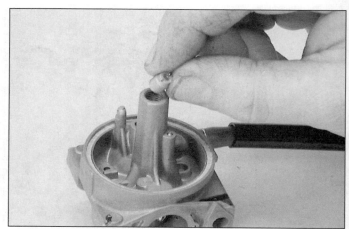

33 Screw in the main jet.

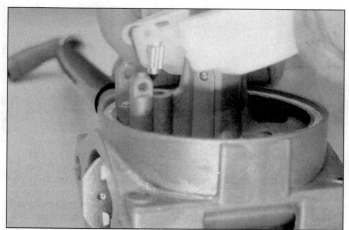

34 Re-attach the needle valve to the float, and insert the valve into its seat.

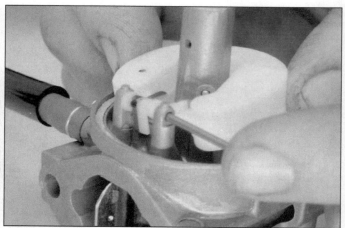

35 Align the float with the pivot hole, and insert the pivot pin. There is no provision for adjusting the float height.

36 If necessary, fit a new float bowl gasket, and refit the bowl.

37 Check the condition of the fibre washer, and secure the float bowl with the retaining bolt.

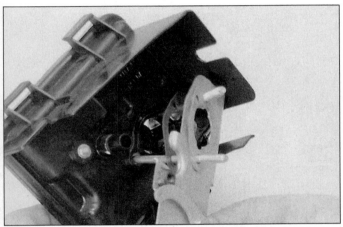

38 The carburettor, linkage plate and air filter housing must be fitted as one assembly. Using a new gasket, fit the air filter housing to the linkage plate, finger tighten the retaining bolt.

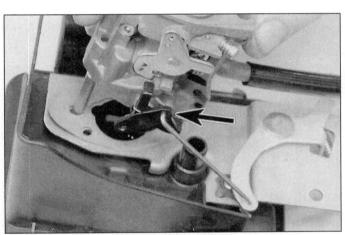

39 Insert the two carburettor mounting bolts through the assembly to assist in aligning the gaskets. Engage the choke linkage with arm on the carburettor (arrowed), and the operating lever on the linkage plate, and slide the carburettor onto the retaining bolts.

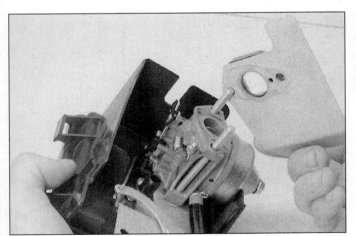

40 Using new gaskets, slide the heat shield and insulator block onto the carburettor retaining bolts.

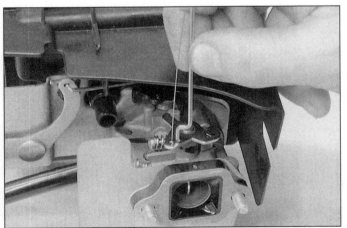

41 Reconnect the governor linkage and spring to the throttle arm and governor lever.

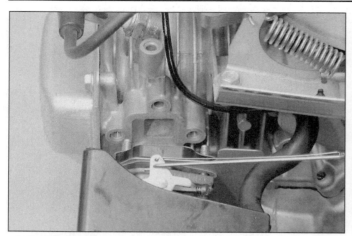

42 Engage the carburettor mounting bolts with their holes in the cylinder head, but do not tighten at this stage.

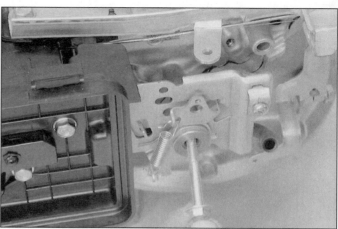

43 Fit the linkage plate retaining bolt. Tighten all four carburettor/linkage plate/air filter housing bolts securely.

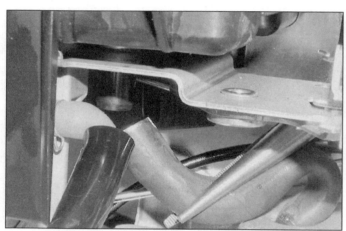

44 Turn the engine on its side, and from underneath, reconnect the engine breather pipe to the air filter housing.

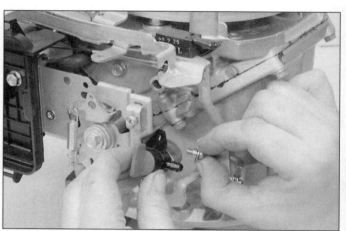

45 Refit the fuel tap to the end of the linkage plate, tighten the retaining screw, and reconnect the carburettor-to-fuel tap pipe. Secure the pipe with the retaining clip.

46 Fit the air filter element into the housing, and clip the filter cover into place.

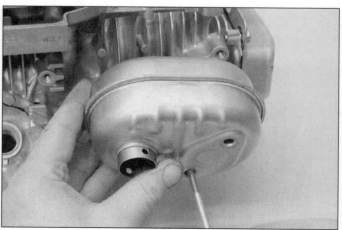

47 The exhaust system mounts onto the cylinder head without a gasket. Fit the system and tighten the two retaining bolts securely.

48 Refit the exhaust shield. Tighten the three retaining bolts securely.

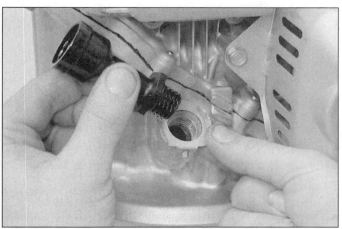

49 Place the tab washer over the oil filler hole in the crankcase, ensuring that the locating lug engages correctly. Screw in the filler spout, and secure it in place by bending the tabs against the nut.

50 Refit the fuel tank/cowling over the mounting studs, ensuring that the HT lead engages with the slot on the underside of the cowling.

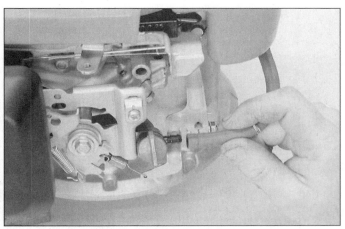

51 Reconnect the fuel tank-to-tap pipe, and secure with the retaining clips.

52 Fit the starter assembly over the mounting studs, and tighten the three retaining nuts securely.

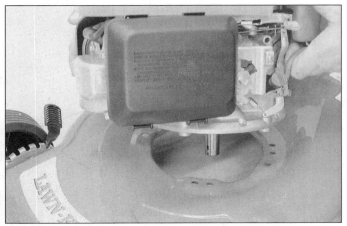

53 Place the engine on the mower body, and align the three mounting holes. Insert the mounting bolt beneath the exhaust system from underneath. The remaining mounting bolts are inserted from above. Fit and tighten the three self-locking nuts.

54 Working under the mower, fit the Woodruff (half moon) key to the shaft, align the key way, and slide on the blade mounting flange. Locate the blade over the two lugs. Fit the dished washer concave side against the blade. Tighten the retaining bolt securely.

55 Engage the end of the inner throttle cable with the lever on the linkage plate (arrowed). Fit the out cable into the clamp and tighten the screw. Check for correct operation.

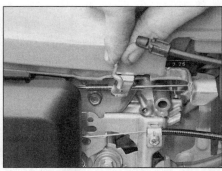

56 Engage the end of the engine stop cable with the flywheel brake lever, and the outer ferrule with the retaining bracket. Again, check for correct operation.

57 Remember to add the correct grade and quantity of engine oil.

Starter repair

1 Undo the three retaining nuts, and lift the starter assembly from the engine cowling.

2 Pull the rope to its full extension, and lock the pulley in place by inserting a screwdriver (or similar) through the spokes of the pulley and one of the slots of the outer cover.

3 To replace the rope: Where the rope goes through the pulley, cut off the knot and pull the rope from the starter. Feed the new rope through the hole in the outer cover, and through the hole in the pulley. Tie the knot. Feed the other end of the rope through the hole in the starter handle, again tie the knot. Tension the rope and remove the screwdriver from the pulley spokes. Br prepared for the spring to violently rewind the starter rope. Refit the starter assembly to the engine cowling.

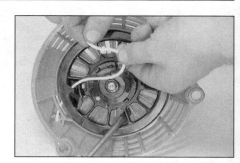

4 To replace the starter spring: Where the rope goes through the pulley, untie the knot and pull the rope from the starter. The Torx screw that secures the guide plate has a left-hand thread. Undo the screw, lift off the guide plate, and remove the spring and starter pawls.

5 Carefully lift out the pulley, noting the locating slot for the end of the starter spring. Lift out the spring.

6 Fit the new starter spring to the underside of the pulley. Ensure that the outer end of the spring engages correctly with the locating slot in the pulley (arrowed).

7 Refit the pulley to the outer cover, engaging the inner end of the spring with the locating lug in the centre of the cover (arrowed).

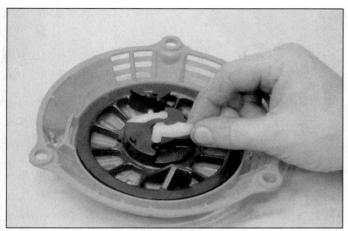

8 Check the starter pawls for damage or excessive wear, and refit them to the pulley. Insert the central spring.

9 Refit the guide plate onto the pawls, ensuring that the pawls locating pins engage with the slots on the underside of the guide plate. Tighten the retaining Torx screw (**left-hand thread).**

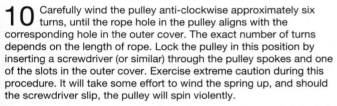

10 Carefully wind the pulley anti-clockwise approximately six turns, until the rope hole in the pulley aligns with the corresponding hole in the outer cover. The exact number of turns depends on the length of rope. Lock the pulley in this position by inserting a screwdriver (or similar) through the pulley spokes and one of the slots in the outer cover. Exercise extreme caution during this procedure. It will take some effort to wind the spring up, and should the screwdriver slip, the pulley will spin violently.

11 Feed the rope through the hole in the outer cover and the hole in the pulley. Re-tie the knot. Tension the rope and remove the screwdriver from the pulley spokes. Allow the spring to rewind the rope. Check for correct operation. Refit the starter assembly to the engine cowling.

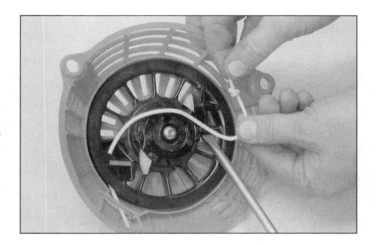

Notes

Chapter 11
Tecumseh LAV 1 53 4-stroke engine

Model/spec. number on engine: E-40

Mower application

Every effort has been made to make the list of models that use this engine as comprehensive as possible. Due to model and engine supply changes, you may have a mower that is not listed. Refer to *Engine Identity* on page 7 to identify the engine that you have, or contact an engine supply dealer to assist with identification.

AL-KO (various)
Castel (various)
Flymo (various)
Harry (various)

Hayter (various)
Kompact 90
Mountfield Emblem
Mountfield Empress

Oleomac G43
Qualcast Quadtrak 45
Qualcast Trojan

Technical Data

Spark plug gap	0.60 to 0.70 mm (0.024 to 0.028 in)
Points gap	0.50 mm (0.020 in)
Armature air gap	0.38 mm (0.015 in)
Valve clearances (Inlet and exhaust)	0.25 mm (0.010 in)
Crankshaft end float	0.13 to 0.70 mm (0.005 to 0.028 in)
Ring gap	0.18 to 0.43 mm (0.007 to 0.017 in)
Oil	SAE 30 or SAE 10W-30
Oil capacity	0.6 litres

Dismantling

Before starting to dismantle, read Chapter 2. The procedures outlined apply to all engines and if adopted, will ensure an orderly and methodical approach that will make both dismantling and reassembly much easier.

1 Disconnect the plug lead. Drain the oil from the engine.

2 Loosen the throttle cable clip at the carburettor, free the cable sheath and unhook the cable from the engine control plate lever. Make a note of which hole the throttle cable was attached to.

3 Remove the cutter from the end of the crankshaft, using a ring spanner on the bolt. Withdraw the blade boss from the crankshaft, taking care not to lose the Woodruff key in the crankshaft slot.

4 Remove the two engine attachment screws and the nut and bolt near the oil filler hole, and lift the engine off the deck.

5 Pull the petrol pipe off the fuel tank connector fitting and lift the tank from the slide-off attachment slots on the engine cowl.

6 Pull the snap-on lid off the air cleaner housing and remove the foam element.

7 Remove the engine cowl.

8 Remove air filter house, held by 2 bolts to the carburettor.

9 Note the position of the holes in which the throttle butterfly link and the governor spring link fit. Remove the carburettor inlet manifold screws, lift the manifold and carburettor free, disconnect the links then remove the carburettor and manifold.

10 Remove the exhaust silencer.

11 Remove the flywheel and rotating screen *(see Chapter 2 for advice on removing flywheels)*. Remove the crankshaft key.

12 Check that the ignition armature and coil unit is index marked for spark timing purposes (if not, mark it as shown in Reassembly later in this Chapter) then remove the unit.

13 Remove the cam sleeve from the crankshaft.

14 Remove the cylinder head and gasket.

15 Remove the breather assembly from the valve chest.

16 Remove the crankcase end cover. Remove the thrust shim from the crankshaft. Remove the oil pump body and plunger from the camshaft.

17 Clearly mark one side of the big end cap and the big end of the connecting rod to ensure that the cap is reassembled the correct way round, then remove the cap. Marking is essential as the cap will fit either way.

18 Remove the valves.

19 Remove the camshaft.

20 Remove the cam followers.

21 Remove the step of carbon at the top of the cylinder with a soft tool. This allows the piston to slide out easily during removal without damaging the piston rings.

22 Slide the piston and connecting rod out through the top of the cylinder, taking great care not to allow the connecting rod to scratch the cylinder bore.

23 Remove the crankshaft.

24 If the governor appears worn, remove it for inspection as follows:

24a Remove the top C-clip.

24b Lift the spool off the governor shaft.

24c Remove the bottom C-clip.

24d Lift the governor plastic gear assembly and the spacer ring underneath it from the shaft.

Reassembly

1 To fit a new crankcase magneto bearing oil seal, prise out the old seal with a screwdriver blade. Take care not to damage the bore into which the seal fits, as this could prevent the new seal from seating properly and may cause oil seepage. Smear the new seal with oil and tap it evenly into place, with the sharp lip of the seal pointing towards the inside of the engine.

2 Check the condition of the magneto bearing, the camshaft bearing and the cylinder bore for wear, scores or cracks. The cylinder bore is unsleeved aluminium and the bearings are unbushed aluminium. If the bore is worn oval or oversized (refer to the Technical Data at the beginning of this Chapter) then professional skills and special equipment will be necessary to repair it. The same applies to worn or damaged bearings. These can be reamed out to accept bushes obtainable from the spares stockist, but special reaming equipment and a knowledge of how to use it are essential. Check all threaded holes for stripped threads and repair if necessary by fitting a thread insert of the correct size.

3 Smear oil on the crankcase magneto bearing and fit the crankshaft into the crankcase.

4 Fit the piston rings and assemble the gudgeon pin and connecting rod the same way round as noted during dismantling. Space the piston ring gaps at 120° from each other. The rings must be fitted the same way up and in the same grooves of the piston as when originally fitted. The photo shows the numbers cast on the web of the connecting rod facing upwards for clarity. These must face the flywheel end of the engine when installing the piston and connecting rod, i.e. the opposite way round to that shown in the photo.

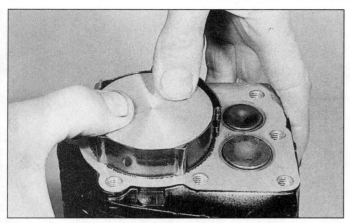

5 Smear oil around the cylinder bore and on the crank throw journal. Using a piston ring clamp, fit the piston and connecting rod into the cylinder from the top. Do not scratch the bore with the big end as the connecting rod passes through. Press the piston firmly into the cylinder, sliding it out of the piston clamp as the rings enter the bore. If necessary, tap the piston gently with a piece of wood or a hammer handle, but stop and investigate any undue resistance.

7 Turn the crankshaft to Top Dead Centre. Oil the cam follower stems and fit the followers into the same holes in the crankcase from which they were removed.

9 Mesh the camshaft gear and the crankshaft gear with the index mark on the cam gear aligned with the marked tooth of the crankshaft gear.

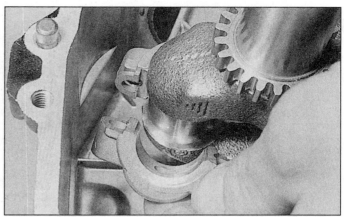

6 Engage the connecting rod big end with the bearing journal on the crankshaft throw. Fit the big end cap and secure with the two bolts and tabwashers. Tighten the bolts firmly and bend the tabs tight against the bolt flats. Rotate the crankshaft to ensure free movement.

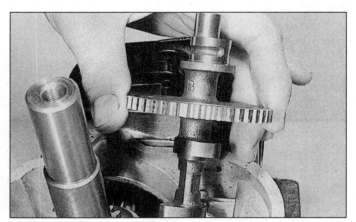

8 Smear some oil in the camshaft bearing and fit the camshaft into the crankcase.

10 Fit the oil pump body onto the eccentric drive on the cam-shaft, with the chamfered side of the hole in the body facing the cam gear. Remove the plunger, fill the body with oil and replace the plunger; this primes the pump for initial engine starting. The pump should be swung to the position shown in the photo so that the ball end of the plunger enters the slotted housing in the crankcase cover when the latter is fitted.

11 Fit the thrust shim onto the crankshaft.

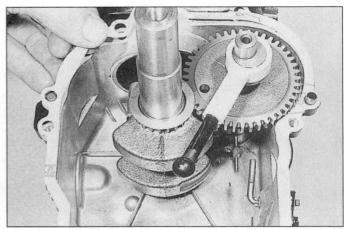

12 Fit a paper gasket onto the crankcase.

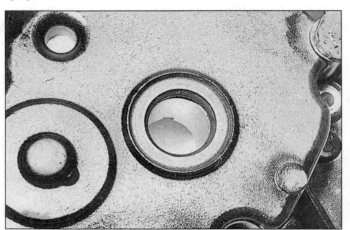

13 To fit a new oil seal for the main bearing in the crankcase cover, prise out the old seal with a screwdriver blade and fit the new seal in the same way as previously described for the crankcase magneto bearing. Be careful not to damage the bore into which the seal fits or oil seepage may result.

14 Fit the engine speed governor plastic gear onto the stub shaft in the crankcase cover and retain it with a C-clip in the lower of the two grooves on the shaft. Check that the pivoting links move freely.

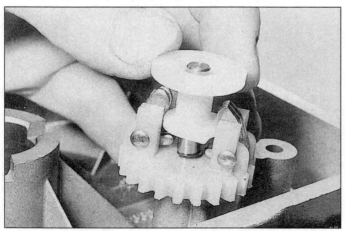

15 Fit the spool over the shaft, with the protrusion on the lower flange located into the space between the two pillars of one or other of the links; this ensures that the spool rotates with the gear. As the spool is fitted, check that the small lobe of each link is below the bottom flange of the spool and the large lobe is above the flange.

16 Secure the spool with a C-clip in the top groove of the shaft. Slide the spool up and down the range of movement between the two circlips and check that movement is free and that the two links pivot correctly. If movement is not free, investigate the cause as the governor will not operate correctly and may allow the engine to overspeed. Worn or damaged parts are best rectified by fitting a complete new governor assembly.

17 Smear oil in the main bearing and camshaft bearing.

18 Check that the Woodruff key has been removed from the power take-off end of the crankshaft. Fit the crankcase cover carefully onto the crankshaft and slide it down onto the crankcase, guiding the oil pump plunger ball head into the slotted housing in the cover as the cover fits into place. Ensure that the governor gear teeth mesh correctly with the camshaft gear and that the crankcase cover locates correctly onto the dowels on the lip of the crankcase. Secure the cover with the six bolts, tightening them gradually in diagonal order to avoid distorting or cracking the cover.

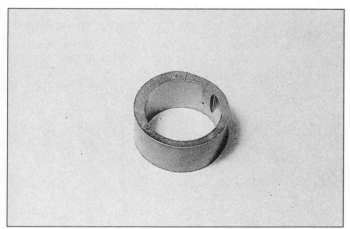

19 Inspect the cam sleeve for signs of wear or grooving on the cam face. Check that the key machined in the bore of the sleeve is not worn, burred or otherwise damaged. Renew the sleeve if necessary.

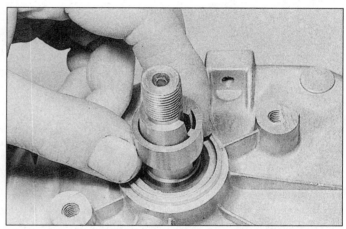

20 Fit the cam sleeve onto the tapered end of the crankshaft, with the key on the sleeve aligned in the crankshaft groove and facing away from the engine.

21 Fit the contact breaker and coil unit assembly onto the engine. Make sure that the heel of the moving breaker point does not catch on the cam sleeve as the unit is offered into place; if this happens, pivot the breaker heel a little until the whole unit seats cleanly onto the lipped end of the crankcase.

22 Secure the breaker and coil unit with the two bolts and flat washers, ensuring that the timing mark on the unit is aligned with the index mark on the crankcase.

23 Turn the crankshaft until the heel of the moving point is resting on the highest point of the cam, then check with a feeler gauge that the breaker gap is as given in Technical Data. If necessary, loosen the fixed point locking screw, move the point to the correct setting then tighten the locking screw. Put a small blob of grease on the heel of the moving point carrier. Re-check the setting, and readjust if necessary.

24 Fit the dust cover over the contact breaker housing and secure with the spring clip.

25 Fit the flywheel drive key into the groove in the tapered end of the crankshaft. The key must be free from shear marks or other damage; renew it if necessary.

26 Fit the flywheel onto the taper of the crankshaft with the slot aligned with the drive key.

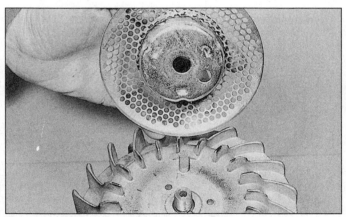

27 Fit the rotating screen onto the threaded end of the crank-shaft. Make sure that the three small grooves pressed into the bottom edge of the screen hub locate onto the nose of the three finger-shaped keys cast on the face of the flywheel. When the starter cord is pulled, the hub takes the recoil starter drive and transmits it to the engine through these keys. It is therefore essential that the hub is properly seated onto the keys and lies flush on the face of the flywheel.

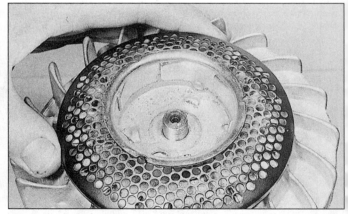

28 If, on examination, the ratchets formed on the internal wall of the screen hub are found to be worn or burred, renew the screen. These ratchets are engaged by the starter pawl when the cord is pulled.

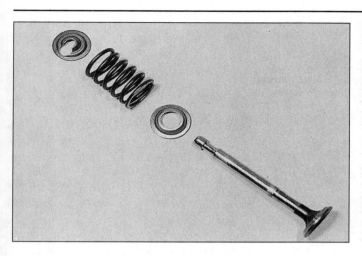

29 The valve components are shown in the photo. The spring retainer, which can be identified by the large symmetrical hole, must be fitted with its dished centre projecting into the middle of the spring coils. Note the two adjoining holes in the centre of the collar that form an offset slot. This allows the larger hole to be fitted over the end of the valve stem. The shallow notch in the rim of the collar points in the direction in which the collar must be moved when removing the valve. Installing the valves is made easier if this notch is pointing outwards from the valve chest.

30 Before fitting valve springs, check valve clearance with piston at top dead centre on the firing stroke (both valves closed). Hold down the valve head securely with finger or thumb and measure clearance between valve stem and cam followers with feeler gauges. The clearance should be as given in Technical Data for both valves. If clearance is too small the end of the valve will have to be filed off to give correct clearance as described in Chapter 2.

31 Fit the valve into the guide. Note that the exhaust valve being fitted above has a much smaller head than the inlet valve shown already fitted. The difference in size is so obvious that inadvertent assembly onto the wrong seat is virtually impossible. The valve seats are not removable and if badly burnt or pitted beyond recovery by normal valve grinding, they will have to be professionally recut. Valve guides can be renewed if worn, but will need reaming using special tools.

32 Place the spring retainer over the valve stem and onto the end of the valve guide projecting into the valve chest. Fit the spring over the valve stem and seat it onto the retainer. Position the collar under the spring. Prise the collar up with a screwdriver so that the offset hole passes onto the valve system, then when level with the shoulder on the valve stem, move the collar sideways so that its smaller hole engages under the shoulder.

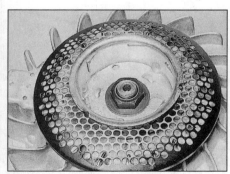

33 Secure screen with nut and domed washer (dome side up)

34 Fit a new cylinder head gasket.

35 Place the cylinder head on the cylinder and fit the five cylinder head bolts shown in the photo, but do not tighten them until the remaining three (which hold the cowl on) are fitted later.

36 Check the disc valve on the inward facing side of the breather body. It should move freely and be undamaged. Fit a gasket to the valve chest and another to the outer face of the breather body, as shown above, then position the breather in the valve chest.

37 Rinse the breather filter in clean petrol, shake out the excess then fit the filter into the body.

38 Fit the cover onto the breather and secure with the two bolts.

39 Renew the carburettor float if it is perforated, damaged or shows signs of leakage. Examine the tip of the needle valve; if ridged, renew the valve. The synthetic rubber valve seat can also be renewed if worn. It can be pulled out of the hole in the carburettor body immediately above the needle valve by using a piece of hooked wire. The new seat should be smeared with oil, then pressed into the hole with a flat ended punch. Make sure that the grooved face enters the hole first, leaving the plain face outward for the needle valve to seat against.

40 The fixed jet need not be removed unless it is obviously dirty. Check that the emulsion holes are clean by blowing through them, then screw the jet back into the body. Never use a pin or wire to clean a dirty jet. If blowing fails, use a thin nylon bristle, or something equally soft.

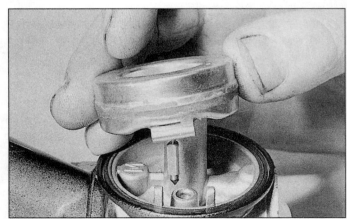

41 Place the float in position between the hinge lugs, ensuring that the needle valve enters the seat housing and seats correctly.

42 Push the pin through the lugs and float hinge bracket. Gently swing the float about the hinge to check that it moves freely. Do not apply force at the end of travel or the stop will be bent out of place and upset the fuel level.

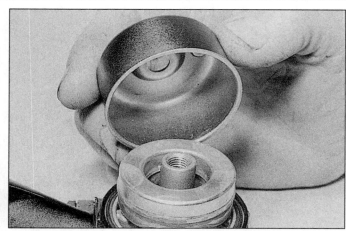

43 Check that the float bowl seal is not damaged or distorted and is seated properly in its groove. Fit a new one if necessary.

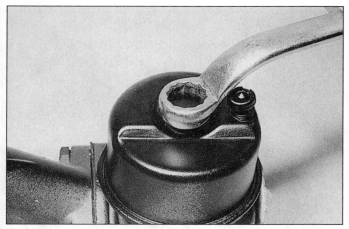

44 Fit the bowl nut. Before tightening, ensure that the flat surface on the base of the bowl is positioned on the same side as the fuel inlet pipe, this allows full float travel.

45 Place a gasket on the inlet port.

46 Connect the throttle butterfly link to the hole in the tip of the governor lever while the carburettor and inlet manifold are still free. Connect the spring link to the second hole from the tip of the control lever on the engine control plate. Connect the spring to the third hole from the end of the governor lever.

47 Fit the inlet manifold and secure with the two shakeproof bolts.

48 Connect the magneto earthing lead to the spade connector on the engine control plate.

49 Attach the exhaust silencer to the exhaust port. Note that no gasket is provided.

50 Run the HT lead to the sparking plug inside the right hand hole for the cylinder head bolt. The cooling fin here is specially shortened to accommodate the lead.

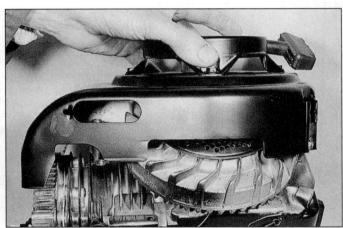

51 Place the cowl onto the engine.

52 Fit the remaining three cylinder head bolts, then tighten down all the cylinder head bolts a little at a time, in diagonally opposite rotation to prevent warping or cracking the cylinder head.

53 Fit the two bolts at the rear of the cowl near the fuel tank attachment slots.

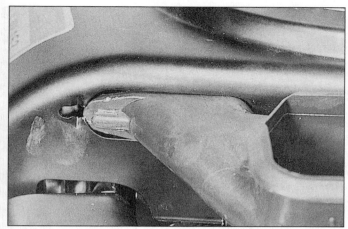

54 Enter the air cleaner intake into the slot in the cowl and press it into the cut-out in the end of the slot.

55 Secure the air cleaner outlet elbow to the carburettor inlet with the two bolts.

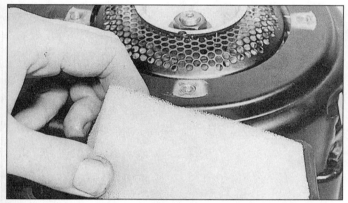

56 Fit the foam filter into the air cleaner housing. If the foam is dirty, wash it out thoroughly in a solvent solution, squeeze it out (but do not twist it) until it is dry, then oil it thoroughly with clean engine oil. Squeeze it vigorously to disperse the oil and remove the excess. Ensure the housing is clean and dry. A foam filter that has gone solid or lost its resilience should be renewed. Press the cover onto the housing until it snaps over the lip.

57 Mount the fuel tank on the cowl by pressing the slotted mouldings on the fuel tank onto the carriers on the cowl.

58 Connect the fuel pipe to the fuel tank and the carburettor; the pipe is a push fit at both ends. If the pipe is kinked or split (especially at the ends) or otherwise damaged, renew it.

59 Mount the engine on the deck and secure it from underneath with two bolts and one separate nut and bolt. The bolt is fitted in the hole near the oil filter hole and secured from underneath by the nut and washer.

60 Fit the Woodruff key in the slot in the crankshaft.

61 Fit the spacer on the crank-shaft with the groove in the spacer aligned with the Woodruff key.

62 Position the cutter on the spigot on the end of the sleeve and secure with the bolt, collar and domed washer. Note that the blade must be fitted the correct way round, i.e. with the two cutting edges leading anti-clockwise rotation of the cutter, viewed from underneath the mower. The domed washer must be fitted with its concave face to the cutter.

63 Hold the blade using a thick rag to avoid injury from the cutting edge and tighten the blade firmly. Use a ring spanner, as a flat one is likely to slip and damage the head of the bolt. Try to tighten by pulling the spanner rather than pushing it, as injury to knuckles and fingers is much less likely if the spanner slips.

64 Connect the throttle cable to the carburettor and secure the sheath behind the clip. The sheath should be positioned to open the throttle butterfly to the full throttle position when the handle bar lever is at the fast run position (shown by the symbol of a hare). The cable sheath will probably show a mark where it was previously clamped; it should be reclamped in the same position.

65 If the adjustment setting of the needle valve has been lost, screw the needle very gently right in and stop as soon as it touches the seat. Do not overtighten or the valve seat and the needle will be damaged. Unscrew the needle one turn. This setting will enable the engine to be started and warmed up later for fine tuning of the needle valve.

66 Set the throttle stop until it barely touches the throttle butterfly lever, then screw it one turn clockwise. This will give sufficient throttle opening at idling for fine adjustment to be made later.

67 Set the stop screw to give a full travel position of the engine control lever which coincides with the full choke position of the choke butterfly, when the handle bar control lever is fully forward in the start position.

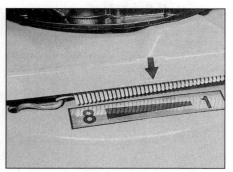

68 Check the condition of the height adjustment spring. The coils should be evenly spaced. A stretched, weakened or damaged spring increases the effort needed to adjust the height of the cut.

Starter repair

If the recoil starter assembly has been dismantled due to the need to replace a broken spring (the most usual cause of the cord failing to wind back onto the rewind housing after being pulled), proceed with the reassembly as follows:

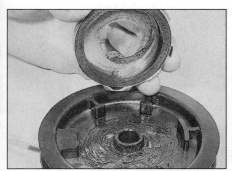

1 Fit the spring into the keeper. This is best achieved by hooking the outer end of the spring into the slot on the side of the keeper, then coiling the spring clockwise into the keeper, from outside to inside. Put a dab of grease in the keeper, place the keeper in the pulley and turn it until the two special tabs enter the slots under the pulley ribs.

2 Place the starter pawl on the pivot pin in the curved slot of the pulley while holding the leg of the dog return spring clear, so that it fits on the outside of the pawl.

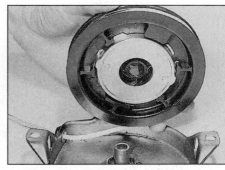

3 Place the pulley on the shaft in the starter housing. Turn the pulley anti-clockwise until the hook on the inner end of the recoil spring engages with the detent in the housing; a slight resistance can be felt when this happens.

4 Continue turning the pulley anti-clockwise until a positive return force is felt (about one turn should be enough) then hold the pulley at this tension. Wrap the cord anti-clockwise round the pulley until about 15 cm (6 in) are left free. It may be necessary to ease the pulley up the shaft to do this, but not too far or the recoil spring may jump out of engagement.

5 Maintain pulley tension, thread the cord out through the hole in the starter housing, then through the handle and metal cleat. Tie a figure-of-eight knot in the cord and heat seal the end to prevent fraying. Press the cleat into the handle and release the pulley tension.

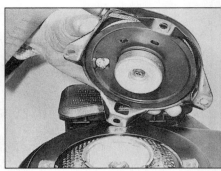

6 Place the coil spring in the recess in the housing shaft.

7 Fit the retainer hub over the dog pawl and tighten the cross head locking screw firmly. Pull the starter handle and check that the pawl emerges freely and that the starter turns freely. Relax the pull and check that the cord rewinds fully and positively.

8 Place the assembled starter on the cowl with the handle pointing towards the right hand end of the fuel tank, and secure it with the four screws.

Chapter 12
Tecumseh 3.5 hp/Vantage 35 4-stroke engine

Model/spec. number on engines: E-31, E-41, E-36, E-46, E-56

Mower application

Every effort has been made to make the list of models that use this engine as comprehensive as possible. Due to model and engine supply changes, you may have a mower that is not listed. Refer to *Engine Identity* on page 7 to identify the engine that you have, or contact an engine supply dealer to assist with identification.

AL-KO (various)
Castel (various)
Efco LR series
Flymo 42cm/46cm
Harry (various)
Hayter Hobby

Kompact 90
Mountfield Emblem
Mountfield Empress
Mountfield M3
Mountfield Laser

Oleomac G43
Qualcast Quadtrak 45
Qualcast Trojan
The Club 470 T35/40
Valex Daytona

Technical data

Spark plug gap . . . . 0.8 mm (0.031 in)
Armature air gap . . . . 0.37 mm (0.015 in)
Valve clearance:
   Inlet and exhaust . . . . 0.25 mm (0.010 in)
Piston ring gap . . . . 0.18 to 0.43 mm (0.007 to 0.017 in)
Oil . . . . SAE 30 or SAE 10W-30
Oil capacity . . . . 0.6 litres
Note: *SAE 10W is an acceptable substitute.* ***Do not use SAE 10W-40***

Dismantling

Before starting to dismantle, read Chapter 2. The procedures outlined apply to all engines and if adopted, will ensure an orderly and methodical approach that will make both dismantling and reassembly much easier.

1 Disconnect the plug lead. Drain the oil from the engine.

2 Disconnect the power drive clutch cable from the drive casing.

3 Remove the cutter, the drive sleeve and the key. Remove the exhaust box.

4 Disconnect the throttle cable from the carburettor.

5 Remove the engine mounting bolts. Remove the engine from the deck by unscrewing the bolts in the power drive cover mounting bracket, and have some assistance to pull sideways on the drive cover while the engine is moved sideways to disconnect the power drive. Lift the engine clear when the power drive is disconnected. Remove the plastic dust shield from the power drive shaft.

6 Disconnect the fuel pipe from the tank.

7 Disconnect the air cleaner housing from the carburettor inlet.

8 Remove the engine cowling complete with the air cleaner housing, leaving the fuel tank and recoil starter behind on the engine.

9 Remove the recoil starter from the engine. Remove the fuel tank with the starter handle in it.

10 Note the positions of the governor spring and the link from the governor lever to the throttle butterfly lever, so that they can be reassembled in the same holes. Disconnect the spring and the link and remove the carburettor.

11 Grip the engine drive shaft in a soft jaw vice and remove the flywheel nut. Do not overtighten the vice. If the shaft turns while loosening the flywheel nut, replace the cutter sleeve and key on the drive shaft and grip the sleeve in the vice.

12 Remove the flywheel from the taper (see Chapter 2).

13 Remove the offset key from the drive shaft; remove the plastic sleeve from the shaft.

14 Remove the valve cover.

15 Remove the cylinder head.

16 Remove the crankcase cover disengaging the power drive pinion as it is withdrawn. Remove the oil pump from the camshaft.

17 Remove cam shaft.

18 Mark the big end cap for reassembly in the same position, then remove it.

19 Withdraw the piston upwards from the cylinder. Ensure that the connecting rod does not score the bore as it passes through.

20 Mark the cam followers for reassembly in the same holes, then remove them.

21 Remove the valves.

22 Remove the breather assembly from the lower part of the crankcase.

Reassembly

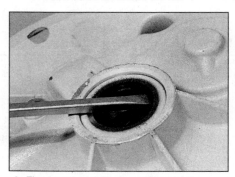

1 Fit new oil seals in the crankcase if necessary.

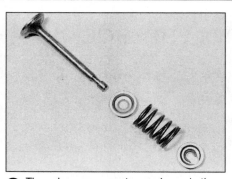

2 The valve components are shown in the photo in order of assembly.

3 The valve marked with an I in the centre is the inlet valve. Be careful not transpose the valves.

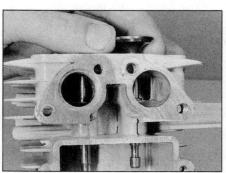

4 Insert the valve into the guide.

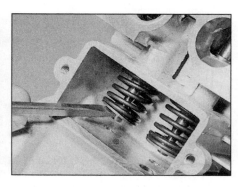

5 Fit the plain hole collar onto the valve stem, dished side to the valve chest. Place the spring against the collar. Fit the slotted collar onto the valve stem, dish into the spring, and offset to allow the valve stem through the wide end of the slot. Lever up the collar and move it sideways so that the narrow end of the slot engages under the shoulder on the valve stem, this locks the spring onto the valve. Fit both valves in an identical manner (this picture shows an exhaust valve).

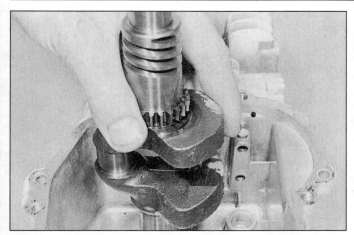

6 Smear crankshaft with oil and insert into the crankcase bearing.

7 Assemble the piston rings and connecting rod on the piston. The rings must be fitted the same way round in the same grooves as when removed. The gudgeon pin and connecting rod must be the same way round as when removed. Ensure circlips are located securely. When assembled in the cylinder, the serial numbers on the connecting rod must face the open end of the crankcase.

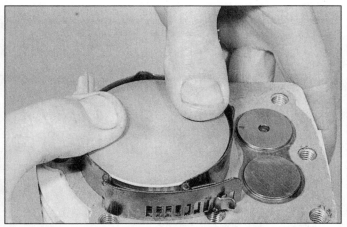

8 Fit a piston ring clamp to the piston. Oil the cylinder walls. Insert the piston from the top, taking care not to scratch the bore with the connecting rod. Press the piston out of the clamp, tapping gently with a piece of wood if necessary. If an obstruction occurs, do not force the piston in, stop and investigate.

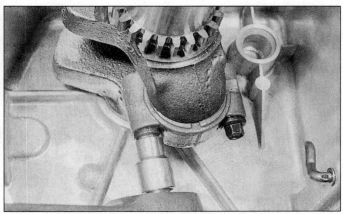

9 Oil the crankpin and engage the big end on it. Fit the cap the correct way round, as marked during dismantling. Tighten the two bolts firmly.

10 Oil the cam followers and insert them in the same holes in which they were originally fitted, as marked during dismantling.

11 Oil the camshaft bearing and insert the camshaft into the crankcase. Mesh the cam gear timing mark in line with the mark on the crankshaft gear.

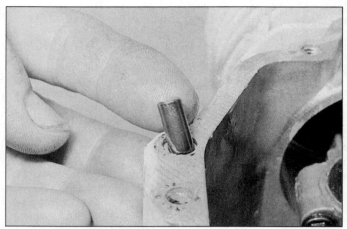

12 Fit the two dowels into the holes in the crankcase.

13 Fit a new crankcase gasket.

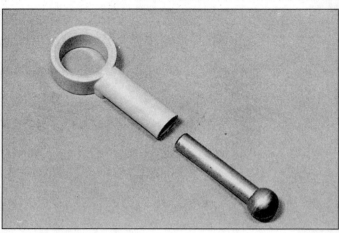

14 Insert the oil pump plunger into the housing.

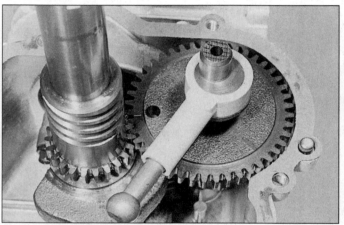

15 Fit the pump onto the camshaft, with the chamfered side of the hole in the white plastic housing facing down onto the cam gear.

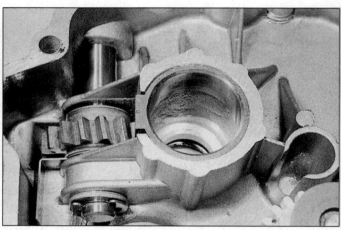

16 The final drive shaft and pinion assembly is held in the crankcase by a circlip with a flat washer behind it.

17 The pinion is keyed to the shaft and has a thrust washer on either side of it, one with an anti-spin angled leg. Removal and installation to fit a new pinion or shaft is straightforward and can be carried out from the picture.

18 Check the governor slider and weights for freedom of operation and signs of wear. If faulty, the governor should be renewed as a complete unit. To remove the governor, prise the C-clip out of the groove in the shaft, withdraw the spool, remove the second circlip and lift off the gear assembly and the washer under it. Reassembly is the opposite sequence.

19 The crankcase cover ready for installation is shown in the picture.

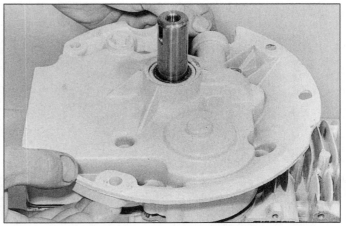

20 Oil the crankshaft and the camshaft bearings, then slide the cover onto the crankshaft. Turn the pinion shaft slightly to engage the pinion with the worm on the crankshaft if necessary. Locate the cover on the dowels. Check through the engine breather hole that the oil pump plunger ball-end is correctly in its housing, and that the governor lever is resting correctly against the governor spindle. Fit and tighten diagonally the six bolts and spring washers that secure the housing.

21 Check the valve clearances. Both valves should have a clearance of 0.25 mm (0.010 in). Adjustment of valve clearance is by grinding the tip of the valve stem to increase it or grinding in the valve seat to reduce it, but there are limits to the amount of seat grinding possible. In bad cases, new valves may need fitting. This requires professional attention and the use of special tools.

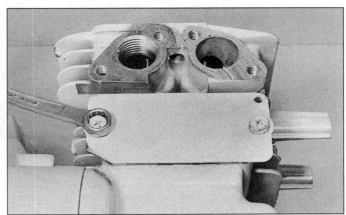

22 Replace the valve cover with the chamfered corner in the bottom left position.

23 Check the engine breather assembly. The valve in the bottom of the cup must be free, clean and undamaged. Wash the steel wool element in solvent and dry it. Place the circular baffle on the shoulder half way down the cup. Insert the element onto the baffle.

24 Insert the baffle cup assembly into the hole in the crankcase. Fit a new gasket...

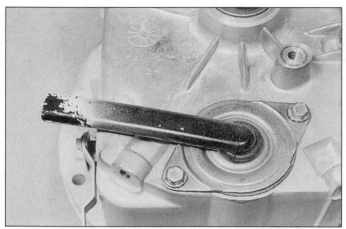

25 ... then fit the cover and tube and secure with the two bolts and shakeproof washers. Ensure that TOP stamped on the cover is towards the top of the engine.

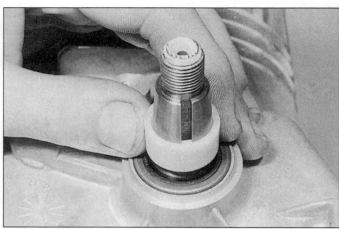

26 Fit the plastic sleeve on the crankshaft with its key in the crankshaft groove.

27 Fit the offset key in the slot as shown in the photo, with the longer offset to the left.

28 Fit the flywheel onto the crankshaft aligned with the key...

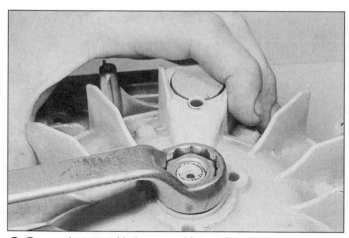

29 ... and secure with the nut and flat washer.

30 Fit the ignition unit and using a non-ferrous feeler gauge...

31 ... set an air gap of 0.37mm (0.015 in).

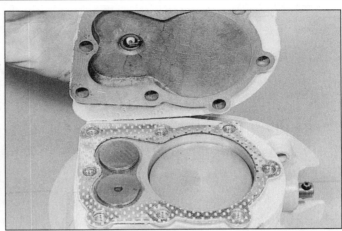

32 Fit a new cylinder head gasket and fit the cylinder head, tightening down a little at a time on each bolt in a diagonal sequence.

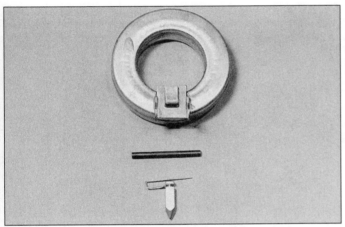

33 The float components are shown in the picture. Check the end of the needle valve for ridging or other damage and renew if necessary.

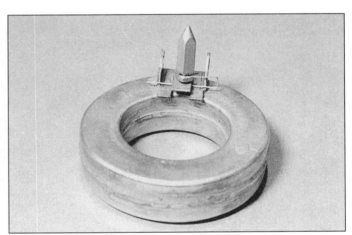

34 Assemble the needle valve on the float with the clip.

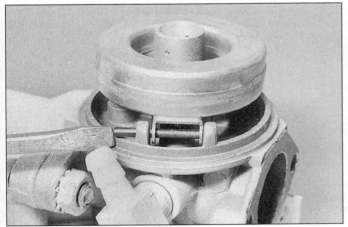

35 Position the float hinge between the carburettor hinge lugs, with the needle valve inserted in the fuel entry hole. Insert the hinge pin.

36 Inspect the float bowl seal for damage or distortion and renew if necessary. Fit the bowl onto the carburettor.

37 The bowl is secured with the threaded main jet. Check the main jet for cleanliness and damage. Rinse and blow to clean it. Do not use a pin or wire on the metered holes or they will be damaged and accurate metering lost.

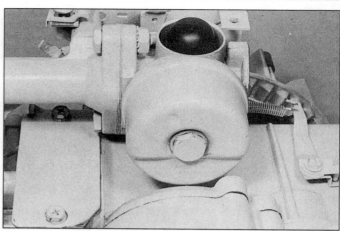

38 The step on the float bowl must be located as shown in the photo to allow full movement of the float.

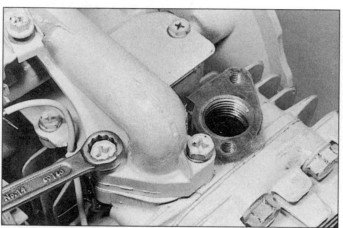

39 Fit the carburettor and linkage plate to the engine using a new gasket. Two screws and spring washers are used to secure the carburettor.

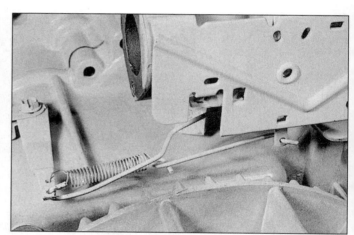

40 Connect the link from the throttle butterfly to the hole at the tip of the governor lever. Connect the spring to the next hole in the governor lever, and the link to the lever on the control plate.

41 Connect the earth lead to the spade connector on the linkage plate.

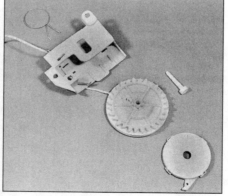

42 Connect the fuel pipe to the carburettor. If the recoil starter needs attention, this should be carried out now as it is difficult to deal with the starter cord after the fuel tank and engine cowl have been installed. The main components of the starter are shown in the picture.

43 Drive the central pin out by tapping on the chamfered end, then remove the pulley and recoil spring capsule.

44 Lift the capsule off the pulley.

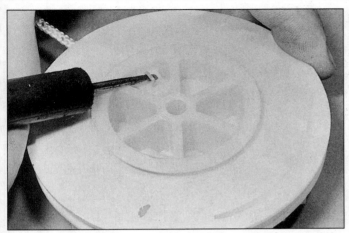

45 To free the cord, prise out the staple in the pulley. Fit the new cord and tap the staple in again.

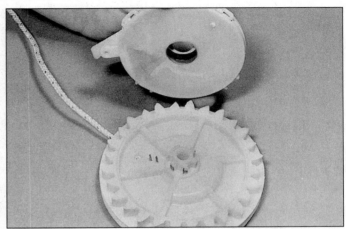

46 Fit the new spring capsule onto the pulley and turn it anticlockwise until the hook on the spring engages in the slot on the pulley hub. This can be verified by increasing tension when turning the capsule.

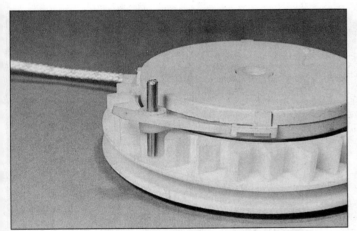

47 Turn the capsule about four turns to tension the pulley. Use a pin through the hole in the stop lever to hold the tension. Wind the cord clockwise onto the pulley when viewed from the capsule side. Leave enough cord free to pass through the hole in the fuel tank and fit the handle.

48 Fit the large clip onto the pulley. Enter the pulley assembly into the housing, ensuring that the legs of the clip are located either side of the divider plate.

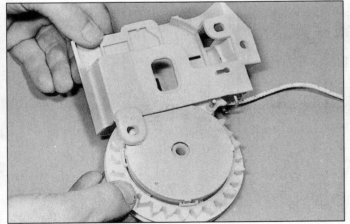

49 Seen from the other side, the photo shows the pulley assembly being entered into the housing with the pin still in the stop lever. Thread the cord under the wire guide.

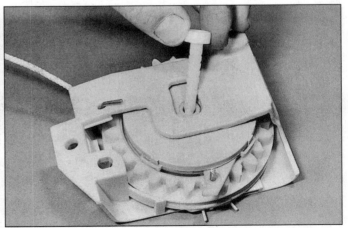

50 Fit the central pin. Do not withdraw the pin from the stop lever yet.

51 Install the recoil starter on the engine with the two bolts and shakeproof washers, fitting the engine fairing plate at the same time, as it is secured by the same screws. Take the pulley tension, withdraw the temporary pin from the stop lever. Pull out some more cord then anchor it temporarily.

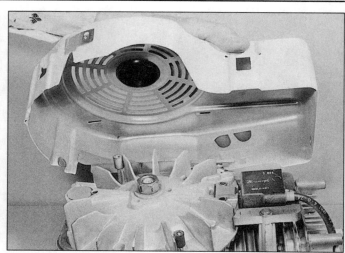

52 Fit the engine cowl with the four bolts and shakeproof washers.

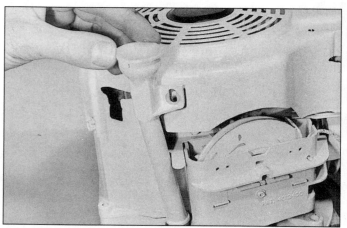

53 Fit the dipstick tube and secure it to the cowling with the bolt.

54 Thread the cord through the fuel tank hole...

55 ... slide the fuel tank into the slides on the cowl and secure it with the three bolts. Fit the handle to the cord with the removable staple. Free the cord from its temporary anchorage. Pull the starter handle to check correct operation and a positive return action.

56 Connect the fuel pipe to the tank and secure it with the spring clip.

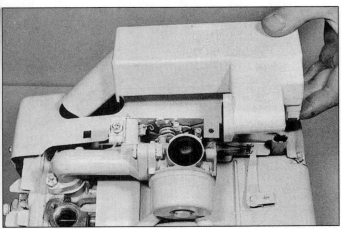

57 Insert the air cleaner inlet duct through the hole in the cowling.

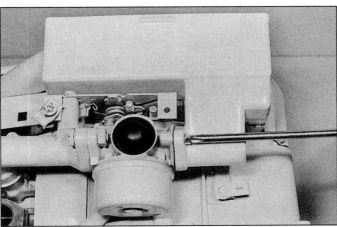

58 Check that the rubber ring is in position on the air cleaner housing elbow duct. Connect the engine breather pipe to the tube on the corner of the air cleaner housing. Position the housing elbow on the carburettor inlet flange and secure with the two screws.

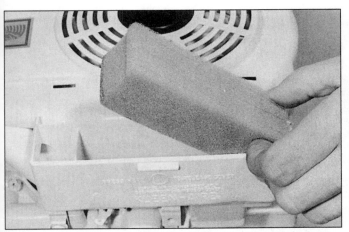

59 Wash the air cleaner foam element in solvent and squeeze it dry. Place it in the housing.

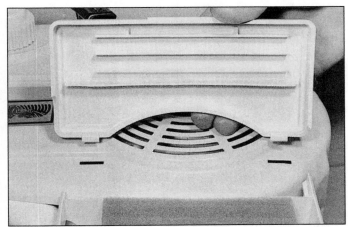

60 Fit the press-on lid.

61 If the power drive unit needs removing, turn the front left-hand wheel backplate until the hole in it exposes the roll pin. Drive the roll pin out and remove the wheel. Withdraw the complete drive unit from the axle.

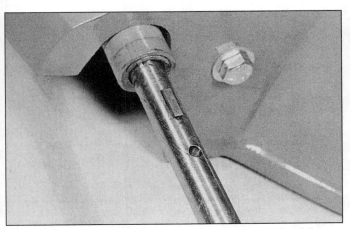

62 To re-install the drive unit or fit a new one proceed as follows: fit the Woodruff key into the slot in the axle.

63 The groove in the power drive shaft engages the key on the axle.

64 Place the washer on the plastic bush. Place the bush on the power drive sprocket shaft; push the shaft along the slot until the flats on the plastic bush enter the slot in the drive unit casing. Repeat this operation for the other face of the casing.

65 Slide the housing onto the axle, engaging the groove with the key on the axle.

66 Enter the roll pin into the wheel hub, fit the wheel onto the axle and align the pin with the hole in the axle. Drive the pin into the axle with a hammer and punch, taking care not to damage the pin. Fit the wheel cover plate.

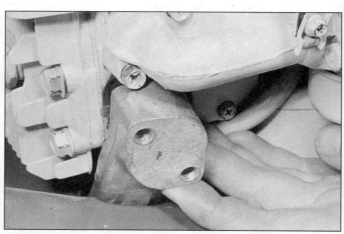

67 Fit the exhaust manifold to the engine, using a new gasket.

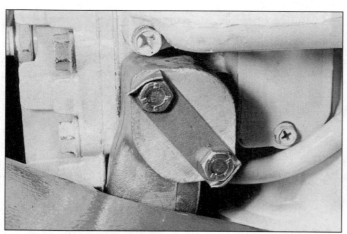

68 Secure the manifold with two bolts and a locking tab.

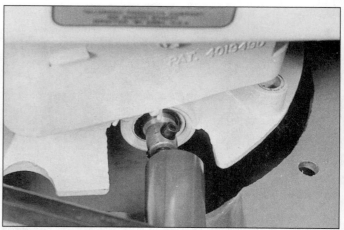

69 Lower the mower to the minimum cutting height position. Place the engine on the deck. Fit the plastic sleeve on the power drive unit shaft. Enter the engine shaft into the sleeve and engage the drive dogs in the drive unit shaft slots.

70 Bolt the power drive unit to the decking.

71 Fit three of the engine mounting nuts, bolts and flat washers. Connect the exhaust silencer into the manifold pipe and secure it with the fourth engine mounting nut, bolt and flat washers.

72 Fit the Woodruff key in the engine drive shaft, then...

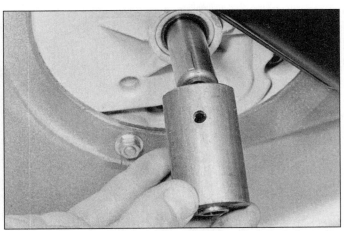

73 ... fit the drive sleeve onto the shaft aligned with the key and fit the cutter using the shouldered spacer, flat washer and bolt.

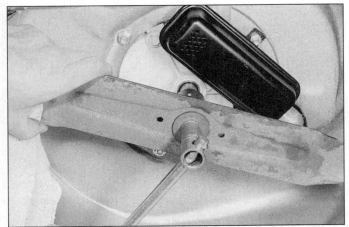

74 Use a rag to hold the cutter while tightening it to protect your hand from the cutting edge.

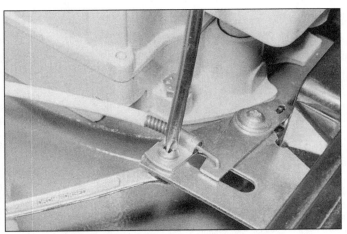

75 Connect the clutch cable to the lever and quadrant.

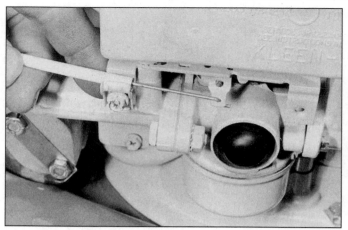

76 Connect the throttle cable to the lever on the linkage plate.

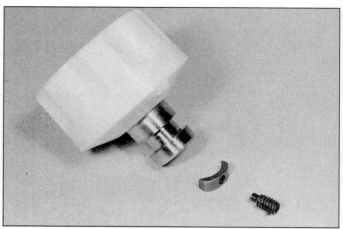

77 The height adjusting knob attachment fittings are shown in the photo.

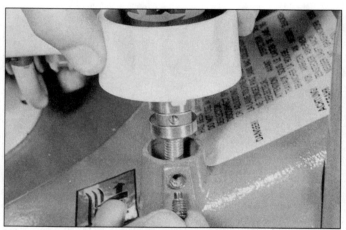

78 Screw the knob onto the threaded rod until the shoulder nears the edge of the casting. Place the half collet in the groove. Continue screwing the knob and collet down into the hole in the boss until the hole in the collet aligns with the threaded hole in the boss, then screw the grubscrew into the boss so that it intercepts the hole in the collet. Tighten the grubscrew, and...

79 ... operate the knob to check for free rotation and correct operation of the height adjustment.

Chapter 13
Tecumseh MV100S 2-stroke engine

Model/spec. number on engine: E-16
Mower application

Every effort has been made to make the list of models that use this engine as comprehensive as possible. Due to model and engine supply changes, you may have a mower that is not listed. Refer to *Engine Identity* on page 7 to identify the engine that you have, or contact an engine supply dealer to assist with identification.

Allen 216/218   Flymo L50/L38/L47/L470

Technical Data

Spark plug gap	0.6 to 0.7 mm (0.024 to 0.028 in)
Spark plug type	NGK B4LM
Magneto armature air gap	0.3 to 0.4 mm (0.012 to 0.016 in)
Torque wrench settings:	
Big-end bolts	7 Nm
Cylinder head bolts	11 Nm
Flywheel retaining nut	47 Nm

Dismantling

Before starting to dismantle, read Chapter 2. The procedures outlined apply to all engines and if adopted, will ensure an orderly and methodical approach that will make dismantling and reassembly much easier. Remove the engine from the mower, and proceed as follows:

1 Turn the fuel tap to the 'Off' position. Release the retaining clip and remove the fuel pipe from the carburettor and fuel tap. Be prepared for fuel spillage.

2 Using pliers, pull the retaining clips up and disengage them from the fuel tank and engine cowling.

3 Slide the fuel tank up and out of its locating slots in the engine cowling.

4 Unscrew the four retaining bolts, and remove the starter assembly from the engine cowling.

5 Remove the engine cowling by unscrewing the four retaining bolts. Note the longer bolt with washer that also secures the exhaust system.

6 Disengage the throttle return spring from the throttle lever and bracket.

7 Unscrew the two retaining nuts, and remove the carburettor.

8 To dismantle the carburettor, undo the float bowl retaining bolt. Be prepared for fuel spillage. Remove the float bowl and rubber gasket.

9 Push out the pivot pin, and carefully lift out the float with the needle valve still attached.

10 The main jet/emulsion tube is located in the centre of the carburettor body. Unscrew the jet/emulsion tube and remove. No further dismantling of the carburettor is advised

11 Check the condition of the needle valve and seat for any damage or wear (*refer to Chapter 2*). Examine the float bowl rubber gasket for any cracks, etc. Check that the holes of the jet/emulsion tube and carburettor body are clear. If necessary, clear the holes by blowing or use a thin nylon bristle. Never use a needle or wire to clean a jet. Check the float for damage or cracks.

12 The two exhaust mounting bolts are locked by means of a tab washer. Bend back the tabs, unscrew the bolts, and remove the exhaust system. Recover the gasket.

13 Carefully pull the HT cap from the spark plug.

14 Disconnect the ignition magneto earthing wire, unscrew the two mounting bolts, and remove the magneto. Remove the magneto earthing wire.

15 The flywheel retaining nut is extremely tight. In order to prevent the flywheel from turning, have an assistant jam a large screwdriver (or similar) between the teeth at the back of the flywheel, and the cast lug of the crankcase end plate. Undo the retaining nut, remove the bevelled washer, starter flange and mesh.

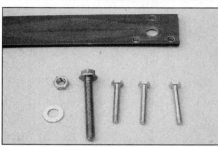

16 To remove the flywheel a puller is required. This can be obtained from a local mower specialist, or one can be fabricated as follows: Using a piece of 6mm thick mild steel plate, drill three 6.5 mm holes, approximately 38 mm between centres, in the shape of an equilateral triangle. These holes should align with the holes in the centre boss of the flywheel. In the centre of the triangle, drill a 10 mm hole to align with the crankshaft. Assemble the puller using three 6 x 40 mm bolts, and one 8 x 65 mm bolt with nut and washer.

17 Regardless of which puller is used, it is necessary to tap the centre holes in the flywheel boss to accept the three 6 mm bolts.

18 Position the flywheel retaining nut flush with the end of the crankshaft, insert the three 6 mm bolts of the assembled puller. Make sure that

the centre 8 mm bolt of the puller acts squarely on the end of the crankshaft, and turn the 8 mm nut to apply a strong pulling force. It may be necessary to encourage the flywheel with a light tap from a soft hammer on the rim opposite the magnets. Take care to only strike the flywheel on the reinforced section of the rim. Once freed from the crankshaft taper, remove the flywheel, puller, and retaining nut. Recover the nylon collar and square-sectioned key.

19 Remove the spark plug.

20 Unscrew the four retaining bolts, and remove the reed valve housing from the base of the crankcase. To remove the reed valves, unscrew the two retaining bolts, lift off the retaining plate, and remove the valves.

21 In a diagonal sequence, loosen evenly and remove the six cylinder head bolts.

22 Working through the hole in the base of the crankcase left by the reed valve block, unscrew the big-end bolts. Carefully remove the big-end bearing cap. The big-end bearing is made up of 37 needle rollers, which will fall into the crankcase unless great care is taken when removing the bearing cap. Recover the needle rollers.

23 Remove any carbon build-up at the lip of the cylinder bore using a soft tool, and gently push the connecting rod and piston assembly up and out of the cylinder bore.

24 If required, remove the piston rings from the piston by carefully expanding the rings at their ends and sliding them from the piston. Note the orientation of the rings for reassembly. Remove the circlips and push the gudgeon pin from the piston.

25 Unscrew the four crankcase end plate retaining bolts, but do not attempt to remove the plate at this stage. A hot air gun (or similar) will greatly assist the removal of the crankshaft from the crankcase. Ensure that the crankshaft is free of dirt and rust. Heat up the area of the crankcase that surrounds the main bearing on the drive (parallel) end of the crankshaft. Using a soft hammer, carefully drive the crankshaft (with the bearing still fitted) and end plate assembly from the crankcase.

26 Heat up the area of the end plate that surrounds the main bearing, and using a soft hammer, drive the crankshaft and bearing from the end plate.

27 If required, prise the oil seals from the crankcase and end plate, noting which way round they are fitted.

28 Use a bearing puller, or hydraulic press, to remove the bearings from the crankshaft.

29 Check the condition of the cylinder bore for wear, scores or cracks. If the bore is damaged, worn oval or oversized, then professional skills and special equipment will be necessary to restore it. Check all threaded holes for damaged threads, and repair if necessary by fitting a thread insert of the correct size.

Reassembly

1 If removed, fit new ball bearings to the crankshaft using a hydraulic press. The bearings are fitted with the lettering on the rim facing outwards. Press the bearings right up to the shoulder of the crankshaft webs. The bearing fitted to the drive end (parallel) of the crankshaft is a type 6005, whilst the flywheel end (tapered) is a type 6203.

2 Fit new oil seals to the crankcase and end plate using appropriate sized sockets. The seals should be fitted with the sharp lip facing inwards.

3 Using a hot air gun, heat up the bearing housing in the end plate. Take care not to damage the oil seal. Smear the inside lip of with two-stroke oil.

4 Fit the crankshaft, tapered end first, into the end plate. Carefully drive the crankshaft and bearing into place using a soft hammer, or hydraulic press.

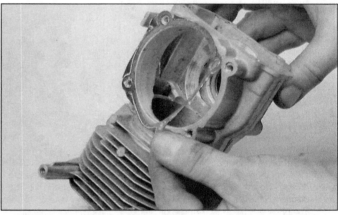

5 Heat up the bearing housing in the crankcase. Again, take care not to damage the oil seal. Smear the inside lip of the seal with two-stroke oil. With a new gasket in place…

6 … insert the crankshaft/end plate assembly into the crankcase.

7 Position the flywheel retaining nut flush with the end of the crankshaft, and drive or press the bearing into place. Insert and tighten evenly the four end plate retaining bolts. Rotate the crankshaft a few times to check for freedom of movement. Remove the flywheel retaining nut from the end of the crankshaft.

8 Refit the gudgeon pin to the connecting rod and piston using new circlips. Ensure that the notch on the piston crown is on the opposite side to the cast mark at the big-end of the connecting rod.

9 Fit the piston rings to the piston. If re-using the old rings, ensure they are fitted to their original locations. The rings are symmetrical in cross section, and can therefore be fitted either way up. Fit the lower compression ring first by carefully expanding the ring just enough to slide it down over the piston, and into the lower groove. Repeat this procedure for the top compression ring. Piston rings are very brittle. If they are expanded too much, they will break.

10 Smear the piston rings and cylinder bore with two-stroke oil. Arrange the piston ring end gaps so that they are approximately 30° apart on the notched side of the piston (arrowed).

11 Using a piston ring clamp, insert the connecting rod and piston assembly in to the cylinder bore, with the notch in the piston crown towards the tapered end of the crankshaft. Slowly push the piston down into the bore, making sure that the connecting rod does not scratch the cylinder walls. Press the piston firmly into the cylinder, sliding it out of the clamp as the rings enter the cylinder bore. If necessary, use a hammer handle or piece of wood and gently tap the piston out of the clamp and into the cylinder, but stop and investigate any undue resistance.

12 Smear the big-end journal with two-stroke oil. Engage the connecting rod big-end with the crankshaft journal, but leave enough room for the needle rollers to be inserted. One at a time, using tweezers (or similar), insert the needle rollers into the gap between the connecting rod and crankshaft journal.

13 Once the gap between the connecting rod and journal is full, carefully add the remaining needle rollers to the journal until all 37 rollers are in place. This is a very delicate operation, and some patience will be required.

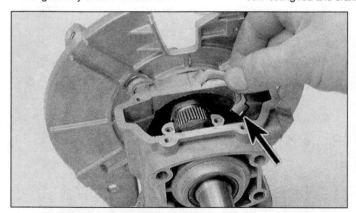

14 Smear the bearing face of the big-end bearing cap with two-stroke oil and carefully place it over the needle rollers, aligning the cast mark on the cap with the matching mark on the connecting rod (arrowed).

15 With a drop of thread locking compound on their threads, insert and tighten the big-end bolts securely. If a suitable torque wrench is available, tighten the bolts to the torque given in Technical Data. Put a drop of two-stroke oil in to the hole in the end of the big-end cap, and rotate the crankshaft a few times to ensure freedom of movement.

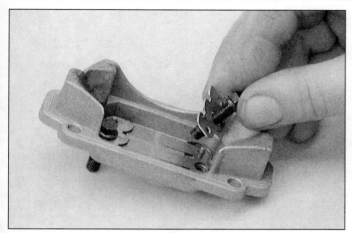

16 If previously dismantled, refit the reed valves in to the housing. Secure each valve in place with the retaining plate, and tighten the retaining bolt securely.

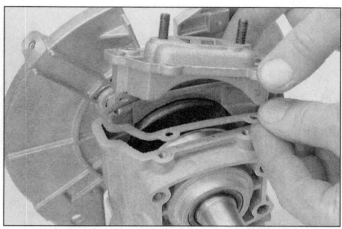

17 Using a new gasket, refit the reed valve housing to the base of the crankcase. Tighten the four retaining bolts securely.

18 Place a new gasket onto the cylinder head, and refit the head to the cylinder. Tighten the six cylinder head bolts evenly, in a diagonal sequence, securely. If a suitable torque wrench is available, tighten the bolts to the torque given in Technical Data. Refit the spark plug.

19 Slide the nylon collar over the tapered end of the crankshaft, ensuring that the nylon tab engages with the keyway of the shaft. Install the square-sectioned key in the crankshaft keyway.

20 Fit the flywheel over the tapered end of the crankshaft, aligning the keyway in the flywheel with the key previously fitted.

21 Install the starter flange and mesh.

22 Fit the bevelled washer with the concave side against the starter flange. Have an assistant jam a large screwdriver (or similar) between the teeth on the back of the flywheel, and the cast lug of the crankcase end plate. Tighten the flywheel retaining nut, with its shoulder inside the bevelled washer, to the torque given in Technical Data.

23 Route the ignition magneto earthing wire as shown.

24 Refit the magneto. Before tightening the two mounting bolts, turn the flywheel so that the magnets are next to the magneto. Use non-ferrous feeler gauges to measure the air gap between the magneto's armature legs and the flywheel. The correct gap is given in Technical Data. The holes in the armature legs are slotted. Move the armature until the correct gap is achieved. Tighten the bolts securely. Refit the HT cap to the spark plug.

25 Using a new gasket if necessary, refit the exhaust system. The two retaining bolts fit through a tab washer and reinforcing plate.

26 Tighten the bolts securely, and lock them by bending the tabs of the washer. The bracket on the exhaust silencer is secured with an engine cowling bolt at a later stage.

27 Insert the main jet/emulsion tube assembly into the carburettor body. Tighten the jet carefully.

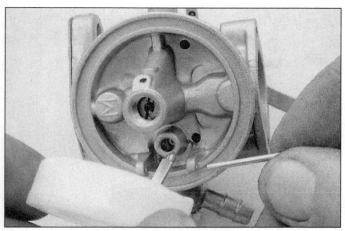

28 Refit the needle valve into its holder in the float, and carefully lower the assembly into place. Align the float with the pivot, and insert the pivot pin. There is no provision for adjusting the float height.

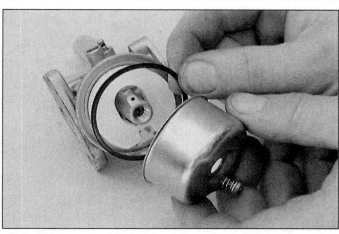

29 Using a new rubber gasket if necessary, refit the float bowl and secure with the retaining nut and fibre washer.

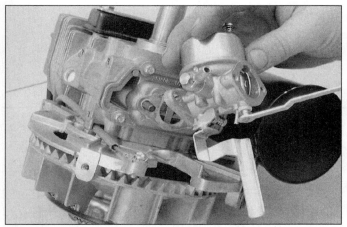

30 With a new gasket in place, refit the carburettor to the reed valve housing. Tighten the two retaining nuts securely.

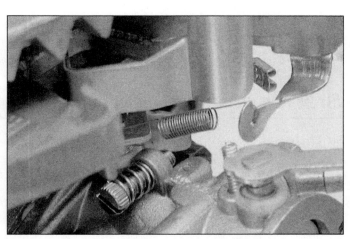

31 Refit the throttle return spring to the throttle arm and bracket.

32 The engine cowling is secured with four bolts. The longer bolt and washer also retains the exhaust silencer bracket.

33 Install the starter assembly onto the engine cowling, and tighten the four retaining bolts securely.

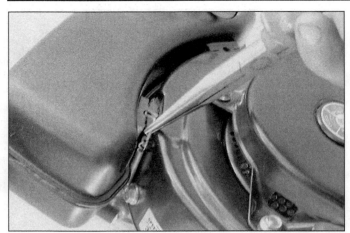

34 Slide the fuel tank into its locating slots in the engine cowling. One end of the retaining clips engages with the underside of the cowling, whilst the other end fits into the locating hole in the fuel tank.

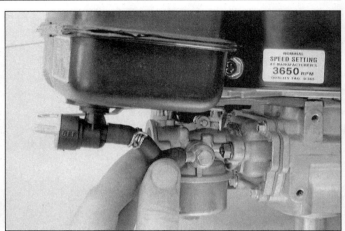

35 Reconnect the fuel pipe to the carburettor and fuel tap. Secure the pipe with the retaining clip.

Starter repair

1 Undo the four retaining bolts, and remove the starter from the engine cowling.

2 Pull the rope to its full extension, and clamp the pulley in place with a self-grip wrench (or similar).

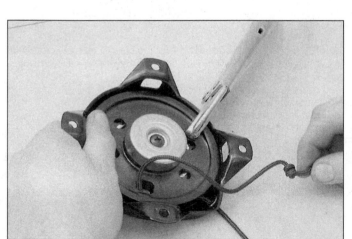

3 To replace the rope: Where the rope goes through the pulley, cut off the knot and pull the rope from the starter. Feed the new rope through the hole in the outer cover, and through the hole in the pulley. Tie the knot.

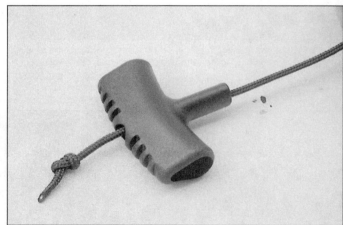

4 Feed the other end through the hole in the starter handle, again tie the knot. Tension the rope, remove the self-grip wrench, and allow the starter spring to rewind the rope.

5 To replace the starter spring: Where the rope goes through the pulley, untie the knot and pull the rope from the starter. Unscrew the central screw, and carefully lift off the pawl cover. Note the spring fitted centrally under the cover.

6 Lift out the starter pawl. Note the 'hair' spring under the pawl. Lift out the pulley. Turn the starter spring retaining cover clockwise to release it from the pulley. Remove the spring.

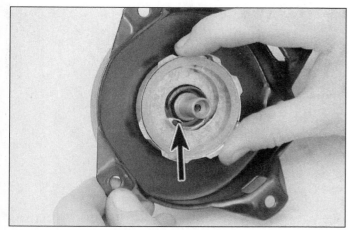

7 The new starter spring should come already fitted into the retaining cover. Place the spring and retaining cover in the starter outer cover, engaging the inner end of the spring with the lug in the outer cover (arrowed).

8 Align the pulley with the spring retaining cover as shown. Fit the pulley over the spring/cover, and twist it anti-clockwise to lock.

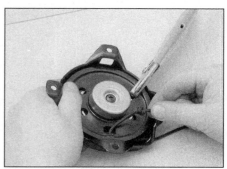

9 Refit the 'hair' spring into the pawl-locating hole and refit the pawl. Ensure that the leg of the spring is on the outside of the pawl (arrowed).

10 Insert the spring into the centre, and fit the pawl cover, engaging the pawl with the slot in the cover. Tighten the screw securely.

11 Wind the pulley approximately five and a half turns anti-clockwise to tension the starter spring, and align the rope holes in the outer cover and pulley. The exact number of turns is dependent on the length of the rope. Clamp the pulley in place by using a self-grip wrench (or similar).

12 Feed the rope through the holes in the cover and pulley, and tie the knot. Tension the rope, remove the self-grip wrench, and allow the starter spring to rewind the rope. Check for correct operation. Refit the starter to the engine cowling using the four retaining bolts.

Notes

Which engine is fitted?

Every effort has been made to make this list of models as comprehensive as possible. Due to model and engine supply changes, you may have a mower that is not listed. Refer to *Engine Identity* on page 6 to identify the engine that you have, or contact an engine supply dealer to assist with identification.

AL-KO	
Engine: E-40	Tecumseh LAV 1 53
Engines: E-31, E-41, E-36, E-46, E-56	Tecumseh 3.5 hp/Vantage 35
AL-KO 42/48	
Engine: GJAF	Honda OHC GCV135 4.5 hp (3.3 kW)
AL-KO Euroline 4200/4700	
Engine: GJAF	Honda OHC GCV135 4.5 hp (3.3 kW)
Allen 216/218	
Engine: E-16	Tecumseh MV100S
Ariens LM series	
Engines: 128802, 127702, 12H802, 12F802	Briggs & Stratton Quantum 55 'L' Head
Atco	
Engines: 110700, 111700, 112700, 114700	Briggs & Stratton MAX 4hp
Atco Admiral	
Engines: 128802, 127702, 12H802, 12F802	Briggs & Stratton Quantum 55 'L' Head
Atco Club	
Engine: 135232	Briggs & Stratton I/C horizontal crank 'L' Head 5 hp
Atco Royale	
Engine: 135232	Briggs & Stratton I/C horizontal crank 'L' Head 5 hp
Atco Viscount	
Engines: 128802, 127702, 12H802, 12F802	Briggs & Stratton Quantum 55 'L' Head
Bearcat BC series	
Engines: 128802, 127702, 12H802, 12F802	Briggs & Stratton Quantum 55 'L' Head
BRILL Hattrick	
Engines: 128802, 127702, 12H802, 12F802	Briggs & Stratton Quantum 55 'L' Head
Castel	
Engine: E-40	Tecumseh LAV 1 53
Engines: E-31, E-41, E-36, E-46, E-56	Tecumseh 3.5 hp/Vantage 35
Efco LR series	
Engines: 9D902, 10D902, 98902	Briggs & Stratton 35 Sprint/Classic 2.6 kW
Engines: E-31, E-41, E-36, E-46, E-56	Tecumseh 3.5 hp/Vantage 35
Efco LR/MR series	
Engines: 128802, 127702, 12H802, 12F802	Briggs & Stratton Quantum 55 'L' Head

Flymo
Engine: E-40 — Tecumseh LAV 1 53
Engines: 110700, 111700, 112700, 114700 — Briggs & Stratton MAX 4hp

Flymo 42cm/46cm
Engines: E-31, E-41, E-36, E-46, E-56 — Tecumseh 3.5 hp/Vantage 35

Flymo L50/L38/L47/L470
Engine: E-16 — Tecumseh MV100S

Harry
Engine: E-40 — Tecumseh LAV 1 53
Engines: E-31, E-41, E-36, E-46, E-56 — Tecumseh 3.5 hp/Vantage 35

Harry 302/C48/322/C49C50/424
Engines: 128802, 127702, 12H802, 12F802 — Briggs & Stratton Quantum 55 'L' Head

Harry 313
Engines: 9D902, 10D902, 98902 — Briggs & Stratton 35 Sprint/Classic 2.6 kW

Hayter
Engine: E-40 — Tecumseh LAV 1 53
Engine: GXV120 — Honda GXV120

Hayter Harrier
Engines: 110700, 111700, 112700, 114700 — Briggs & Stratton MAX 4hp

Hayter Harrier 2
Engines: 110700, 111700, 112700, 114700 — Briggs & Stratton MAX 4hp

Hayter Harrier 41
Engines: 128802, 127702, 12H802, 12F802 — Briggs & Stratton Quantum 55 'L' Head

Hayter Harrier 48
Engine: 121602 — Briggs & Stratton Intek/Europa OHV

Hayter Hawk
Engines: 110700, 111700, 112700, 114700 — Briggs & Stratton MAX 4hp

Hayter Hayterette
Engines: 128802, 127702, 12H802, 12F802 — Briggs & Stratton Quantum 55 'L' Head

Hayter Hobby
Engines: E-31, E-41, E-36, E-46, E-56 — Tecumseh 3.5 hp/Vantage 35

Hayter Hunter 48
Engines: 110700, 111700, 112700, 114700 — Briggs & Stratton MAX 4hp

Hayter Jubilee
Engines: 128802, 127702, 12H802, 12F802 — Briggs & Stratton Quantum 55 'L' Head

Hayter Ranger
Engines: 128802, 127702, 12H802, 12F802 — Briggs & Stratton Quantum 55 'L' Head

Honda HR17
Engine: GV100 — Honda GV100

Honda HR173
Engine: GV100 — Honda GV100

Honda HR194
Engine: GXV120 — Honda GXV120

Honda HRA214
Engine: GXV120 — Honda GXV120

Honda HRB423 Engine: GV100	Honda GV100
Honda HRB425C Engine: GJAF	Honda OHC GCV135 4.5 hp (3.3 kW)
Honda HRG415C Engine: GJAF	Honda OHC GCV135 4.5 hp (3.3 kW)
Honda HRG465C Engine: GJAF	Honda OHC GCV135 4.5 hp (3.3 kW)
Honda HR214 Engine: GXV120	Honda GXV120
Husqvarna Engines: 110700, 111700, 112700, 114700	Briggs & Stratton MAX 4hp
IBEA 4221/4237/4238/4204/4704/4721 Engines: 128802, 127702, 12H802, 12F802	Briggs & Stratton Quantum 55 'L' Head
IBEA 5361 Engine: 121602	Briggs & Stratton Intek/Europa OHV
IPU 400 series Engine: GXV120	Honda GXV120

Kompact 90
    Engine: E-40
    Engines: E-31, E-41, E-36, E-46, E-56
	Tecumseh LAV 1 53
	Tecumseh 3.5 hp/Vantage 35

Kompact 90S Engine: 135232	Briggs & Stratton I/C horizontal crank 'L' Head 5 hp
Lawn-Boy 400 Engines: 128802, 127702, 12H802, 12F802	Briggs & Stratton Quantum 55 'L' Head
Lawnflite by MTD 383 Engines: 9D902, 10D902, 98902	Briggs & Stratton 35 Sprint/Classic 2.6 kW
Lawnflite by MTD 384 Engines: 128802, 127702, 12H802, 12F802	Briggs & Stratton Quantum 55 'L' Head
Lawnflite by MTD 991 SP6 Engines: 128802, 127702, 12H802, 12F802	Briggs & Stratton Quantum 55 'L' Head
Lawnflite by MTD GE40 Engines: 9D902, 10D902, 98902	Briggs & Stratton 35 Sprint/Classic 2.6 kW
Lawnflite by MTD GES 45 C Engines: 128802, 127702, 12H802, 12F802	Briggs & Stratton Quantum 55 'L' Head
Lawnflite by MTD GES 53 Engines: 128802, 127702, 12H802, 12F802	Briggs & Stratton Quantum 55 'L' Head
Lawn-King NG series Engines: 9D902, 10D902, 98902	Briggs & Stratton 35 Sprint/Classic 2.6 kW
Lawn-King PA/NP/T484 series Engines: 128802, 127702, 12H802, 12F802	Briggs & Stratton Quantum 55 'L' Head
McCulloch ML857 Engines: 128802, 127702, 12H802, 12F802	Briggs & Stratton Quantum 55 'L' Head

Mountfield Emblem
    Engine: E-40
    Engines: E-31, E-41, E-36, E-46, E-56
	Tecumseh LAV 1 53
	Tecumseh 3.5 hp/Vantage 35

Mountfield Emblem 15 Engines: 9D902, 10D902, 98902	Briggs & Stratton 35 Sprint/Classic 2.6 kW
Mountfield Emperor Engines: 110700, 111700, 112700, 114700 Engines: 128802, 127702, 12H802, 12F802	Briggs & Stratton MAX 4hp Briggs & Stratton Quantum 55 'L' Head
Mountfield Empress Engines: 110700, 111700, 112700, 114700 Engines: E-31, E-41, E-36, E-46, E-56 Engine: E-40	Briggs & Stratton MAX 4hp Tecumseh 3.5 hp/Vantage 35 Tecumseh LAV 1 53
Mountfield Empress 16 Engines: 128802, 127702, 12H802, 12F802	Briggs & Stratton Quantum 55 'L' Head
Mountfield Empress 18 Engines: 128802, 127702, 12H802, 12F802	Briggs & Stratton Quantum 55 'L' Head
Mountfield Laser Engines: E-31, E-41, E-36, E-46, E-56	Tecumseh 3.5 hp/Vantage 35
Mountfield Laser Delta 42 Engine: GV100	Honda GV100
Mountfield Laser Delta 42/46 Engines: 9D902, 10D902, 98902	Briggs & Stratton 35 Sprint/Classic 2.6 kW
Mountfield M3 Engines: E-31, E-41, E-36, E-46, E-56	Tecumseh 3.5 hp/Vantage 35
Mountfield MPR series Engine: 121602	Briggs & Stratton Intek/Europa OHV
Oleomac G43 Engine: E-40 Engines: 9D902, 10D902, 98902 Engines: E-31, E-41, E-36, E-46, E-56	Tecumseh LAV 1 53 Briggs & Stratton 35 Sprint/Classic 2.6 kW Tecumseh 3.5 hp/Vantage 35
Oleomac G47 Engine: GJAF Engines: 128802, 127702, 12H802, 12F802	Honda OHC GCV135 4.5 hp (3.3 kW) Briggs & Stratton Quantum 55 'L' Head
Oleomac MAX 53 Engines: 128802, 127702, 12H802, 12F802	Briggs & Stratton Quantum 55 'L' Head
Partner 431 Engines: 9D902, 10D902, 98902	Briggs & Stratton 35 Sprint/Classic 2.6 kW
Qualcast Quadtrak 45 Engine: E-40 Engines: E-31, E-41, E-36, E-46, E-56	Tecumseh LAV 1 53 Tecumseh 3.5 hp/Vantage 35
Qualcast Trojan Engine: E-40 Engines: E-31, E-41, E-36, E-46, E-56	Tecumseh LAV 1 53 Tecumseh 3.5 hp/Vantage 35
Rally 21/MR series Engines: 128802, 127702, 12H802, 12F802	Briggs & Stratton Quantum 55 'L' Head
Rover Engine: GXV120	Honda GXV120
Rover 100 Engine: GV100 Engines: 9D902, 10D902, 98902	Honda GV100 Briggs & Stratton 35 Sprint/Classic 2.6 kW

Rover 100/200/260 Engines: 128802, 127702, 12H802, 12F802	Briggs & Stratton Quantum 55 'L' Head
Rover 200 18" Engine: GJAF	Honda OHC GCV135 4.5 hp (3.3 kW)
SARP 484 Engine: GJAF	Honda OHC GCV135 4.5 hp (3.3 kW)
Stiga Multiclip Pro 48 Engine: GJAF Engines: 9D902, 10D902, 98902	Honda OHC GCV135 4.5 hp (3.3 kW) Briggs & Stratton 35 Sprint/Classic 2.6 kW
Stiga Turbo 48/55 Engines: 128802, 127702, 12H802, 12F802	Briggs & Stratton Quantum 55 'L' Head
Suffolk Punch P16 Engines: 9D902, 10D902, 98902	Briggs & Stratton 35 Sprint/Classic 2.6 kW
Suffolk Punch P19 Engines: 128802, 127702, 12H802, 12F802	Briggs & Stratton Quantum 55 'L' Head
Suffolk Punch P19S Engines: 128802, 127702, 12H802, 12F802	Briggs & Stratton Quantum 55 'L' Head
The Club 470 T35/40 Engines: E-31, E-41, E-36, E-46, E-56	Tecumseh 3.5 hp/Vantage 35
TORO Re-cycler 20776 Engines: 128802, 127702, 12H802, 12F802	Briggs & Stratton Quantum 55 'L' Head
TORO Re-cycler 26637/20791/20789/20826/20827 Engine: 121602	Briggs & Stratton Intek/Europa OHV
Tracmaster Camon Engine: GXV120	Honda GXV120
Valex Daytona Engines: E-31, E-41, E-36, E-46, E-56	Tecumseh 3.5 hp/Vantage 35
Viva PB seies Engines: 128802, 127702, 12H802, 12F802	Briggs & Stratton Quantum 55 'L' Head
Yardman by MTD YM series Engines: 128802, 127702, 12H802, 12F802	Briggs & Stratton Quantum 55 'L' Head

Glossary

Bellville washer
A domed spring steel washer used as a locking device.

Breather valve
Due to the constantly changing pressures in the crankcase whilst an engine is running this valve is needed to equalise the pressure and stop the oil being expelled from the engine.

Bush
A thin tube used to form the outside of a plain bearing. Usually used in soft metal castings to improve the life of the bearing.

Cam followers (tappets)
Shaped metal rods which fit between the cam lobes of the camshaft and the valves to open the inlet and exhaust valves.

Circlip
A spring steel retaining device located in a groove in a shaft or hole which has lugs at each end to allow compression with special pliers for fitting.

Contact breaker points
A set of electrical contacts operated by a cam on the crankshaft to ensure that the fuel-air mixture is ignited at the correct moment in the engine cycle.

Crankcase
The main body of an engine which can consist of two or more parts. The crankcase houses the crankshaft and most internal engine components.

Dowels
These are close fitting pegs used to align parts of an engine accurately.

Feeler gauge
Usually a set of steel fingers of specified thickness, for setting gaps between parts i.e. spark plug contacts, ignition contact breaker points.

Governor
Most small engines have a speed governing device. This limits the maximum speed of the engine. The two most common types are the pneumatic governor and the mechanical governor.

The pneumatic governor controls the carburettor according to the air flow generated by the cooling fan of the flywheel effecting a vane or paddle placed under the engine.

The mechanical governor is a device inside the crankcase with weights which spin; the centrifugal force pushes the weights into position to control the carburettor.

On both types the speed at which the engine runs is determined by a spring attached to the throttle link.

Gudgeon pin
The gudgeon pin is a metal pin used to connect the piston to the connecting rod.

Ignition coil
An induction coil that supplies the high voltage to the spark plug.

Magneto
A combination of coil and flywheel magnets used to generate the electricity to fire the spark plug.

Oil splasher
An internal engine part which disperses oil from the sump around the inside of the crankcase. To lubricate the bearings and the piston.

Pawl
A pivoted lever shaped to engage with a ratchet to prevent motion in a particular direction i.e. recoil starter.

Piston ring clamp
A tool that consists of a steel band which is tightened up to hold piston rings compressed against piston for assembly purposes.

Recoil starter
A rope based starting device in which the rope is returned onto the pulley by a spring. When the rope is pulled a ratchet engages drive to the engine, drive is disengaged when the rope is returned by the spring.

Shim
A thin washer or strip used for adjusting clearances i.e. crankshaft end float.

Split pin
A wire pin with an eye at one end and two parallel shafts making up the pin. When fitted the legs are bent to retain the pin in position.

Spring washer
A split spring steel washer used to prevent bolts or nuts vibrating loose.

Throttle butterfly
An oval plate in the carburettor which pivots on a shaft to control the air flow through the carburettor and thus the speed of the engine.

Top dead centre (TDC)
This is the point when the piston is at the highest point of its travel. It occurs twice in one cycle of a 4-stroke engine. At the top of the compression stroke (when the spark ignites the fuel) and between the exhaust and inlet cycles.

Wire gauge
Usually a set of steel wires of specified thickness, for setting gaps between parts i.e. spark plug contacts, ignition contact breaker points.

Woodruff key
This is a special type of semicircular key which fits into a slot of the same profile. The slot is in a shaft and is there for locating purposes.